ALTERNATIVE
PRINCIPLES
OF
ECONOMICS

ALTERNATIVE
PRINCIPLES
OF
ECONOMICS

Stanley Bober

M.E. Sharpe

Armonk, New York
London, England

Library of Congress Cataloging-in-Publication Data

Bober, Stanley.
    Alternative principles of economics / Stanley Bober.
        p. cm.
    Includes bibliographical references and index.
    ISBN 0-7656-0553-8 (hc. : alk. paper)
    1. Economics. II. Title.

HB171.B5418 2001
330—dc21   00-041966

Printed in the United States of America

The paper used in this publication meets the minimum requirements of
American National Standard for Information Sciences
Permanence of Paper for Printed Library Materials,
ANSI Z 39.48-1984.

                                   ∞

BM (c)   10   9   8   7   6   5   4   3   2   1

To Sharon and Mitchell

Contents

Preface

This book was undertaken to introduce "new" economic reasoning along several topical lines, which should cause some discomfort with the continued reliance on the accustomed "tools of the trade." There has developed over recent decades a cohesive alternative approach to the conventional— neoclassical (marginalist)—framework that has, indeed, posed a challenge to the core understanding of what the study of economics is about.

This heterodox alternative considered under the broad umbrella title of post-Keynesian or postclassical economics, takes an opposing view to the idea (usually the opening thought to start a Principles of Economics course) that all economic questions and problems arise from scarcity. This, at the center, is the notion that economics is the science of rational allocation in the presence of scarcity or limitation of resources—a limitation imposed on society mostly by the forces of nature.

While not denying the existence of a choice problem, the post-Keynesian approach would reorder the problem out of the center and relegate it to the status of a minor consideration. Students are aware of their world as being one of continuous technological change, and realize that the modern world is more and more a man-made world where the elements of knowledge and innovations leading to the reproduction of economic resources and the introduction of different types of resources are developed from within the society, thus essentially freeing "man" from the "imprisonment" of nature. Whatever economic constraints a society faces, thinking here in terms of growth of production, it results greatly from perverse institutional and economic arrangements, rather than from the commonly understood vision of resources given by nature. We do not give the subject of economics much credence, certainly in the skeptical minds of introductory students, by placing them in a Robinson Crusoe world at the very outset.

What our alternative approach would then consider as the central theme in economics is an understanding of how a society can maintain the reproduction of levels of production and employment and over time realize appropriate growth rates of levels of them. It is a problem of production and growth, and not that of an optimal allocation of scarce resources, that should constitute what economics is about, for a key driving force behind political change in much of the world is to put in place economic and social institutions that will yield economic betterment to a wide range of society.

Taking this tack, then, leads us to propose a different reasoning regarding many neoclassical constructions, which removes or significantly downgrades the marginalist calculation as the basic explanatory principle. It is very prevalent in economics that propositions that have been proven "wrong" and to be without sound theoretical foundation are still widely used in the practice and teaching of the subject. Economists become attached to, or let us say blinded by, particular theoretical principles that have led to the present morass in our thinking and have prevented a correct analysis of many real-world economic events. And this is all the more serious for many if not the majority of students on the level of the Principles of Economics, which is their first and last formal learning exposure to the subject. And while some students may very well appreciate the elegance and inherent consistency of particular conventional models, when it is all said and done, they are unable to understand or make sense of the outcomes of the functioning economy, because to a large degree those supposedly explanatory models do not reflect the institutional realities.

This book calls into question and offers an alternative approach to some conventional (neoclassical) ideas, such as the following. There is the universal applicability of the law of diminishing returns, specifically its use as the foundation for a firm's cost-curve construction, or its use in the construction of the "well-behaved" production function, or what we would consider that grand notion of miseducation—that an understanding of income distribution is but a facet of price theory, so that one explains income in terms of the usual market mechanism with a price-clearing outcome. In addition, the book questions whether a realistic understanding of consumer behavior can be found within the demand-curve construction, be it based on the ordinal or cardinal foundation, or that the rate of interest is determined in a money market composed of independently standing money supply curves and demand curves.

Overall there is a serious problem with the continuing adherence to the most fundamental of economic tools, which is the market model, with its conventionally sloped supply and demand curves, that permeates the entire body of orthodox theory as the explanatory instrument of prices and quantities. While it is often useful to separate matters influencing the quantity demanded from those operating on the supply side, one must not assume that the two will be brought into balance with one another through a change in the price level. It is the latter error that has led to the intellectual bankruptcy of economics. As will be made clear, whether one thinks of the goods market in terms of industrial products or of the market for labor or of the credit market, the idea of specifying a supply curve that is separate and independent of the demand curve, which then determines the prevailing price in that market, is generally wrong, thereby preventing a realistic interpretation as to how prices are formed. But is this not one of the first ideas that students are imbued with, which they encounter again and again?

To cleanse one's thinking of this error in such a basic mechanism, and to jettison what one has been accustomed to teaching, will not be easy; though hopefully, as a result of going through the analysis here, one will feel comfortable in loosing the bonds and be amenable to adopting a heterodox viewpoint in various areas. After encountering the different approach to the matters of pricing, production, and income distribution, the reader will then find them pulled together into a supportive framework for sustaining economic growth (encompassing as well a discussion of money) that, to reiterate, should be the core idea of what economics is about.

This "little" book is not designed to replace the standard Principles text (which these days has grown quite voluminous); its coverage is limited to a few essential topics. And we are not asking, nor really expecting, the professor (particularly in the introductory economics course) to put aside accustomed presentations. All that is asked is for the professor to take that bold step to question conventional wisdom and introduce alternative explanations. The reader will notice that with regard to the topics of distribution, consumption, and the labor market, the respective chapters first set out the standard analysis in some detail, so as to have the usual model right there, to which questions are then put and alternatives presented. Should this book be helpful in bringing about some changes in what we normally teach in our economics classes, it will have done its job.

Acknowledgments

There have been many discussions with colleagues about the need for an entry-level book on the alternative economic paradigm, as well as about the topics to be covered and the nature (depth) of the analysis. In particular I thank Professors Ed Nell of the New School for Social Research and Ingrid Rima of Temple University for their comments and encouragement about this book. Of course, any misconceptions are entirely my responsibility.

On the preparation for publication side, I acknowledge a debt of gratitude to my two helpmates at Duquesne University: Karen Plack and Guozhu (Patrick) Zhu. Karen has helpfully solved many e-matters in smoothing the way for computerizing the manuscript. Patrick has patiently performed a necessary task that, at times, must have been somewhat frustrating—transforming the illegible hand of the author into finished typescript and actually producing the disk form. Also, Patrick's computer genius has produced professional draftsmanlike diagrams from the author's crude hand-drawn pictures. Life was made less stressful because of their commitment to this book.

ALTERNATIVE PRINCIPLES
OF
ECONOMICS

1

An Alternative Introduction
to Economics

We begin with what is, by now, the universal way to introduce the study of economics and convey what it is supposedly all about. The wide range of issues and problems that people associate with being "economic" is understood to have its grounding in this widely accepted core approach of discipline to which we will then offer an alternative.

The conventional approach is to see society in a continuous state of confrontation between a virtually unlimited desire for material things and services and the "fact" of an inherent limited capability to satisfy this desire. While it is also a fact that from time to time society realizes a condition of unused resources and productive capacity, the attitude, at least in introductory Principles, is that the insufficiency of demand is an anomaly, and that basic understanding comes through the vision of society in a state of limitation of supply. This limitation is seen as resulting from a scarcity of resources or "factors of production" that are the inputs to all production processes to produce the output satisfying those diverse material wants. One can simply say that economic activity is the actions of society, is what people do to cope with this scarcity problem.

What is this activity composed of? What kinds of decisions result from societal action to deal with the limitations placed upon it? As is normally portrayed, there is the necessary decision as to what types of goods are to be produced and in what quantities they are to be produced. An immediate associated question is whether society allows this decision to be arrived at privately, that is by organizations or individuals who own (have legal entitlement to) or control the productive capability of what has been referred to as the means of production of society. Or is this decision somehow vested in society as a whole through the community ownership of the means of production? To what degree is society reflective of a middle way in which this decision is entered into by the government as an agent of the community, as well as by private owners? Students are told that what is being studied is the operation of a capitalist market system in which practically all of the means of production is privately owned, and that it is the decision outcome of this private sector that generates employment and income in the society and that allocates resources to the production of the different kinds of output, thereby determining the composition of the aggregate level of production.

The term "market" as part of the description of the economic system is conceived of as an operating mechanism on a day-to-day basis that guides the economic decisions of society. We ask whether a market-clearing concept, which is espoused to be the essential determining process, is indeed a description of the way the economy really works. Or are we dealing primarily with an emotional term that, while it may have descriptive significance for a particular economic-political arrangement, bears very little on actual economic outcomes.

Now let us mention two other economic decisions. One deals with the choice of technique involved in the production process, and the other is the mechanism at work that results in a societal decision regarding the distribution of income, which itself is greatly related to the "how" decision entered into by the individual producing units of the system. As we are told, the three questions of the economic system—the what, how, and for whom (the distribution question)—are coordinated and answered through market operations that yield outcomes dealing with quantities and types of goods produced, while simultaneously determining selling prices and costs (input prices) of production.

Yet all of the above questions arise out of the accepted condition of scarcity characteristic of the material and human inputs of production. This gives rise to a definition of economics as a discipline concerned with administering scarce resources so as to bring about the maximum fulfillment of society's unlimited wants, or as one textbook by McConnell and Brue puts it: "Economics is concerned with doing the best with what we have."[1] The fundamental aspect of economics is the problem of an optimum allocation of scarce resources; that is, to study the mechanics of the market procedure that reflects rational choice leading to this optimum outcome.

So we have individual (atomistically behaving) economic units—individual consumers or producing entities—entering into an ever constant exchange process, through which individuals maximize their utility subject to the constraint of a given distribution of income among them, and firms maximize their profits (or minimize losses) subject to the constraints of existing selling prices and production costs. The economic problem is to understand how the society determines those prices that bring about this optimum outcome, which simultaneously reveals the combination of goods produced and consumed. Of course the endowment of resources by individuals is simply a reflection of the exchange process entered into by producing units in their quest to purchase that combination of inputs that minimizes production costs. We are given to understand that the workings of an economy are the working of markets that set factor prices, thereby determining the level of income and, greatly, its distribution, and that set the prices of produced goods and services. As is made clear, it is through interplay of these markets that society solves the what, how, and for whom issues. They are solved in a manner that leads to a maximization of the utilities of the economic constituents so that no single element can become better off without some other being made worse off. There has been, in other words, an optimum allocation of existing scarce resources. But how do these prices (equilibrium prices) come into existence? To say that they are determined by the free market or by competition is to propose a largely mythical concept, because the institutional basis for such an explanation is, generally, nonexistent.

Yet such descriptions serve as propagandizing tools for a particular organization of society. One popular view is that political democracy is linked to market capitalism and may even be an essential underlining of it. A society in which voters determine the government, where all voters have equal power, where the central administrative authority is prevented from excessive power by a checks-and-balances structure, and where the government must earn its mandate, could only exist in concert with an economic structure where there is great diffusion of economic power among the producing and consuming units and where all constituents interact with generally equal influence in their respective markets, leading to price and quantity outcomes that reflect that optimum allocation of resources.

The lack of coercive political power manifests itself in the workings of the competitive market structure with the free enterprise of large numbers of independent agents. In determining a government of democratic policy, voters bring into being an organization that maintains the legal and institutional structure of competitive markets. From this point of view (and it is only one view) the political and economic arrangements are reflective; where you find political democracy, you should also find free competitive markets. And where you do not find the one, you will not find the other. Though the emphasis placed on the microfoundations of competitive market-clearing exchanges is, I would say, a misguided attempt at a comfortable fit between the "economy" and the "political" of democratic capitalism. One is aware that the economic system operates overwhelmingly upon a foundation of highly imperfect competitive arrangements where prices do not continuously adjust to clear markets. Indeed, in the reality of matters economic, agents trade at what is labeled as false prices—prices that are nonequilibrium and not competitive-market determined. We will, in a subsequent chapter on pricing, examine this phenomenon in some detail.

Yet the way this reality is handled is to see it as a departure from some "normal" or "desirable" state (and as calling upon the central authority to restore "competition"), rather than to consider the organizations operating in this false environment as the normal structure representative of the current development of modern capitalist society—if indeed one could upon hindsight find a period of time where the perfectly competitive market generally held sway. One must bring to the forefront of study the price determination and production arrangements of noncompetitive (in the traditional sense) economic agents. One must also understand the role of prices in this pervasive environment.

If we may reiterate the point here: For a realistic understanding of the economic workings of our society, we must eschew the "vulgar economics" (to use a Marxian term) that views the economy through the lens of appearance rather than that of reality—the appearance being the continuous presence of exchanges between atomistic independent-acting agents within a structure of competitive markets characterized by the separability of supply-and-demand schedules. These exchanges then, allocate the given resources between competing ends and give rise to the price and quantity outcomes. Now this allocation is presumed subject to constraints imposed by "nature" and technical knowledge. The latter constraint is, as well, usually thought of as given but not immutable; from time to time the state of knowledge is acknowledged to have changed, but it is invariably seen to impact the system from outside. It is normally not thought of (as indeed it should) as the driving force of economic activity, and the internal operation of the economy is not analyzed in terms of a cause-and-effect relationship to technological change itself.

Luigi Pasinetti has been much involved in propagandizing for and developing an alternative approach to the current (marginalist competitive) model of economic analysis. He overviews the existing state as follows:

> We may say that the marginal economic theorists have chosen to look at the real world through the lens of the scarcity model. All aspects of reality have been magnified or eliminated according to whether they did or did not fit into the pattern of a scarcity world. The conception that has thereby arisen is that of a world where the material goods which are the object of man's desire, and technical knowledge have been shaped by some external agents. Let us simply call it 'nature' and given to man in scarce quantities, with a haphazard distribution and in immutable form. Of course some changes in the state of technical knowledge may now and then suddenly

come in from the outside; but this is not the model's concern. . . . All that concerns to be done, or to be talked about, is a possible series of exchanges of the existing goods. In other words, the only economic problem that the members of society are facing is a problem of rational behavior in order to increase when possible the enjoyment they obtain out of what is given and immutable. By combining and exchanging the existing goods on the basis of their given preferences and knowledge they may reach a better allocation than the one which happened to be given to them by nature at the beginning.[2]

Now we are proposing a Principles of Economics that discards this marginalist schematization. The economy is more, indeed it must be more, than a mere allocating mechanism. The reality of the world as we look back over long periods of time is the secular rise in real output experienced by industrial societies (i.e., advanced capitalist economies). Societies have experienced capability that is largely the result of the cumulative effects of technical changes, that is, of the growth and infusion of such knowledge into the production process, thereby freeing man from the constraints of nature.

Again from Pasinetti:

A cursory look around us is enough to perceive this most clearly. The constantly advancing technology in the more modern parts of the world has by now freed entire populations, for the first time in history, from the yoke of hunger and starvation. Technical change has made and is constantly making men less and less dependent on nature and more and more dependent upon themselves. The commodities that nowadays men produce and the surroundings in which they live are more and more shaped by them; the product of their own decisions. Even the raw materials and the traditional sources of energy, which at the beginning of the industrial revolution absolutely conditioned the rise of industries, are becoming less and less important, as men themselves learn how to make, in whatever place they like, a great part of the raw materials (or their synthetic substitutes), and are moreover developing entirely new sources of energy. . . . The world of the future is going to become more and more a man-made world.[3]

So the goods that are consumed and exchanged, and have positive prices, are not scarce goods reflecting nature's constraints on the ability of society to produce them as a result of some niggardly endowment of resources. They are goods that can be produced in practically whatever quantity is desired, provided the society decides it is worthwhile to devote the amount of effort that is required by the given technology. And the quantity and type of resources required (the effort involved) is itself always changing as a result of the ongoing technical knowledge.

In an overall way, then, the different starting point for an introduction to economics is that of a world of abundance. But let us again be clear about this world. In terms of produced physical inputs to a productive process, these inputs can be generally manufactured without limit. So that all other resources besides land, normally considered as given by nature, are not so at all—they are not scarce. One may encounter a scarce condition, but it would only be temporarily so. Given the technological know-how in land reclamation, water treatment, and the so-called green revolution, our agricultural capability is being enlarged more and more. It is questionable whether we should even consider land in the sense of agricultural capability as being fixed.

But in an operative economic way, abundance means that the system will, as a matter of course, have at its disposal a degree of excess capacity of output in a structural sense and a not fully employed labor force. This is generally what characterizes the economic environment: The society always has the capability to increase output overall. It is not a central matter, or as it is put, "the research program" of the society, as to how to allocate a fully employed limited amount of resources. What is the real research program is how to bring about the increase in production at any point in time so as to utilize the available capability. The related longer-term issue is how to keep production growing in line with society's capability (its abundance, if you will), which is itself greatly driven by ongoing changes in technical knowledge.

One need only recall those early discussions in introductory economics to realize how different our proposal is concerning the core issue of the discipline. Those lectures are wrapped around the production-possibilities curve as illustrative of the basic allocative function of the system. The student is told repeatedly that this structure is based on the idea of a given quantity of resources that is not unemployed or used inefficiently and that the level of technology is constant. And while one does allude to the possibility of the curve shift and some causal factors therein, this is rather quickly put aside in favor of the analyses of the stationary state of the society and the allocative mechanics of a market.

Yet upon observing the world as it is, looking out the classroom window, the student does not find an operating market as the term is understood resulting from those introductory lectures (some in very particular circumstances), nor does the student find an operating competitive production environment, and the student is well aware of how rapidly technological change has altered the availability and types of jobs. Certainly the cost curves of the firm that form the bases of much of the introductory micro setting are, as we will make clear, very unrealistically based, causing a misunderstanding between prices and demand changes.

What I believe the instructor has in mind when tracing out the cost-production curves is a vision of the family-run firm supposedly subject to the "inexorable" law of diminishing returns. And one accepts these curves as the reality; one does not inject any doubt. The question is not asked whether a production function extracted on this basis (even if we were to accept its existence in the agricultural sector) is applicable to the industrial component of modern society. What is done is to generalize those cost curves as they are promulgated to represent the competitive (the agricultural firm again being the mind-set) as well as those "aberrant" noncompetitive arrangements. We consider this approach as another example in the Principles of Economics that removes much reality from our understanding.

As we begin to recast some of the Principles, let us propose that theory and accompanying explanatory models be based on realistic hypotheses. One should take an epistemological position on a stand of realism and eschew the approach whereby one abstracts from reality supposedly for the purpose of simplification, only to systematically add helpful pieces of reality to the initial design. The incorporation of different assumptions will in all likelihood cast aside the original model altogether as a basis for a realistic understanding of what is happening. Our approach is that the analyses of the economy be constructed of elements that, in the words of Lavoie, an unorthodox economist, are "observable and objective rather than metaphysical and subjective."[4]

In the following chapter we confront the Principles with the heterodox reasoning concerning the law of diminishing returns and the cost curves of the firm.

Notes

1. Campbell McConnell and Stanley Brue, *Economics*, ISO ed. (New York: McGraw-Hill, 1996).

2. Luigi Pasinetti, *Structural Change and Economic Growth* (London: Cambridge University Press, 1981), p. 20.

3. Ibid., p. 21.

4. Marc Lavoie, *Foundations of Post Keynesian Economic Analysis* (Aldershot, UK: Edward Elgar, 1992), p. 9.

2

Returns and the Costs of Production

Initial Thoughts

An analysis of the cost curves of the firm as a prelude to the decision outcome regarding production and prices is usually preceded by impressing the student with the operation of the law of diminishing returns. This is the procedure because the law is seen to be the foundation of the unit cost curve and, importantly, the rational for the conventional upward-sloping marginal cost curve and resulting rising supply price curve for the commodity in question.

The law is promulgated as a natural law similar in its universality to a law of physics. It is, of course, supposed to tell us about the flow of output as successive units of a variable resource are added to a fixed resource, with examples of the latter being either land or capital, thereby emphasizing its general applicability.

Even if one were to illustrate this with the most likely agricultural example—that "famous" plot of land of given fertility upon which one places an increasing number of labor units—the more telling illustration would be in relation to capital. And here, in an attempt to provide some framework of reality, the professor might tell of a plant with an array of different types of equipment where a unit of labor moves from one workstation to another, consuming much time in the process and severely restricting the output flow. But as more labor is added, each unit of labor works more machines, thus reducing lost time and increasing productivity (there is the unspoken assumption that all additions to the labor force are equally adept at working each type of machine). One then moves to the point where each piece of equipment is manned by a unit of labor. Beyond this condition productivity increases begin to deteriorate when additional inputs of labor are added. A particular task divided by too many people begins to offset whatever gain is accomplished by reducing the fatigue factor. Output may actually fall and per-unit costs increase—thus at some point, diminishing returns and eventually absolute declines begin to set in.

Yet in relating this diminishing returns story (if it is told this way) the professor has escaped production reality, though the story is viable on an imaginary basis. The question that is normally not posed is, what kind of production facility would actually engage labor in this way? Well, perhaps a response would be a home-based cottage industry; but it would not be the reality of large market-production facilities. In the latter environment production would be carried on within a context of having as much labor as is technically required to operate each piece of equipment (or perform a particular task) and, as required, adding additional capital units with the necessary associated labor units. Or, should negative demand conditions prevail, one would idle capital stocks with the associated labor input or work the productive facility less intensely with a corresponding reduction in labor hours.

The professor would perhaps be nonplussed to come up with an example of labor units being added to or withdrawn from a "fixity of capital" notion akin to the variability of labor operating on a fixed plot of land.

Yet such doubt about the law's applicability is invariably not brought up as the student is quickly moved on to the numbers exemplifying the short-run cost curves. But we do want to raise such doubt, which would then have us undertake a brief foray into the history of economic thought for a look at how the law came into being and what was its original intention, and to understand how it was adopted as an underpinning for the supply-curve construction. We will conclude that such an adoption was, in the least, a misplacement of economic thinking. We then will construct cost curves on a different foundation, bringing us in line with the reality of production mechanics. As Sraffa makes the point:

> We are disposed to accept the laws of return as a matter of course because we have before our eyes the great and indisputable services rendered by them when performing their ancient functions, we often neglect to ask whether the old barrels are still able to hold the new wine.[1]

A Look Back and a Problem

The original intent of the law of diminishing returns was to explain the distributive variable of rent with reference to agricultural land. And it was the Malthusian theory of population, which focused attention on the scarcity of land as the overriding ingredient limiting the "means of subsistence," that was identified with foodstuff. While the Malthusian propositions did not directly deal with the relationship of land rent and diminishing returns, both of these connecting concepts were reactions to Malthus's *Essay on Population.*[2]

Malthus argued that attempts to relieve poverty among the masses will eventually be of no avail, as policies such as state subsidies and private charities will come to be overwhelmed by the proclivity of the population to increase its numbers in a geometric progression. And this increase in population growth will, as a matter of a natural consequences, outpace the economy's ability to provide the necessities that would maintain the greater numbers of people at a higher-than-subsistence level of existence. Malthus argued that, at best, additional food would increase arithmetically; that the rapid increase in foodstuffs is not possible since the supply of land is limited and technical improvements in agriculture will not come fast enough. Indeed, the policies designed to better the condition of people would be thwarted, ironically, by altering the behavior of these same people by removing the restraint to procreate based upon the fear of hunger and ultimately the presence of a higher death rate. In Malthusian language, to reduce the essential "positive" check to population growth, that of "misery," is a consequence of removing the necessity of each person to fend for himself and to bear the responsibility of his own improvidence.

Malthus spoke of "preventive" checks to population growth in terms of lowering births, which he attributed to moral restraint, and of "positive" checks in terms of raising deaths, which he ascribed to vice and misery; however, his major assertion was that the ultimate check to reproduction capacity lay in the limitation of the food supply. And as Blaugh stated, "the magic phrase that was subsequently used to sanction this assertion is the Law of Diminishing Returns."[3] We want to be clear as to what the classicists believed was subject to the law and what was not. Malthus, Ricardo, and others agreed that there was no law of diminishing returns to technical progress, but that it was applicable to agricultural output despite the presence of capital accumulation and technical change. Ricardo's belief was that "the necessity of having recourse to land inferior to that already in tillage, or of cultivating the same land more expensively, tends to make labor in agriculture less productive in the progress of improvement which more than counteracts the effect of machinery and the division of labor in agriculture."[4] Thus in its static framework the law asserted something about returns to varying input proportions under given technical conditions, but there was an overall belief that even in a dynamic setting of tilling land under improved technology, society would not escape the effects of the law in its agricultural sector.

What we have is an assertion about diminishing returns that, as Blaugh tells us, "was regarded as a simple generalization of everyday experience that can be verified looking at the real world."[5] And what was observable in the early years of the nineteenth century during the Napoleonic wars were high prices of foodstuffs and the extension of cultivation to less fertile and less accessible land, with the classical economists taking the position that the underlying explanation for this lay in the phenomenon of diminishing returns. Indeed, this was a point in Ricardo's argument for free trade developed in conjunction with the theory of comparative costs. The idea was that the consequence of diminishing returns could be avoided by importing agricultural products from countries with abundant land, where agriculture is not subject to diminishing returns. In this way the price of foodstuffs and thereby land rent is kept low, which means that wages will not be increasing, allowing the rate of profit to be maintained at high levels, which serves to continue a rapid rate of capital accumulation.

So we come to the essential point that the law in its original understanding was intended to provide a theory of ground rent, and that the foundation of the law, to reiterate, was with reference to land. It was not at all understood in terms of the production mechanics of a manufactured good. Certainly what is not verifiable by simply glancing at the real world, is the now commonly accepted modern version of diminishing returns, which is a statement of what would happen if we increase the amount of one input while all other inputs remain fixed, with the reference here being the manufacturing sector. Classical economists, of course, never assumed the latter reference, as we can see by a quotation from Edward West that "in the progress of the improvement of cultivation the raising of rude produce becomes progressively more expensive . . . each equal additional quantity of work bestowed on agriculture yields an actual diminished return. Whereas it is obvious that an equal quantity of work will always fabricate the same quantity of manufacturers."[6] The classical economists asserted the presence of "constant return" in manufacturing, that is, where the scale (size) of output of a good makes no difference to factor proportions, which is saying production is carried on with fixed proportions between inputs. We will come back to this notion in our construction of a modern production function and related cost curves.

The notion of diminishing returns was conceived of as a macroeconomic tool intended to explain the nature of ground rent, with rent being an aggregative category of income along with wages and profits. Thus the law has to be placed within the context of aggregate production belonging, as Robinson said, "to the department of output as a whole,"[7] which has nothing to do with the rising supply price of a particular commodity of a single firm or industry.

Now let us see how this land rent comes into being and its basis in diminishing returns. The fact of population growth is seen to inevitably require society to cultivate less productive soil. That is, land of a particular fertility is being used at a certain point in time, with less fertile land coming into production at a future point; thus with a sufficient lapse in time, different grades of soil are simultaneously cultivated. The aggregate level of rent is then the payment for the utilization of the whole of that productive resource (land) at a particular time in the production of total foodstuff output. In classical thinking, rent was agricultural rent for land having only a single use. One did not differentiate between land in use for growing foodstuffs and land in use for grazing of animals. Thus labor and capital could move from one grade of land to another (and we want to see the economic forces at work here) but land itself is not movable from one type of activity to another. Society is considered to be able to freely take up additional agricultural land as needed; therefore the payment (rent) for the next unit of land is not a payment to bid it away from an alternative activity for which it is already receiving a payment. So we are dealing with a factor of production (land) that is of a specialized nature (agricultural use) whose supply is fixed in the aggregate. Additional units of this supply are brought into production as the price of the output makes it profitable to do so, which then leads to a reward to the landlord in the form of a rent payment for making available additional land for cultivation. This is the reasoning behind the idea that rent is price determined, not price determining. As Ricardo put it, "Corn is not high because a rent is paid, but a rent is paid because corn is high."[8] Thus rent is not a direct cost of production to the farmer that enters into the determination of price.

Now we look at an example that will illustrate the law and its relation to rent. Our example is one of differential rent, where it is assumed that while all land is identical in the sense of the use to which it is put, it is differentiated in quality (fertility) into many classes, say running from highest fertility (A) to lowest fertility (E), whose use exhausts all of the land resource. Now in the application of productive resources one normally refers to the trio of capital, labor, and natural resources (here meaning agricultural land), but these separate identities (corresponding to the distribution variables of profits, wages, and rent) can leave us with the sense that each can be applied individually to a productive process while holding the others constant. Certainly this has been the conventional handling of capital and labor, which has caused much difficulty in forging greater realism in economic analysis (the modern construction of the law and its use being a case in point). Yet long ago, classical thinkers understood that realism called for the consideration of capital and labor in a fixed relationship as applied to a production process both in manufacturing and agriculture. So their model is in actuality a two-factor model consisting of capital (thought of as seed corn and other capital goods) and labor combined in a fixed set for the production of foodstuffs (corn). In the illustration of diminishing returns, they considered the

Table 2.1

Input	Total output from land				
	A	B	C	D	E
0	0	0	0	0	0
1	180	170	160	150	140
2	350	330	310	290	
3	510	480	450		
4	660	620			
5	800				

effect of an application of a homogeneous dose of capital and labor in successive increments on different grades of land (one can think of this as men-with-shovels doses to which we would attach a preset amount of seed). Yet the bringing into production of different grades of land occurs over time, where we can expect technical change to be a ongoing presence, but as indicated, the classical economists acknowledged its impact but reasoned that it was not strong enough to thwart the workings of those "fundamental influences."

In Table 2.1 we note five grades of land of varying fertility from A to E. We see that with an equal employment of the input dose of capital and labor the production of corn per acre decreases when the quality of land utilized is lower. But more to our point, Ricardo tells us:

> It often, and indeed, commonly happens, that before inferior lands are cultivated, capital can be employed more productively on these lands which are already in cultivation. It may perhaps be found, that by doubling the original capital employed on No. 1 [on land A], though the produce will not be doubled, will not be increased by 100 quarters [in our case 180 quarters], it may be increased by 85 quarters [we see an increase of 170].[9]

Ricardo's words imply that the marginal productivity of land A will diminish when it is cultivated more intensely, that is, when more capital is invested on the same land and similarly for the other grades of land as well. And here we have the original framework for the use of the law of diminishing returns.

We translate our physical quantities into money values with the assumptions of a $1 sale price per bushel of corn and that the cost of a dose of the capital-labor input is $140. Our capitalist-farmer using grade A land will increase production levels under intense cultivation as long as the value of output resulting from the unit of input exceeds its cost. To keep matters on a

Table 2.2

Input	A	B	C	D	E
			Marginal output		
1	180	170	160	150	140
2	170	160	150	140	
3	160	150	140		
4	150	140			
5	140				

rather simple level since we want to highlight the rent distributive variable, we can assume that the profits to the farmer are part of that input cost of $140. Thus for an intense cultivation of 2 units of input we have a combined surplus of $70; for an input level of 3 units the total surplus increases by $40, and for a fourth input the surplus increases by $10. Beyond this point the landlord will not, let us say, permit any additional cultivation, since the land will not earn any rent payment. The realized surplus at a given level of cultivation becomes the rent payment to the individual who has legal title to the land; it is, as Ricardo says, a payment for "the use of the original and indestructible powers of the soil."[10]

With the pressure of population increasing the need for greater levels of foodstuffs, there will be recourse to poorer grades of land, and as we see, these lands will be cultivated less intensely and yield smaller rent levels. We can see this more clearly with the use of Table 2.2, which shows the incremental output on the different lands per units of additional input.

Reading across Table 2.2 reveals a movement extending outward from the richest to the poorest land at a given level of cultivation, thereby summing to the total rent payable on all lands. For a single dose of input on all grades the aggregate rent comes to $100, with land E generating zero rent. Land E is seen as the outer-fringe land or land at the extensive margin of cultivation, where it produces a value of output equal to the cost of capital and labor expended upon it. But surely if it pays to apply resources to the worst grade and at least generate a value equal to costs of production, then it would make sense to apply these resources to more intensely cultivate the more fertile land to produce a value in excess of costs and to keep doing so on any grade until an intensive margin equal to the extensive margin is reached—at a level of 140. The reader will note that, for example, a third unit of input on land A is as productive as that third unit would have been if applied to the third-best land, and so forth. It is not the capability of the inputs that is the problem, it is the inherent fertility of the land that is the difficulty and that is seen in the operation of diminishing returns and yielding differential units (rent calculated as a residual).

Table 2.3

Input	Output	Average product	Marginal product	Marginal cost
1	180	180	180	140
2	350	175	170	140
3	510	170	160	140
4	660	165	150	140
5	800	160	140	140
6	930	155	130	140

Yet one need not necessarily consider a context of abundant land of different levels of growing capability. We could presume land being of limited supply of a particular grade, say we are dealing only with grade A. The output of corn becomes a function of capital and labor only while the role of land in production is implicit; let us reposition our numbers for an explanation of rent in this framework. Thus for 2 units of input the payment to this capital-labor dose is 340, yielding a surplus of 10 as payment "to land" (in classical rent theory the variable input can be thought of as receiving a reward equal to its marginal product, but this feature, in common with conventional marginal productivity distribution theory is acceptable here because of the nature of the fixed factor of production). And for an application of 3 doses of the variable input the total earnings will be 480 (equal on a per input-dose basis to its marginal contribution) thereby generating an intermarginal surplus appropriated as rent equaling 30. Now with the fifth unit of input we find land A being cultivated at the intensive margin, where it generates an additional value of output that, after the payment of the intermarginal surplus of 100, is equal to the costs of production. On this homogeneous land, aggregate rent is calculated as the difference between the value of the output of all the inputs applied to it (800) and the product of the final input at the intensive margin (700). The landlord would certainly not countenance a more intense cultivation beyond this margin as it would lead to a reduction in the rent payment. Carrying Table 2.3 forward to an input dose of 6 units, we find that an output of 930 necessitates a payment to the variable input of 780, which is less than what is required to bring about the level of output; this difference of 60 would need to come out of the return to the landlord, reducing the rent to 90. And we can see the workings of the law in determining the surplus (rent), since for equal applications of the input the rent is equal to the value of the output and the payment to the capital-labor dose, which is itself determined by the declining marginal product.

We can appreciate all this in more exact form with the following notation.

Let

> N = Input dose
> Y = Aggregate output
> R = Rent

Then:

$$Y = f(N) \tag{2.1}$$

Subject to

$$f'(N) > 0, f''(N) < 0 \tag{2.2}$$

telling us that output is increasing at a decreasing rate.

Keeping with the notion of a composite input dose being paid its marginal product, we have the rent payment as

$$R = f(N) - Nf'(N) \tag{2.3}$$

Thus for an input dose of 4, the rent is

$$R = 660 - 4(150) = 60 \tag{2.4}$$

And the share of rent in total output is

$$\tag{2.5}$$
$$\frac{R}{Y} = \frac{f(N) - Nf'(N)}{f(N)}$$

For an input dose of 2 the share of rent is:

$$R = 350 - 2(170) = 10$$
$$R/Y = 10/350 = 0.029 \tag{2.6}$$

And for the greater intensity of cultivation reflective of input doses of 3, 4, and 5, the rent share comes to 0.058, 0.09, and 0.125; rent increases absolutely and as a proportion of the total value of output with its maximum being achieved at the point of intensive margin.

Having mentioned rent in terms of a proportional share, it behooves us to look again at Table 2.3 and extract the shares of output going to labor in terms of total wages and that going to our capitalist-farmer in terms of profits. The idea of a composite dose, while useful to highlight the understanding of the rent share, needs certainly to be pulled apart, and it will again show up diminishing returns in its relation to the aggregate distribution of output.

Now if we presume that the marginal costs (MC) number equals the natural real wage rate ($\overline{w}$), then for an input level of 3 units, the level of output minus rent comes to 480, of which total wages amounts to 420, leaving profits of 60. With an intensity of cultivation of 4 input doses, wages come to 560 with profits shrinking to 40; and at the intensive margin all of the difference between output and rent has been taken up by wages, reducing profits to zero. So in an overall view, the greater the level of employment the higher the total rent payment; as well, increasing levels of employment mean higher total wages. All this goes to reduce the profit share of production while increasing the share accruing to the landowner. And what is at work here is that output increases correspondingly less than employment, and with rent levels and total wages increasing with employment, it is clear that the profit portion shrinks as production enlarges. We see the profit level as

$$P = f(N) - [f(N) - Nf'(N)] - N\overline{w} \tag{2.7}$$

We will have more to say toward an understanding of income shares, and will appreciate that distribution is largely conditional upon the institutional class arrangements of the production process interplaying economic, technical, and social factors. For now we reiterate that the law of diminishing returns in its original use was seen as a tool that can be helpful for this understanding. As such it was thought of as a macro notion in the analysis of what happens to aggregate output shares over time. In particular, in terms of a simple Ricardian exposition, all of the essentials can be put forth within the confines of the one-sector corn model (viewing the economy as one gigantic farm). However, in a more astute approach Ricardo's analysis was in terms of a two-sector economy, where one sector produced wage goods (necessaries), which were congealed into the one commodity—corn production—and a second sector produced a "luxury" good—say cloth—this being the manufacturing sector. This two-sector approach was necessary when Ricardo entered into the theory of valuation. And the two-commodity analysis does not remove the basic conclusions that can be gleaned from the one-commodity model. For example, the rate of profit for the system as a whole, the wage rate, and the price of the wage good depend upon the function $f(N)$; that is, they are all governed by the production in the agricultural sector that, as we know, was assumed to be operating under diminishing returns. Once again we note the aggregate influence of the diminishing returns property; to paraphrase Ricardo, it is the profits in the agricultural sector that regulate the profits of all other trades.

But in modern times the notion of diminishing returns was taken up in a micro setting, serving to underpin cost curves of the firm and the normally constructed production function. And while the latter is talked about in terms of an aggregate relationship between output per capita and capital per capita, it does rest on the individual firm's presumed ability to vary one input while holding other inputs constant. But this was more than simply setting the mechanics of production; it brought forth an understanding of the distribution of output based on marginal productivity considerations. The idea of taking the law of diminishing returns as an operative relationship on the firm level led to an aggregate production function that was used to account for the distributive shares of wages and profits based on factor marginal productivity. In addition, going back to its micro application, the law of diminishing returns served to account for the rising supply price of a particular commodity.

So the question before us is what are the assumptions or modifications that positioned the law in its micro stance, being a cause of variation in the relative price of individual commodities? It is important to reiterate that diminishing returns in its original usage was understood to affect not only rent but also the cost of production in terms of a total sector, that is, agriculture as a whole. Thus even in its relation to costs, the analysis dealt with output as a whole and not with the relation between cost and quantity produced of an individual producing unit.

Yet in its modern role, diminishing returns is involved in the theory of competitive pricing through its impact on the firm's supply curve construction. All that was necessary was to generalize the particular case of agricultural land to a situation where, in the production of a particular commodity, a firm employs a considerable portion, if not all, of a productive input, the amount of which is fixed or can be increased at considerable cost. Consider then that we are dealing with firm alpha; an increase in the demand for alpha commodities will necessitate a more intense use of that input, resulting in the diminishing returns outcome with increasing costs and the usual upward-sloping supply curve.

But this image of a single firm or industry using all of an input factor that is unique only to its production is rather unreal or very particular. What is more to the point is to presume that other firms, say beta and gamma, also utilized this input in some proportion to their output. Now assuming full employment and the competitive model equilibrium, an increase in the demand for alpha output will reflect a reduction in the demand of, let us presume, both the output of beta and gamma. Thus some of this fixed input will be transferred from firms in general (beta and gamma) to the alpha firm.

What happens to costs of production in alpha in response to an increase in production then depends on the magnitude of the transfer. Again, the general context is that if a firm or an industry employs only a small portion of the "constant" factor, it is more likely to meet an increase in its production by drawing "doses" of the constant factor from other industries than by intensifying its own use of it.

Now should alpha employ this fixed input in proportion to its output in a manner identical to that of beta and gamma (i.e., akin to industry in general), then alpha will increase its employment of this input in the same proportion as it is "released" due to the decline in the other sector's demand. Under these circumstances the increase in alpha's output is produced under constant costs.

But we should suppose that industries are idiosyncratic, so it is natural to presume that alpha uses inputs not in proportions in which they are employed in the other industries (i.e., in terms of the average proportion in the system), but in proportions particular to itself. Now if it does so in a proportion greater than the average, then an increase in alpha's demand will entail an increase in total demand for this fixed input, and its cost will go up relative to other input, causing a higher level of production to be associated with higher supply prices.

But this possibility brings up other considerations. Here we have that a change in levels of production by the individual firm or industry will alter relative input prices. So we are no longer in a competitive framework (which is usually the backdrop for the introduction to the cost-curves construction). Certainly if a single producing unit can change factor prices in response to its demand, then it is not a nondescript bit player in the market.

And still a further consideration: Why are we to suppose that the alpha industry would adhere to the same input proportion after a change in relative prices as it was employing initially, unless we presume technologically determined fixed input proportion. But this is not the presumption in the conventional story about least-cost production, where firms are seen to alter input proportions in response to changes in relative costs. One does assume a high degree of elasticity of substitution, and if this is so, the alpha industry can be expected to adjust its input proportion to bring it in line with that of the average input employment. This would minimize, if not eliminate, any change in relative factor prices and greatly eliminate any increase in supply price.

As Robinson pointed out in her very trenchant article over fifty years ago:

> A markedly unaverage selection of factors and a low elasticity of substitution between factors are necessary conditions for an appreciable degree of rising supply price. Even a very large industry will show a small rise in

supply price if its selection of factors is near the average, or if it is nearly indifferent as to what factors it employs. On the other hand, a very small industry may enjoy sharply rising supply price if it has very specialized requirements.[11]

Then in order to maintain the competitive nature of the discussion and to allow a capability of altering input proportions, but simultaneously to subject the firm and industry to rising supply price as related to diminishing returns, implies a most unusual situation. Namely that the alpha industry is employing essentially the whole of a unique or rare factor that is not used in other industries; for example, an input reflecting an unusual human skill or the employment of a particular mineral. This special input is not reproducible, and the industry employing it is indeed carrying on the production with a selection of factors that is very much apart from the way production is carried on generally. An increase in alpha production will necessarily entail a more intense use of this input.

The whole theory of diminishing returns has developed around this type of case, which we could readily accept in the agricultural sector, assuming production taking place on a fixed acreage of a very special soil. But it does require a great stretch of reality to suppose a similar situation in the manufacturing sectors of the economy; it is simply too peculiar a condition for a generalized explanation of the supply curve construction. So what is implicit in the mind of an instructor when explaining the cost curves of the firm is, to reiterate, the agricultural case or the image of the firm utilizing a very unique input that is not used in other industries.

One can perhaps rescue the diminishing returns and increasing supply-costs image by presuming a case where the demand for alpha is increased while the demand for beta and gamma outputs remain the same. On the surface this odd circumstance can be brought about by alpha intensifying its own use of a particular input, and this implies the artificial assumption that the input being more intensely utilized is fixed in supply, while the other input being "injected" to it is increasing in supply (in this case there are no factors being released by the other industries). However, a net increase in demand, assuming full employment, presupposes an increase in resources generally. So even in this particular case we cannot say whether diminishing returns will or will not show up until we know what inputs have increased in supply and to what extent. The tendency to a rising supply price will be stronger the less elastic the total supply of inputs required by the expanding alpha industry—having admitted to an increase in resources overall.

We would conclude that the usual supply-curve construction, with its diminishing returns underpinning, is representative of very particular circumstances and is to be found, if at all, in the agricultural and perhaps the mining industries where the required inputs are highly idiosyncratic, where there is the likelihood of zero elasticity of substitution between employed inputs, and where the total supply of the factors of production is highly inelastic. These are industries where production is carried on within a context of essentially natural-made conditions that can give rise to diminishing returns.

But this is not the condition of the manufacturing or secondary industries where the environment is man-made. Here the inputs are not rare but common, are in elastic supply, and are, as Robinson puts it, "not cranky"[12] but adaptable. So for the general run of manufacturing industries the construction of the cost curves and the elaboration of the supply schedule cannot, with a degree of realism, be anchored in production subject to diminishing returns.

An Alternative Construction

An alternative cost analysis would then be based on production mechanics that yield cost curves of a constant supply price, which overall is reflective of the operation of the modern manufacturing unit. And we must, as an overall observation, conceptualize the workings of the economy within the realism of a system composed of imperfectly competitive oligopolistic industries consisting of a small number of large "organizational entities."

At a later point we elaborate somewhat on the nature of this organization in its difference from the conventional representation of the firm. We would also add that this alternative analysis has important implications for an understanding of a theory of price, for it allows a separation of costs of production and product demand from the price to be determined.

But to the matter at hand, which is to understand the production function that supports the "stylized facts" of constant marginal costs and a constant supply price now that we agree that a production relationship built upon diminishing returns is simply not capable of yielding a general explanation of costs and supply price.

Consider a manufacturing plant that at the time of its construction and implacement of capital equipment embodied the then most recent technological advances. This design necessitates a particular fixed capital-to-labor input ratio per unit of output. Increases or decreases in production levels will then correspondingly change the combined volume of input use, but one cannot bring about a change in output as a function of altering the input ratio, which, to reiterate, is inherent in the technology built into the plant.

Figure 2.1 illustrates this fixed coefficients or L-shaped "isoquants" production process. An isoquant is a curve in input space showing all possible

Figure 2.1

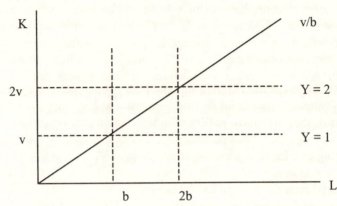

combinations of inputs capable of producing a given level of output. We are proposing that production is such that there are no possible combinations but only that a single combination can produce a specified output in any given operating plant. Now one can argue for the logic of supposing various fixed-proportion processes in the production of a level of output, but we need to keep in mind that each of these processes is reflective of a different age or "vintage" operating plant. Under particular conditions an organization may decide to activate an older plant, thus having its output produced under different cost conditions or, as a result of increasing capacity by building a new plant, may then deactivate older plants because the new technology and associated input ratio makes obsolete the older vintage plant due to the latter's too high costs of production relative to the organization's administered price of the output. But this is far different from the usual assumption of an isoquant that allows much flexibility in the combinations of inputs within a single operating plant.

We should add an additional piece of realism to our thought process: The technology embodied in the capital of the most recent operating plant cannot as a usual procedure be passed back to an existing older plant. The unit of most recent vintage can be expected to have a smaller ratio of wage costs to total costs than that of an older vintage. And the technology inherent in the investment to bring the new plant online is particular to it and is not adaptable to an operating older facility. This situation is characterized as one of putty–clay. The term putty refers to the choice of a plant embodying a particular technology (there is ex ante flexibility in production coefficients), while clay refers to the condition that once the equipment has been put in place, it hardens into the clay state in that input coefficients become fixed.

The point here is that an existing structure cannot normally be modified to incorporate the latest technology.

But let us not stray too far from our isoquant image of a single plant. The production function representing the input–output relationship of Figure 2.1 is

$$Y = \min (K/v, L/b) \tag{2.8}$$

where v and b are the required inputs of capital and labor respectively per unit of output. And minimum (min) means that the output (Y) equals the smaller of the two ratios. A firm with fixed input proportions is viewed as being a "black box," where inputs are fed in and outputs are spewed out according to a fixed engineering formula.

Some numbers will be helpful here. Suppose the coefficient ratio to be 4 units of labor and 2 units of capital per unit of output ($v = 2$, $b = 4$), and say production is at 4 units of output. We find

$$\frac{\overline{L}}{\overline{K}} = \frac{b(4)}{v(4)} = \frac{4(2)}{2(4)} = \frac{2}{1}$$

and $\overline{L} \cdot v = \overline{K} \cdot b$

$$\overline{L} = \frac{b}{v}(\overline{k}) \tag{2.9}$$

$$= \frac{4}{2} \cdot (8) = 16$$

Thus if the capital stock is given at 8 units then the maximum level of employment that this can give rise to is 16 units of labor (assuming the utilization of all the capital stock). Clearly any labor supplied in excess of 16 units will have a marginal productivity of zero and be unemployed. Thus unemployed labor results of $K/L < v/b$. Similarly

$$\overline{K} = \frac{v}{b}(\overline{L})$$

$$= \frac{2}{4} \cdot (16) = 8 \tag{2.10}$$

A capital stock in excess of 8 units of capital, that is, a condition of $K/L > v/b$, will result in unemployed capital.

For an existing amount of capital and labor to be fully utilized requires that

$$\overline{K}/v=\overline{L}/b$$

or

(2.11)

$$8/2=16/4$$

Thus the 8 units of capital, given the capital coefficient v, permits the production of 4 units of output with the corresponding employment of the available 16 units of labor, and this is the required level of employment given the b value. But in a situation of

$$\overline{K}/v>\overline{L}/b$$

(2.12)

say $10/2>16/4$

then part of an existing capital stock ($\overline{K}=10$) will be excessive. The level of capital would allow the production of 5 units with a corresponding labor requirement of 16, given the labor coefficient b. However, the available labor force accommodates the employment of only 8 units of capital, yielding an output level $Y=4$. We find an excess supply of 2 units of capital with the level of output being determined by the ratio of the labor force to the labor coefficient, that is, by the smaller of the two ratios, so that $Y=\overline{L}/b$. In other words, the level of output will be the result of capital being employed up to the full utilization of the labor force.

Perhaps a more realistic vision would have the employment of labor being limited by the availability of capital. Suppose

$$\overline{K}/v<\overline{L}/b$$

(2.13)

such that $6/2<16/4$

and with similar reasoning we would find an excess labor supply of 4 units, with the limit of output being determined by the smaller ratio ($\overline{K}/v$). This gives an explanation of the min term in the production function in Equation 2.8.

We are considering the matter of the prevailing type of production function on a micro level of an organization operating one or more plants of different vintages. Let us think in terms of a single plant embodying a capital stock of a particular technology that is being utilized to produce the 4 units of output. Based on our input coefficient values, this means, as we said, the employment of 8 units of capital and 16 units of labor. A decision to increase production by 50 percent would require an increase in employment of both capital and labor by 50 percent. We are relating a constant returns-to-scale situation whereby if all inputs are increased by α percent, output increases by α percent as well; by returns to scale we mean the effect on output of an equal proportionate change in all inputs. Perhaps it would be easier to think of the change in all inputs as bringing into a production mode an additional quantity of the capital stock with the associated required labor units. The variable costs would involve the additional labor content plus the material and running costs related to the additional capital usage, where these costs relate to the technology built into the capital stock itself. And these costs would change in proportion to the change in output levels.

Now what does this type of production process mean for our cost-curve construction? Surely that average variable costs, and hence marginal costs, will remain essentially constant over a wide range of production levels up to full capacity operation of the plant. And we may assume that the plant maintains a level of overhead or fixed costs associated with its operation in addition to its direct labor and material costs. Thus its average overhead costs will decline steadily due to the greater volumes of output over which they can be spread, while its average direct costs remain constant. Overall, the total cost per unit will fall continuously over the entire range of production levels that will be undertaken within the particular plant—there is no saucer-shaped average total cost (ATC) curve. We have to keep in mind that in the reality of the modern plant, unit prime or direct costs do not depend on the degree of plant utilization.

But what is the "optimal" production level, or degree of capacity usage, we would expect from this fixed coefficient process (assuming adequate demand conditions), where engineered design of the facility yields the particular technical coefficients of input, and where, at this optimal usage, costs per unit of production are at a minimum? We identify a most efficient or optimal level of output as resulting from operating the plant at a level of "practical" full capacity or what has been referred to as operating at 100 percent of engineer-rated capacity (ERC). These terms refer to a plant that is running at normal working time, but where the projected output per unit of time must take into account the down time for maintenance and repairs particular to the nature of the equipment. This engineer-rated optimum differs from the theoretical full-capacity operation, which is the optimum level of production attainable where the maintenance shutdown does not interfere with the smooth running of production or where the plant was operating in excess of normal time and would not suffer any breakdowns due to excessive use of equipment.

We need to think of a realistic range of production levels that would extend capacity use up to 100 percent of ERC and where marginal costs would remain constant for levels of output to this point. This level of production at 100 percent of practical capacity is one that the plant was indeed designed for. Yet in its operational plans the organization would deliberately want to maintain a reserve capacity so that the relevant production range would not exceed 80 to 90 percent of ERC as the normal optimum capacity use.

Now assume that circumstances bring about a decision to use up this excess capacity, and even to carry production to the theoretical full-capacity level. In this latter condition we will see prime costs per unit begin to increase as overtime payments are realized as well as see more than the usual costs for maintenance and repairs resulting from a speeding up or an excessive use of equipment. These increasing marginal costs can be expected to overcome the ongoing spreading of the overhead, causing increasing total costs per unit, but we stress that, distinct from conventional cost-curve thinking, this does not occur over the normal operating range of the plant, and when it does occur, it is based on entirely different reasoning.

If a plant is operating under conditions of rising costs, management may very well bring up discussions regarding the possibility of constructing additional capacity and about how this investment is to be financed, which in turn could cause a change in its administered price arrangement. Of course, one must expect that the modern corporate organization will have at its disposal many operating plants, perhaps dispersed in different countries, of reasonably similar vintage to the plant realizing high-cost production levels. A possible decision could be to increase capacity use in other plants as one curtails production levels in the high-cost plant as an interim step until additional capacity comes online. This entire image is very different from the neoclassical, conventional entrepreneurial family-type business with a singular producing unit. The reality is that the modern corporate organization has much flexibility in managing its aggregate production plans by reopening idle facilities or by reviving capacity use in existing operating units.

We can now consider the cost-curve diagram reflective of our discussion. Industrial organizations will want to avoid producing at levels of output where the marginal costs (MC) and therefore the unit costs (UC) will be rising. This once again highlights the difference between the traditional (textbook) approach and our discussions, since the rising portion of the MC and UC curves so fundamental to orthodox microeconomics is for all practical purposes irrelevant to the cost analysis of the modern producing plant (see Figure 2.2).

Yet there is an additional characteristic of an economic system that one should take note of. We consider that a particular sector would normally consist of a number of firms. Even if we were to assume that each corporate

Figure 2.2

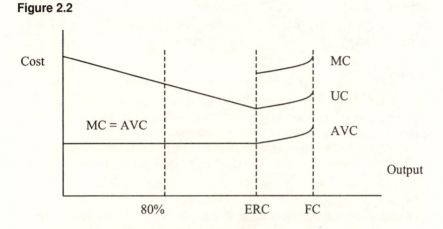

Note: AVC is average variable costs. FC is operations at the full capacity level.

organization has operating plants of similar vintage with nearly alike em-bodied technology, this does not imply that the producing plants of all the firms are of the same technology. Thus it is realistic to suppose that a sector is composed of high-cost as well as low-cost firms, even though all firms have constant marginal costs.

The selling price determined by the firm would be one that covers unit costs and provides an average cash flow or profit (we look at this pricing arrangement in the following chapter). But this unit cost can be taken as being predicated on the level of output needed to supply the market in the absence of unplanned-for surges in demand. Now given such an increase in sector demand, we can reasonably suppose that the resulting increase in out-put will be spread over all the firms. Thus all will realize a decline in unit cost of production as capacity use is enlarged, and this increase in efficiency will mani-fest itself via a higher level of profits rather than in prices. This result stems from what we now understand to be the normal condition of available excess capacity and the price-determining rational of the organization.

Interestingly enough, if we contemplate a fall in overall demand, this will more or less be shared by all the firms, resulting in higher unit costs suffered by all but to different degrees. Here, as well, this shows up in the form of lower profits per unit rather than higher prices. Certainly the least efficient (high-cost) firms will be most severely impacted and may even be forced out entirely should they realize large reductions in production.

What is noticeable is that we do not bring to the fore the notion of price flexibility or responsiveness when the system is confronted with changes in the level of economic activity. Indeed, seeing the real world generally in terms of such a lack of response would have us understand the formation of prices and the role they play within a much different framework than that of the conventional approach. So we turn to this piece of heterodox analysis.

Notes

1. Pierro Sraffa, "The Laws of Return Under Competitive Conditions," *Economic Journal* 36 (1926), reprinted in *Readings in Price Theory*, ed. George Stigler and Kenneth Boulding (London: Allen and Unwin, 1953).

2. T.R. Malthus, *Essay on Population* (1798); reprint, London: J.M. Dent, 1914.

3. Mark Blaugh, *Economic Theory in Retrospect*, 4th ed. (Cambridge, UK: Cambridge University Press, 1985), p. 70.

4. Ibid., p. 77.

5. Ibid., p. 78.

6. Edward West, quoted in Mark Blaugh, *Economic Theory in Retrospect*, p. 77.

7. Joan Robinson, "Rising Supply Price," *Economica* 8 (1941), reprinted in *Readings*, ed. Stigler and Boulding (London: Allen and Unwin, 1953).

8. David Ricardo, *Principle of Political Economy and Taxation*, The Everyman's Library Edition (New York: E.P. Dutton, 1957), p. 36.

9. Ibid., p. 36.

10. Ibid., p. 33.

11. Joan Robinson, "Rising Supply Price," p. 238.

12. Ibid., p. 240.

3

The Formation and
Role of Prices

Introduction

Before we undertake our analysis of a theory of pricing that differs from the
core approach of the standard Principles of Economics, it behooves us to
briefly call attention to some historical economic developments that have
changed the economic landscapes. This will provide the institutional basis in
support of our previous discussion calling for a change in the way we reckon
the firm's cost curves, and will also underpin our nonconventional understanding of pricing policy.

First we must bring to the forefront of our consciousness the nature of the
producing units that in the main comprise the economy. It is not at all helpful
to place them at the end of a line of models beginning with that of pure
competition, and thus end up evaluating them against some ideal or normal
construction. We must appreciate these types of firms as the norm characteristic of this point in time in the evolution of democratic capitalist economies,
and not as a deviation from what should be. And what is representative of
such an economy are large corporate organizational entities that are oliga-
polistic in nature, and more often than not are multinational in scope, and
whose pricing and production decisions flow from one organizational setup
rather than from an individual, and where these decisions have wide ramifi-
cations beyond the firm itself. In our analysis of the behavior of the firm—
whether regarding our previous discussion of the cost curves or the ensuing
looks at the firm's price policy or that of a theory of pricing—we find
ourselves in a framework that puts us a world apart from the accustomed
conventional (neoclassical) environment where we envision many small individually owned enterprises and where it is all too easy to think in terms of
the lone entrepreneur decision maker concerned totally with profit maximization or loss minimization, with these decisions having little if any impact
beyond the enterprise itself.

The modern large oligopolistic firm (referred to as the megacorp) is characterized by the following: The cost-curve construction reflective of approximately constant marginal costs; a particular pricing policy that we simply refer to here as cost-plus pricing; the fact that it operates several plants in the industry to which it belongs and in all likelihood will belong to several industries (and with each plant embodying, in the form of a fixed set of input coefficients, the least-cost technique available at the time of construction—or last modernized); and—what is perhaps most noticeable—the separation of management from ownership. The megacorp must be thought of as an organization rather than an individual; decisions are made through a managerial hierarchy, the uppermost level being the executive group.[1] The key decisions made at this level include the investment projects to be included in the annual budget (and further along we will look at the firm's pricing policy in relation to the financing of these projects), a targeted rate of return on investment, setting the markup on costs price, determining the dividend pay-out policy, and determining which new markets or industries the megacorp shall attempt to enter. And it may be that decisions taken by a management group as the best interest of the organization will not always be the same seen as such by stockholders.

Furthermore, in our quest for a realistic vision we need to jettison the idea that the firm has as its only goal that of profit maximization—a notion that fits fancifully with a small firm in a single line of output run by a manager-owner entrepreneur. But for our "super" multinational firms the most essential objective could very well be to either penetrate a new market or to increase its present share of the market in the industries to which it already belongs. So that if the firm attempts to maximize anything, it is to try and maximize its rate of growth as measured, say, by the growth of sales. This drive to bigness begets power, enabling the organization to wield influence over its suppliers and perhaps to affect the political climate in the area of its operation. There is the observation that technocrats are awarded as much for enhancing the market power of the company as they are for achieving a particular rate of return (if not more so). In order to grow at the highest rate possible, the megacorp is then guided by the following: It attempts to retain its existing market share of its business lines as long as these industries are growing at an acceptable rate, say, equal to that of the overall economy; and it will at times decide to expand into newer more rapidly growing sectors while withdrawing from (or reducing its presence in) those industries where the growth rate of sales is insufficient and the rate of profit has been reduced below the set target rate.

Having glimpsed the nature of the firm that concerns us, we then turn to some developments that have transformed producing entities from a basis of small owner-manager proprietorships linked together by more or less competitive markets, to these "super" oligopolistic organizations. Indeed, it is interesting to see the economic challenges facing these preexisting firms that could only be overcome by their restructuring, which simultaneously transformed generally competitive markets into oligopolistic ones.

One can point to two telling complementary developments that gained momentum in the early years of the twentieth century and have been ongoing. One is the growth of mass markets as the United States was woven together by expanding automobile and rail transport, and the second is the nature of the technology inherent in the later industrial evolution that made it possible to supply these large markets under conditions of declining average costs over a large range of production. We spoke of them in the previous chapter on cost, and here we want to note that the consolidation into oligopoly sectors had a basis in the technological nature of large-scale production. And this "nature" was one of large producing units continuing large amounts of capital with the associated fixed labor input; so that distinct from the earlier time small-market producing firms, what emerged were firms with a very high ratio of fixed-to-total costs.

But this altered cost structure led to a particular difficulty when these large firms confronted those periodic slumps in demand. They could not, one might say, "withdraw" from production by reducing their productive capacity as easily as those earlier small-market firms whose costs, that is, whose capacity, was primarily embodied in the labor input. The condition that one's capacity lies heavily in sunken costs means that one would look to continue production even at prices that did not cover all costs. Within the conventional costs framework the student of the Principles is made aware of what is referred to as the close-down case, where prices are such that losses would be minimized by reducing labor costs to zero. Of course, the assumption (perhaps not even mentioned) is that labor costs are the predominant costs representing the productive capability of the firm, so that, as discussed earlier, reducing them to zero represents minimum acceptable losses. But when capital costs predominate, they obviously would not be reduced to zero when production ceases, and they would come to represent to those "industrialists" of the time unacceptably large losses on their investment. They would not then accept the option of voluntarily stopping production and realizing such losses in that so-called close-down circumstance. As Eichner tells it:

> Here businessmen ran up against the irreversibility of social processes. The heavy fixed or sink costs to which they had been forced to commit themselves by the capital-intensive nature of the new production techniques

made it impossible to respond as merchants had traditionally done to fallen prices by withdrawing from the market. With a high ratio of fixed to total costs, it was best to continue producing even at prices that failed to cover all expenses.[2]

What was needed were agreements among the firms to reduce the burden of these huge sunken costs in the face of slackening demand, and these agreements normally took the form of price maintenance or output restriction arrangements. One thing became quite clear: businessmen could no longer play by the competitive rules of the game of cutting prices whenever demand fell, and, as Eichner said, "found themselves with no choice but to continue to supply the market at prices that failed to cover their long-run average total costs."[3]

However, these agreements to restrict production or maintain prices fell apart almost as quickly as they were formed, as competition between firms emerged in the form of granting special or secret price concessions to customers. Firms found themselves in somewhat of a bind. It was in their common interest to maintain prices for a particular quantity of production and capacity use, but individually each could do better by lowering prices and increasing production, which would be more than compensated for by falling unit costs—providing, of course, that all others did not do the same. So the common interest of having the price level shored up was inexorably undermined by a situation that compelled each individual firm to pursue its own self-interest to the detriment of all.

This type of aggressive competition led some firms into merger arrangements and others into failing. The result was a major consolidation in the manufacturing sectors of the economy that then came to be dominated by a small number of large enterprises, in effect wiping away the relatively competitive environment of the early years of the twentieth century. We are certainly not considering here a structure of a pure competitive nature, but thinking competitiveness along lines of "greater" numbers and/or reduced firm market power with regard, say, to pricing. This was certainly diminished in the early 1900s.

In a sense, what motivated the wave of consolidations was an awareness that the attempt on the part of a particular firm to better one's position, and the response this elicited from others, was in fact expropriating the capital of all. And it bears repeating that the underlying institutional condition was the twin-headed thrust of the transportation revolution creating mass national markets and the new technology that made it possible to supply these markets with long-run falling average costs. One can say that in the burgeoning oligopoly nature of production we find the natural adaption of the producing entity to a changing environment in pursuit of profit-making opportunities and its own survival.

Now having provided a bit of historical background to the emergence of the megacorp organization, let us consider the mechanics of its exercise of power in the realm of a price policy. And in doing so we relate to our previous cost-curve analysis, which is reflective of its operations.

Price Determination and Related Questions

We acknowledge the reality of two categories of rationale for short-term price changes, and by short-term we would accept the conventional understanding of a time frame within which the organization's productive capacity is given. One category refers to price changes determined mainly by costs of production, and the other to those price changes driven essentially by changes in demand. A similar distinction reflective of these designations, respectively, was proposed as between fix-price and flex-price markets. And we want to see the connection, for example, that where the condition of supply (reflective of production costs) is the essential determinant of the selling price, then the price will generally not be responsive to short-term variations in demand and capacity usage. This phenomenon arises out of the related elements of the power of the megacorp to establish and maintain prices, and of the technology inherent in the production process that gives rise to the flat marginal cost curve.

We made the observation in our discussion of costs that the megacorp organization will build into its operations a deliberate degree of excess capacity, thereby providing the capability to rapidly adjust production levels. Increases in demand can be met by a rapid increase in the volume of production, which, when taken with constant marginal costs, cancels the necessity to increase the price level. Indeed, the declining average total cost, as production increases absorb the excess capacity, will increase the profit margin for an existing administered price. Thus for most types of production (reproducible goods produced in those secondary and tertiary sectors that comprise practically all of the economy) increases in supply will be quickly forthcoming so that higher demand levels will be met minimally by inventory depletion with its consequent increase in prices. So as a general observation, the characteristic of this fix-price market is that declines in demand will be absorbed via a decrease in production and employment rather than a decline in prices, and that increases in demand will be met by an increase in production rather than a reduction in inventory levels and higher prices. Of course, prices need not increase because of the production technology that gives rise to the flat marginal cost curve; but should they increase, it will result from a decision process within the organization responding to changes in those very same costs of production.

This should be juxtaposed to those flex-price sectors where production is not of the reproducible-type goods such as the depletion of natural resources, or where production takes a long time (as in agriculture), and/or there is no reserve of capacity. Surges in demand will then be accommodated by a reduction in stocks with a consequent increase in prices.

For this type of output prices are, as a rule, demand determined, and firms can be designated by that Principles of Economics appellation of a price-taker, though we hesitate to add the associated pure competitive description. This is not to be seen as having to do with numbers of sellers, but with a condition outside of the internal cost considerations of the firm. This not only will enable it to raise prices for its existing stocks but will indeed require it to do so as it increases production. This is because the production technology for these kinds of output will yield the conventionally shaped marginal cost curve. Increases in prices of these primary raw material sectors will be transmitted to the price of the secondary finished good sectors through the channel of costs, as the megacorp may adjust its price in response based on its internal policy. An additional observation of the structural change in the economy during the early years of the twentieth century is that with the severe drop in aggregate demand in 1929, leading to the Great Depression that engulfed the economy through most of the 1930s, the large secondary sectors composed of the megacorp firms (e.g., iron and steel, cement, motor vehicles) did not, of course, play by what were heretofore the rules of game, as they chose to maintain prices and absorb the reduced demand in the form of reduced production and employment.

Now we come to the mechanics by which the price is established and a look at the underlying analysis involved—we do want to become acquainted with the overwhelming reality of fix-price markets. And we repeat that what we are doing is heterodox reasoning in that it departs from the conventional Principles of Economics reliance on the equality of marginal cost and marginal revenue determination of the price level.

A pricing policy implies that the firm can determine and maintain a price that reflects a percentage increase or markup over unit costs. One approach is that the organization will mark up its unit variable (prime) costs by a particular percentage, which yields a cash flow per unit of sale sufficient to cover these costs plus the overhead (fixed) costs, and will result in a level of profits per unit. One can think of the price as being composed of an amount obviously equal to prime (direct) costs, plus a percentage increment sufficient to account for the indirect costs, and a further conventional percentage for profit. We can represent this as

$$mu = p - u$$

or

$$m = \frac{p-u}{u} \tag{3.1}$$

where

m = markup
u = unit prime costs
p = determined price

The gross profit portion of the price level is a reflection of the percentage markup on the direct unit costs, and is referred to as the gross profit margin. Suppose we have unit costs of $10 and an existing profit margin of 5 percent; the administered price reflecting this margin will read

$$p = 10 + .05(10) = 10.50 \tag{3.2}$$

The greater the profit share the greater the markup. The markup (m) can be expressed in terms of, or be considered to be a proxy for, the gross margin of profits (θ), since the former can be written as a function of the latter:

$$\theta = \frac{m}{1+m}$$

or

$$m = \frac{\theta}{1-\theta} \tag{3.3}$$

We will now consider the objectives underlying the markup decision, with the reminder that the "representative" firm in the real economy operates in a price-setting regime via its determination of a markup that is the amount by which the price exceeds its average direct costs of production viewed as a percentage of those costs.

One approach is to view the markup as being determined by the short-term goal of profit maximization. In this context the megacorp is not contemplating a change in its overall productive capacity. It expects no change in its costs of production (until the time of its next price review), and we may also add it is not planning to enter new markets. The company will set a price in its own interest and will plan a level of production to equal the anticipated demand at that list price. We want to consider some of the elements that play on the ability of the organization to achieve and sustain a maximum level of average cash flow at the time of the price decision. In terms of the goal it is akin to that proprietorship company of the competitive model. But that is as far as any comparison goes. The price is not set by some anonymous auctioneer or market, and the distinction between the short- and long-term spans has nothing to do with numbers of sellers but with the considerations of that executive group underlying its price determination. And we are calling the goal of profit maximization a short-term price decision. As we will see, there are other concerns such as the enlargement of capacity and/or expanding market share that may impact the price decision differently. If these are overriding factors in arriving at the markup, then the decision is being carried out within the long-term context.

Let us first consider the approach that emphasizes that the firm seeks to gain as much profit as possible at the time of the price decision. Its ability to achieve and sustain such an objective will depend on the degree of its own influence in the industry (what Kalecki refers to as the "degree of monopoly" of the firm's position) and on the extent of price interdependence that it perceives to exist with other firms in its industry, or, more generally, let us say with other firms producing similar products. It is telling to see how Kalecki tries to capture both of these considerations in the same pricing decision equation. His point is the following:

> In fixing the price the firm takes into consideration its average prime costs and prices of other firms producing similar products. The firm must make sure that the price does not become too high in relation to prices of other firms, for this would drastically reduce sales, and that the price does not become to low in relation to its average prime costs, for this would drastically reduce the profit margin. Thus, when the price (p) is determined by the firm in relation to unit prime costs (u), care is taken that the ratio (p) to the weighted average price of all firms ($\bar{p}$) does not become too high.[4]

We have structured the markup equation reflective of the firm's price decision in terms of average prime costs. This assumes that the actual level of those fixed or overhead costs remain stable over what we considered as the relevant range of output, and they do not directly influence the determination of price. Thus the price and production levels that yield the highest gross profit margin will be, as well, most favorable to net profits, when taken with the overheads. But decisions that increase the level of overhead costs in relation to prime costs will reduce profits unless the ratio of prices to unit prime costs are increased through a change in the markup. So overheads here show up as an indirect influence upon price formation; but as we will see, in another approach it becomes a direct component of the pricing equation.

Getting back to those price-setting considerations of interdependence and degree of monopoly, we incorporate them into the following price equation:

$$p = ku + n\bar{p} \tag{3.4}$$

and then restate our markup formula as

$$m = \frac{p-u}{u} = \frac{ku-u+n\bar{p}}{u} \tag{3.5}$$

Or, perhaps more clearly, as

$$m = k - 1 + \frac{n\bar{p}}{u} \tag{3.6}$$

The coefficients k and n relate those considerations that we spoke of in influencing the firm's ability to set and maintain that profit maximizing markup. The k indicates the state of the megacorp's degree of monopoly in the sense of permitting it to determine price and realize profits greater than that of the industry as a whole, let us say in the sense that it feels quite secure in exercising its arbitrary power to mark up unit costs. The value assigned to n is an indication of the limitation to that power, in that when formulating its own price, the organization gives serious consideration to the price response of its rival firms. Our firm may be seen as being sensitive to a possible impact on its market share and is loath to originate a price war in defense of that share.

Certainly a value of $n = 1$ indicates that the firm is severely limited in its price-setting policy, and its markup will be restricted to yielding an average profit flow no greater than that of the industry average. And this is saying that the firm carries no particular power (being either a feature of its size or some particular nature of its product) giving it independent action; in other words it does not possess that "degree of monopoly" allowing it to set a price and earn profits that is out of step with its competitors. This lack of price freedom renders $k = 0$ so that via Equation 3.4 we have the firm markup as

$$m = \frac{p}{u} = \frac{\bar{p}}{u} \tag{3.7}$$

But perhaps more interesting is a vision of the megacorp under a condition of $n = 0$; here the executive decision-making group does not concern itself with the response of other firms, and this is reflective of the possession of a very high degree of monopoly ($k \to \infty$) in setting the markup in pursuit of the objective of highest profits. The extent of an independent pricing policy depends then on the degree to which n is less than one, which is reflective of $k > 1$; these relate overall to that degree of monopoly, or the extent of the capability of an independent price policy, which, within our current discussion, determines the size of the markup.

But let us get a better handle on the firm (let us say on the representative firm) that we are talking about and how it would impact the average price. We could suppose that our megacorp accounts for an overwhelming share of the total sector's output, and on the basis of its size would take the lead to increase the markup. Certainly its action would bear greatly on the weighted average price $(\bar{p})$. The other "follower" firms would in all likelihood adopt a similar pricing policy, not wanting to be out of step with the average price, which, in essence, is not wanting to be out of step with the predominant firm. The smaller firms exist with a relatively large n consideration and will follow, for they do not want to initiate a price rivalry, and/or they may share a similar view of the profit potential of the higher markup. Say the dominant firm's price is not necessarily the average price (in terms of unweighted prices); smaller enterprises, wanting to hold onto their market share, may feel that they are pricing in a fair way if their markup is not too different from that of the leader. If a smaller firm is one that has relatively high costs, then the decline in volume of output and accompanying higher unit costs may overwhelm the higher price level. Though it may be that the sector has in place a price leader/follower characteristic either of being the result of precedent or of a covert agreement. In this tight interdependent circumstance all firms maintain the price set by the dominant megacorp; thus all other firms are in the condition of $n = 1$, $k = 0$, with only the lead firm having the power (the degree of monopoly) to independently set its profit margin (we have a different rationale for Equation 3.7). However, this brings up a cautionary note and a slight digression.

For the nondominant firm Equation 3.7 is akin to the price-taker characteristic of the pure competitive firm. Yet the price-giver is not that anonymous "auctioneer" representing the operations of the market, but the leading firm, which, though it will adjust prices, will do so in the interest of its own strategic goals. As we mentioned previously, and it bears repeating, the constancy of price in the face of demand changes is not an aberration or what the conventional approach would see as a market failure to clear, but an integral part of the workings of a decentralized imperfectly competitive economy. There is an auctioneer, or a price adjustment mechanism, but it is in the decision of the firms (or our lead firm); and it is generally not an adjustment in response to any excess demand or supply. Indeed, the entire notion of an excess demand existing as a result of a "wrong" price and therefore being price cleared is, to say the least, a misunderstanding. What happens is that the megacorp adjusts production levels to the expected demand at the price that it sets, and if demand exceeds expectations (and it is in this sense that demand is "excess") then this excess demand is "cleared" within a short time frame via an increase in the volume of production, that is, an increase in the rate of capacity utilization. It is not that a rigid price is an indication of or a cause for excess demand or supply; it is a reflection of the reality that in general the existence of a particular price is not a manifestation of consumer choice.

Principles of Economics students are inculcated with the view that monopoly is "bad" and that degrees of monopoly inherent in the reality of an imperfect world are bad by degrees, with the less than perfect or bad environment being defined, in the usual respect, as one where consumers are not sovereign in the determination of the price and related production outcomes. Of course they are not, but this does not mean that via their demand behavior they will not have a voice in production outcomes; it is that this voice is not heard through the channel of price-level changes. And to say that this reality is bad or a departure from some desirable norm is to leave the student with a warped attitude. In the next chapter we will reconsider the conventional approach to the theory of household choice and the demand-curve construction.

Now we come back to the cautionary point about the pure competitive look, like Equation 3.7. It is simply that such an interpretation is not workable, for the stability of unit prime costs, which is the basis for setting the markup, is incompatible with pure competition. If the latter prevailed, then the ability to push up the price level in excess of unit prime costs (the MR > MC condition) would drive firms to increase production levels, and do so eventually up to the point of their full capability. We would find a megacorp economy with no excess capacity and higher prices, corresponding to higher levels of capacity utilization that clear the market. And, of course, we do not find what we would find; so Equation 3.7 cannot be read to reflect a competitive market, and the price adjuster in our imperfect megacorp economy is that of the firm itself. This lead firm may or may not be able to adjust prices simultaneously for all firms, and whether prices are indeed altered or not is a matter of a policy decision based on many considerations, and not a natural result of a particular state of the market.

In Figure 3.1 we see the revenue–cost relationship for our representative megacorp, which we can take as the lead firm with a high degree of monopoly. We observe a gross profit margin (m) at price (p_0), resulting from the markup of prime costs or average variable costs (AVC) per unit. There is another version to cost-plus pricing, referred to as full-cost pricing, where

Figure 3.1

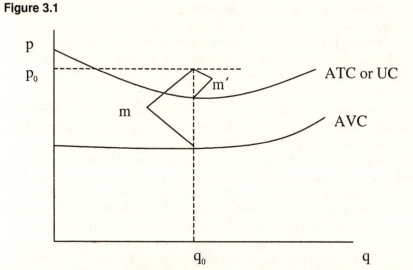

overhead costs are directly incorporated into the unit cost (UC) calculation, and the markup is placed on the full unit cost to yield the desired profit margin, that is, the net profit margin. But the calculation of a maximum rate of return then involves a direct estimation of the rate of utilization as this determines full unit costs. The executive group in making the pricing decision will usually have in mind an estimation of demand that results in what we might call the standard rate of capacity use (we observe such a calculation as m').

However, to suppose that the pursuit of profit maximization is the central objective may be a simplified version of the pricing decision. Recalling our previous discussion, we suggested that what is likely to be the overriding goal for our modern megacorp enterprise is the attainment of an increasing market share and a sense of power or influence in its economic dealings. The organization strives to diminish uncertainty, which may scuttle its plans to increase production levels and/or limit its drive to enlarge its capacity. It would seek to guarantee access to financial capital and to material inputs through "forward contracts," that is, a legal obligation between contracting parties that specifies the future date of delivery and payment at an agreed price. And, as we stated, with the likelihood that our organization maintains productive facilities in many countries, it would look to influence political outcomes in the areas of its operations. A point of view in this regard from Mark Lavoie is:

> Power is the ultimate objective of the firm; power over its environment, whether it be economic, social or political. The firm wants power over its

suppliers of materials, over its customers, over the government, over the kind of technology to be put in use. The firm, whether it be a megacorp or a small family firm would like to have control over future events, its financial requirements, the quality of its labor force, the prices of the industry and the possibility of takeovers.[5]

But for it to be able to exercise this power, to be able to have some influence over events, the organization needs to become big; it needs to become dominant. If it already has achieved this, it is always mindful of maintaining its position. Power, if it is achieved, must be protected, which may mean that the megacorp must not lose any cost advantage that it may possess (maintaining its technological edge). As important, it must maintain its market share, if not look to increase it. That is, the organization must keep at the forefront its capability to grow not only within the market that it is currently selling, but to be looking to enter markets with an even greater potential for expansion. To be able to do this, the megacorp requires another "power" if you will, which is over the availability of the required financial capital. This, to an extent, may be generated through its markup pricing policy. The expected profit resulting from the pricing decisions is not seen as a goal in and of itself, but is calculated as a means to generate the cash flow to support the firm's capital budget. We then propose an alternative view: that it is not the maximization of profits that is the central goal in driving the markup, it is that at the time of the price decision the organization knows the investment required (i.e., its capital budget) to carry out its growth targets, and sets the markup to supply the required amount of internal finance. One does not, in this context, separate the price decision from the investment decision. It is the latter that is the essential driving force, so that at every point of decision, profit margins are adjusted in the light of the finance requirements for investment.

It may be helpful to think of the profit maximization objective as a short-term consideration, and having the markup as unchanged between decision periods and the growth or the capacity enlargement consideration as a longer-term influence on the profit margin. One can suppose that changes in capacity needs and the decision to enter new markets would not be a frequent occurrence in the pricing decision. Given the constancy of unit prime costs with the contractual nature of the money wage and material prices, one could assume that the markup is determined so as to maximize profits given these costs. And in all likelihood one would expect no change in the list price unless there was some unexpected change in unit costs, say due to a change in material prices.

But in the longer term, where the need for investment finance enters into the pricing decision, the markup will exhibit flexibility. Certainly the supply of finance can be drawn from internal and external sources; and in considering a change in the profit margin, the organization has some calculation of the amount of its needs that can be prudently internally generated. In general, one approach is where the markup is set in an effort to fulfill short-run objectives, which, in particular, is to maximize short-run profits; aim the other stresses the links between prices and investment, thus appearing to emphasize the long-term influences.

And we can point to some interplay here. In contemplating its long-term financial needs, the megacorp may opt not to charge a profit maximizing (high) price in any short period if it sees too high a risk of adversely affecting profits in the long term. The organization would need to consider its degree of monopoly, which among other matters involves an estimation of its short-period elasticity of demand. So that a decision as to what markup is optimal in its long-term outlook is really a decision as to what level of profits is maximally sustainable, which is not what is necessarily maximally obtainable within a given short-term decision period.

But let us elaborate a bit more on the factors that could influence the estimation of maximum sustainable profits and thereby affect profit margins and the proportion of the firm's financial requirements to be internally generated—again considering pricing as a decision with long-term investment implications. An important consideration is the reduction in the growth of sales or in the absolute level of sales as estimated by price elasticity of demand at the firm level, that is, the intra-industry elasticity "cost." Another factor, and perhaps more worrisome, is the possible market erosion for the industry as a whole in the face of global competition for virtually every product manufactured. Higher list prices could open the door to new entry; it would be ironic that a higher markup based on the projected need for new capacity may cause the megacorp to find itself with a reduction in capacity utilization and higher total unit costs. Assuming that we have in mind the leading megacorp that sets an industrywide profit margin, then a maintainable level of profits would need to be calculated on the basis of longer term industry elasticity of demand. Of course, the lower the degree of monopoly power the more immediate the concern of demand elasticity at the firm level. But we stress that the more important overall consideration is the possible longer term reduction in the growth of industry sales and disappointment with realized profits.

Another concern, essentially domestic and political, is that the government may look at the higher markup and see the organization as taking advantage of its monopoly power to charge "excessive" prices. A consequence of stretching the profit margin may be triggering government intervention in the form of some restraint on the firm's pricing decision, and perhaps bringing to bear other restrictions to lessen the firm's influence in the industry.

Now these concerns about increasing the profit margin are reckoned in terms of their negative impact on the organization's cash flow and market share. Each possible "happening" would be related to a discount formula that reveals the estimated deterioration of the firm's position over time; thus one is assigning an implicit interest rate (R) to each external response to the markup change, so that in total they tell the organization something about the long-term risk of increasing the list price.

The decision makers would presumably weigh the cost of externally borrowing the needed finance at some interest rate (r) against the cost of raising the funds via a higher markup as given by R. Certainly the smaller the R, the lower the risk of increasing the profit margin, and the organization would like to take the position that its long-term viability is best assured on its being able to finance its investment out of profits. Thus a lower implicit interest rate reflects a greater net result as between the gain of internally generating the cash flow and the longer term loss of doing so. But under reverse conditions the organization would see too great a risk in changing the profit margin, and rely on some form of externally raising its investment funds.

It is then reasonable to assume that in determining the markup, the organization is setting a profit margin that it deems sustainable considering its long-term growth and investment requirements, keeping in mind the ever present concern to maintain—if not increase—its market share. And this understanding is telling us that the price level is not tuned to short-term variations in demand; the firm will normally allow output to deviate from its expected level while maintaining the price in its sustainable position. Certainly we can expect the list price to respond to changes in cost per unit whether we are considering the markup as being placed on full costs (taking into account normal overhead costs) or on unit direct costs or AVC. But given the degree of stability here, based on the constancy of the input coefficients inherent in the production technology and the long-term contractual input prices, we reiterate the fundamental point that once the pricing policy is determined, the margin of profit and the price will not vary with reasonable fluctuations in demand and capacity utilization.

The reader will immediately sense how different this approach is from that of the Principles of Economics. Prices are not driven, on the one hand, by demand shifts. On the other hand, from the cost side, prices need not change to protect profit margins upon increases in production. One can divorce an understanding of the price level or, indeed, a change in the price, from the demand and supply apparatus that, as the Principles instructs one virtually at the very beginning, is the mechanism that establishes the price level in the first place. And students are taught to specify a supply curve that is separate and independent of the demand curve, and to see these schedules as representing separate constituencies that are coordinated via changes in the price level, thereby imbuing the student with the rationing function of prices. But as a result of our analysis of production costs and discussions of a pricing policy, we can appreciate just how wrong this approach is.

Let us again note the obvious. In conventional thinking a measure of scarcity could be obtained from a comparison between the quantity demanded and the quantity supplied at different levels of prices. Yet it is demand that determines supply; a change in demand will bring about a change in output, and it does so independently of the price prevailing in the market for that commodity. For practically all types of production a separate supply curve does not exist; there is no curve linking changes in the amount supplied to associated changes in the price level. To suppose the existence of such a supply curve, students have been taken through stories that are, to say the least, caricatures of reality. An example being that industrial firms are subject to decreasing returns when they expand production. As we observed in chapter 2, the diminishing returns approach to understanding the cost curves of modern firms is a misapplication of an ancient tool.

Necessary Prices and Interdependence

Prices do perform an essential function, but what they do not do, in almost every instance, is to provide an index of scarcity. We must not consider the price level as a market-clearing device that is somehow transmitted to the firm by forces outside of itself. What underlies the message conveyed to students (though seldom stated) is that the firm always knows what the clearing price is; thus its production level is always equal to demand that is forthcoming. Well, as we can now appreciate, it is this kind of imagery that must be put aside.

But we do want to bring up a related point, which is the inconsistent behavior of prices between the micro and macro sections of the Principles course. In the former one emphasizes the market determination of prices and their clearing attribute, while in the latter over- and underproduction is made much of, with reference being made to the nonclearing nature of prices and their ratchet characteristic. And perhaps this illogical position of price flexibility in individual markets but general inflexibility in the aggregate is not even noticed or not understood if it is. However, with our analysis of costs and price setting, we now understand the reality of generally constant prices in individual markets in the light of changes in capacity utilization or—what is essentially the same thing—the level of demand. So what happens at the macro level is reflective of what happens at the micro level; our quest for reality in our understanding of economics must demonstrate consistency at both levels.

Thus actual prices are administered, or fixed, by the megacorp firms and are based on a cost-plus or markup arrangement with the intention of yielding some desired rate of return. To put different words to our point here, we say that the organization in determining the price takes into account the costs of production, assuming a normal rate of capacity use, that is expected to yield a certain cash flow and level of profits. Should demand exceed expectations, the firm then adjusts supply to demand via capacity use at the existing price while it realizes an increase in its profits. Thus actual prices should not be referred to as market prices or market-clearing prices, which is the usual appellation, but should be spoken of as "prices of production" or, to use terms harking back to nineteenth-century classical economics, "natural prices" or "necessary prices."

Again we reiterate the essential point: The function of the price level is to generate a desirable rate of profit for an expected level of production (at operations for a normal level of capacity utilization) taking into account "costs of production," that is, the technical coefficients of production. And, as we now understand, the mechanics of this administered price is that it is set on a cost-plus basis; thus the set price is indeed the necessary price if the firm is to maintain its production level and earn its planned rate of return. Of course, if costs of production increase because their necessary prices have gone up, this will be incorporated into the administered or necessary price of our megacorp without necessarily changing the markup factor.

Prices then arise from a decision-making process within the organization based on an intention to realize a particular rate of return. Should matters work out as expected, the megacorp will continue to reproduce the existing level of production; and if not, it will adjust capacity utilization at the existing administered price. We do understand that prices may change, but not in terms of any direct relationship to changes in demand (we stress the point that demand plays no direct analytical role in price determination). The reader now senses how different this reality is from the Principles' text vision and emphasis on the role of consumer sovereignty and the notion of market-determined prices.

Now the costs of production in consideration of administering the price depend on the technology in place, that is, on the input coefficients and on their prices, which are themselves the necessary or markup prices attached to those inputs. Let us refer to them as "basic goods." By a basic good, we mean a produced good that serves as an input in its own production and which is also an input in the production process of goods produced in all other sectors. If we imagine that the output of all sectors is basic, then we can immediately sense a physical linking up of all sectors, and we must reckon the interdependence of costs. For we cannot calculate the costs of production of, say, sector A without knowing the necessary price of the outputs, say, of sectors B and C, and one cannot know the price of output B without simultaneously knowing the prices of outputs A and C, and so forth. In order to determine the price of a good that is regarded as a means of production, it is necessary to consider the entire system of technical relationships among the various producing sectors. Of course, in actuality not every kind of output utilizes every other output as an input, but what we want to emphasize with this notion of interdependence of production is that relative prices are determined by the conditions of production between outputs and the existence of a level of profits. We want another way to demonstrate our alternative approach, which is that we need to abandon the concept of prices as being determined by supply and demand curves.

As a demonstration let us look at a linkup between two sectors, iron and foodstuffs—placing the latter as a consumer good that we might refer to as the proverbial "corn" that can be used as seed to provide for further production and for consumption purposes. These two sectors comprise the economy and provide the total employment, and this economic system will be depicted, in a first scenario, as a subsistence economy. What we mean is that the output level of each of the two sectors is equal to what is required as necessary input for that sector's output and for the output of the other sectors. In other words, we have a system in which the total amount of each sector's output that goes into the productive processes of the entire economy is the same as what is produced by each sector. A possible set of conditions for such a subsistence economy is as follows:[6]

$$280(t) + 12(t) \text{ iron} \rightarrow 400 \ (t) \text{ corn} \tag{3.8}$$

$$120(t) \text{ corn} + 8(t) \text{ iron} \rightarrow 20 \ (t) \text{ iron}$$

In the corn sector (represented by the first line), 280 tons (t) of corn and 12 tons of iron are required inputs and are used up to produce an output of 400 tons of corn. Similarly in the iron sector (the second line) we set out what is required for the annual production of 20 tons of iron. If we add the amounts of corn and iron used as input in the processes of both sectors, we see that the sums are equal to the amounts that are produced at the end of the production period.

There are some oddities about this sample example. First of all, we do not overtly see any labor input in either production process; it is as if the application of the physical inputs of corn and iron by themselves magically become transformed into output. But what is, of course, hidden is that a proportion of the 280 corn input in that sector is advanced or paid out to purchase the necessary labor at the beginning of production, so that the labor cost gets folded into the material input. Also, we do not see any accounting for profit; here again let us imagine that what remains of the 280, after the payment to labor, is used partly as material input by the corn company (seed) and partly as required payment to the owners of the company (the profit). Again, the profit (if we want to use the term) is reckoned as part of the necessary material input; it is not considered here as a residual.

Now accepting for the moment this way of looking at our production example, at the end of the production period the corn firm will have produced 400 tons of corn, of which 280 will be set aside as necessary input and advances for production in the following period, and the iron firm will have produced 20 tons, of which 8 are similarly set aside. It is clear that the proceeds from the sale of 120 tons of corn must be sufficient to enable the company to purchase 12 tons if it is going to continue to produce the same level of output in the next period. And similarly the iron sector must realize an income from the sale of 12 tons of iron that will enable it to purchase 120 tons of corn if it is to reproduce iron at the existing quantity. In other words, prices of the outputs must be such that 120 tons of corn can be exchanged for 12 tons of iron; thus the necessary price of a ton of iron must be 10 times the necessary price of a ton of corn. And to reiterate, it is a price that allows production to continue at the existing level in both sectors given the technology of the production process, that is, the interrelations among sectors and the requisite advances. So we have a set of unique prices that were determined directly on the basis of the methods of production—demand playing no analytical role.

Starting our example in value terms, we have

$$280p_c + 12p_i = 400p_c$$
$$120p_c + 8p_i = 20p_i$$
$$p_c = \text{price of corn}$$
$$p_i = \text{price of iron}$$

(3.9)

Setting $p_c = 1$, reveals the price of iron:

$$280 + 12p_i = 400$$
$$p_i = 10$$

(3.10)

and

$$280 + 12(10) = 400$$
$$120 + 8(10) = 200$$

(3.11)

Now let us carry our interdependent relationship further along by introducing the reality that profits arise from a surplus created out of the production process; the sector produces a level of output and realizes proceeds from its sale (at an administered price) that exceed costs of production. However, we want to maintain that the reward to labor is still an advance of corn at the beginning of the production period, so that at the end labor receives no part of the surplus output if we think in terms of a physical payment. In terms of a money wage, this tells us that labor will not receive a wage in excess of what is earned in the previous production period by sharing in the generated surplus (profits). In this next vision of our two-sector economy, we will then still keep the wage of labor overtly out of the equations so that it cannot show up as possibly impinging on profits. What will our administered or necessary price look like in this context?

Laying out the system in physical terms we have

$280(t)$ corn $+ 12(t)$ iron $\rightarrow 575(t)$ corn
$120(t)$ corn $+ 8(t)$ iron $\rightarrow 20(t)$ iron

It is the corn sector that now produces a surplus, the value of which accrues to the system in the form of profits. So that in value terms we find that

$$280p_c + 12p_i < 575p_c$$
$$120p_c + 8p_i = 20p_i$$

(3.12)

The necessary price will be such as to cover costs of production that, in this context, is to replace the used-up inputs of the last production period so that output levels can be reproduced, and to allow a level of profits on the value of these inputs. This is our markup price arrangement; and we are simply going to assume that profits will be earned at the same rate in both sectors, though the production process is different in both. Thus

$$(280p_c + 12p_i)(1+r) = 575p_c$$
$$(120p_c + 8p_i)(1+r) = 20p_i$$

(3.13)

Again making the price of a ton of corn equal to 1, we can simultaneously solve for relative prices and the uniform rate of profit. The solutions are

$$p_i = 15$$
$$r = .25$$

(3.14)

Prices that make 1 ton of iron exchangeable for 15 tons of corn will bring about the average rate of profit of 25 percent, and allow for the replacement of inputs to maintain the existing level of production. The natural price is one that maintains a rate of profit under existing technical and demand conditions.

At this point we will close our introductory "technical" analysis of price determination not engaging the more complex case where the wages of labor show up as an explicit cost paid for out of the surplus. What we come away with is that the making of the price is seen to reside in the decision of the organization, as it deals with considerations such as desired rates of return, unexpected changes in unit costs, the need to raise financial capital for additions to capacity in the light of utilization rates, and other matters. What we do not say is that the making of the price resides in the "market." What we now understand is that a change in demand will have no direct effect on the price level, insofar as this reflects what Principles texts herald as the operation of consumer sovereignty. This is not to say that consumer behavior does not impact directly on the economy; of course, the influence is there. But the part it plays, one might say, is in the strategic role of shifting resources (and hence changing capacity utilization) between producing sectors (megacorps) and thereby, perhaps, causing changes in the markup price. The part that it does not play, and which has been the source much misunderstanding, is that of creating a "buying imbalance" that triggers a corresponding price level change to correct the excess or insufficient level of spending. There is, in general, no imbalance–price relationship of this nature. What may exist is a difference between actual and expected demand at the set markup price, which prompts a production or capacity utilization adjustment. To restate a point made earlier: There is, for the most part, no separate or independent supply curve that positively relates production levels and prices. Thus we end this discussion with the overall observation that price is essentially a cost-determined phenomenon, while production is demand-determined. It is through the latter that consumers exercise their role, their sovereignty, in the economy. Their behavior impacts not only the aggregates of employment and production but, importantly, the intra-behavior of these macrophenomena in terms of the types of goods produced and associated levels of employment. In the next chapter we reexamine the conventional approach to understanding consumer behavior and the derivation of the demand curve with the intention of offering a different insight.

Notes

1. See a somewhat detailed discussion in Alfred A. Eichner, *Toward a New Economics* (Armonk, NY: M.E. Sharpe, 1985), pp. 30–32.

2. Ibid., p. 20.

3. Ibid.

4. M. Kalecki, *Theory of Economic Dynamics* (New York: Rinehart, 1954), p. 12.

5. Marc Lavoie, *Foundations of Post-Keynesian Economic Analysis* (Aldershot, UK: Edward Elgar, 1992), pp. 99–100.

6. This approach is based on that very pathbreaking book by Pierro Sraffa, *Production Commodities by Means of Commodities* (Cambridge, UK: Cambridge University Press, 1960). An explication of this involved work can be found in Ronald G. Meek, "Mr. Sraffa's Rehabilitation of Classical Economics," *Scottish Journal of Political Economy* (1961): 119–136. Also, Stanley Bober, *Modern Macroeconomics: A Post-Keynesian Perspective*, chap. 4 (London: Croom Helm, 1988).

4

Consumer Behavior and Demand

The Conventional Reasoning

Introduction

The law of demand, which speaks of the inverse relationship between the quantity demanded of a good and its price, is conventionally explained by the complementary approach, including the presence of an income, or the substitution approach, relating to a price change, and those factors that relate changes in the consumer's optimum purchase of a commodity in response to a price change based on a utility calculation and its effect on consumer preferences. The latter can be greatly understood by reference to the utility-maximizing rule; and there is an additional explanation based on the modern theory of indifference analysis (seeing utility measurement as an ordinal magnitude) but which in all likelihood is not covered in an introductory economics course.

The usual explication is to analyze consumer behavior as congealed in an aggregate or market-demand curve, being a summation of individual demand curves where each consumer's preference is based on that individual's utility calculation. The aggregate curve can then be said to be that of the representative consumer. Now we will argue that our representative consumer pictured as making buying decisions based on isolatedly calculating utility is a very limiting if not simply an unreal vision of consumer motivation and behavior. If one proposes (as is commonly done) that the relation between consumption and utility maximization at the different prices that the consumer faces is a reflection of rational behavior, then we will counter by proposing that in the real world our representative consumer is acting irrationally—that we cannot understand consumer choice behavior and hence construct a demand curve by relying on the conventional notion of what is meant by the consumer's rationality calculation.

There are certainly two issues that make for a degree of skepticism about the conventional approach to household choice. One is that the price level is to be seen as far from the essential factor in influencing behavior, and, relatedly, that individual consumer choice (our representative consumer) should not be understood in terms of the actions of an isolated agent with a built-in or innate utility calculation stemming from one's isolated experience. Our consumer does not appear on the buying scene separated from an understanding of the lifestyle and consumption patterns of other consumers or of a particular social class in society that the individual has come to associate with. This knowledge plays the essential role in determining the demand pattern for different consumer goods. We would propose that it is the role played by social convention, and therefore that of acquired tastes, that is central in forming the household's normal consumption pattern. Consumer preferences are to be understood as being the result of learned social behavior. As Pasinetti tells us, this means that "each consumer is increasingly bound to carry out a preliminary process of discovering his preferences before he (or she) can express them."[1] The acquisition of knowledge, the process of learning, is the more basic or realistic foundation underpinning consumer choice than is the conventional notion of rational behavior, which pictures the individual making consumption choices with the intention of maximizing satisfaction on the basis of an innate set of utility assignments that one attributes to different quantities of various goods. But what if these assignments exercised by an individual are essentially molded by society rather than stemming from instinctive behavior? This will necessitate a rethinking of the very basis of consumer choice and the derivation of the demand curve.

We will set out the conventional model of individual consumer choice in its cardinal (measurable) utility form so as to have before us the picture to be compared with heterodox reasoning on this matter. As well, we will take a look at the more advanced orthodox explanation of the law of demand based on indifference curves and budget lines. This latter approach poses a less stringent requirement for our consumer; here one has simply to specify whether different combinations of goods yield greater or lesser amounts of utility (satisfaction) without having to calculate how much more or less. Thus if one can state a preference for a basket of one combination of goods over that of another—but not by how much—then the individual's utility measurement is said to be of an ordinal magnitude. Quite possibly in Principles classes the students will not have been taken through the analysis supporting the law of demand, being told that the demand curve rests on common sense and is always observable. However, by the end of this chapter we may very well conclude that the common sense explanation resting on conventional utility-choice mechanics is very much uncommon, and cannot adequately explain consumer behavior in the real economic world.

Consumer Choice—Marginal Utility Analysis

There are four basic elements in the solution to a choice problem. The first is to delineate the set from which choices can be made. For the consumption decision the set (in the orthodox form) is comprised of goods that are known, that is, types of goods that the consumer is familiar with and has been purchasing all along. The second is to set out the existing constraints on the choice decision. Here the emphasis is usually on the limitation of the consumer's money income and credit capability (confronting the array of price tags). The third element is to provide a criterion for ranking the results of the possible consumption decisions, with the standard explanation being a subjective arrived-at level of utility or satisfaction. And a fourth element is to determine the behavior rule that guides the choice—again convention tells us that it is to achieve the highest level of utility for a given level of choice expenditure.

Within this framework let us now consider the usual explanation underpinning that law of demand. First, we have the notion that utility is considered a numerical indicator of a person's preference such that a higher level of utility indicates a greater preference. It is also evident that this measure is wholly subjective or, let us say, mythical, for it cannot be identified outside of the consumer's internal psychological judgment. But in wanting to quantify consumer behavior, economists took this unit of subjective satisfaction and proposed that the consumer does indeed assign a numerical value to the satisfaction that is obtained from the consumption of different quantities of goods. For economists who put forth the marginal utility (MU) derivation of the demand curve, this utility number was a concept as real as the commodities themselves.

Our consumer obtains utility (satisfaction) from the possession of a commodity. After some quantity of the commodity has been purchased, the total utility received from the possession of that good will reach a maximum; then the utility obtained from additional quantities will literally fall. But the movement to this saturation point is presumed to be subject to a particular mental construct that says that initially increasing one's consumption (or possession) of a good will yield increasingly greater additions of satisfaction; however, after some level of possession the consumer will sooner or later encounter diminishing marginal utility at all quantities of goods that he is willing to purchase. In the more precise terms of Quirk, let us read the law of diminishing marginal utility as: "After sufficient units of a commodity have been consumed each additional unit consumed provides less additional utility to the consumer."[2] Figure 4.1 shows us the total utility (TU) levels associated with different quantities of the good purchased. The section of the curve AB reflects increasing marginal utility (total utility increasing at an increasing

Figure 4.1

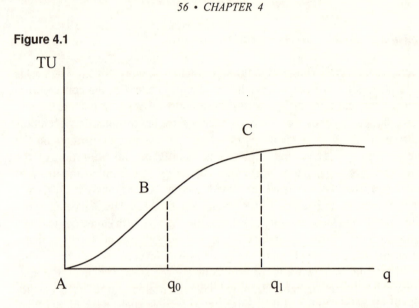

rate), with the section BC representing the concept of diminishing marginal utility (total utility increasing at a decreasing rate).

To see this in operation, we have our representative consumer in a "constrained" condition of limited income, existing product prices (that will not be influenced by the individual's expenditures), and a given utility function constructed out of the individual's psychological relationship to the goods that can be purchased. Then from the array of goods our consumer will choose an expenditure pattern that will maximize total utility—a decision of rational behavior.

Now suppose our consumer to be making purchase decisions as between goods A and B, and the consumer thought process relates to the utility received from a dollar's worth of expenditure on either good. But with prices of the goods (p_A and p_B) given, a dollar's worth represents quantities of A and B, we set out the analysis in Table 4.1 in terms of dollar worth so it would be easier to translate dollar worth into quantities by presuming $p_A = p_B = 1$. Let us give our consumer an income constraint of $13 and see how the attempt is made to maximize utility (we presume that all of income is spent).

Certainly the consumer in making the initial purchase will acquire a unit of good A, since a unit of A yields greater utility than would the acquisition of a unit of B—50 units of satisfaction as opposed to 40. If we make believe that the individual engages in a dollar's worth of buying per day, we now have a day-two spending decision—prices remaining unchanged between day intervals, so a second dollar of spending would also be spent on A, as its utility exceeds that from a first unit of B. As far as the third dollar, the

Table 4.1

	Good A			Good B	
Dollar worth	TU	MU	Dollar worth	TU	MU
1	50		1	40	
2	95	45	2	76	36
3	135	40	3	108	32
4	170	35	4	136	28
5	200	30	5	160	24
6	225	25	6	180	20
7	232	20	7	196	16
8	247	15	8	208	12
9	257	10	9	216	8
10	262	5	10	220	4

consumer (as guided by that "internal" utility function) is now indifferent as between a third unit of A and a first unit of B. Assume that the third dollar is spent on purchasing a unit of B. A fourth decision will have the consumer purchasing a third unit of A, yielding an additional 40 units of satisfaction rather than a second of B, which is calculated to increase one's utility by only 36 units. Continuing on with this line of reasoning, we should find our consumer spending all income and having acquired a combined basket worth of A and B. With this combination, total utility has been maximized; the consumer has behaved rationally to bring about an optimum outcome given the constraints that determine the objective environment. And the maximizing rule is that the consumer's money income should be allocated in a manner such that the marginal utility per dollar's worth of the purchase of any one good is equal to the marginal utility per dollar's worth of the purchase of each of the other goods. The last dollar spent on different goods at a point in time will yield equal amounts of utility from each of the purchases. So

$$\frac{\text{MU of } A}{\text{dollar's worth of } A} = \frac{\text{MU of } B}{\text{dollar's worth of } B} \tag{4.1}$$

Suppose that after having come to this point, the consumer returns and alters the buying pattern, opting to purchase a seventh unit of B, necessitating the giving up of the seventh unit of A. This would be considered a wrong balancing of one's margin, or a nonmaximizing decision, as the individual would be sacrificing 20 units of satisfaction to acquire an additional 16 units.

In our example the quantities purchased are given in dollar's worth rather than physical units, but with similar priced goods, similar incremental expenditures on either good mean the same physical amounts purchased. But let us look at the maximizing problem a little differently. We have an income constraint, say it is now $16; two goods ($A$ and B), but with different price tags of $p_A = \$2$ and $p_B = \$1$; and presume the marginal utility calculations as in Table 4.2, where quantities are directly in physical units. The behavior rule here is in terms of marginal utility per unit price, for the same dollar's worth of spending on either good will not yield the same physical acquisition of goods. The worthwhileness of a purchase will not only depend on the additional utility one gains from purchasing an additional unit, but also on the cost of purchasing the unit (which in essence is the amount of the alternative good that the consumer must give up). Money itself has a marginal utility in terms of the different quantities of the available goods that it can purchase.

We see an example from Table 4.2. Suppose our consumer is indifferent between a third unit of A and a first of B reckoned along physical units and related marginal utilities. Now, on Table 4.2, the cost of a unit of A is $2, while that of B is $1; given this difference, why would the choice be the first of B in the face of identical marginal utilities? The obvious answer is that the utility gain per dollar spent is higher for B, being $30 = \$30/\$1.00$, than per A, where it is $15 = \$30/\$2$ (one is undergoing a smaller level of expenditure to acquire the same addition to one's satisfaction). One could see the matter this way: For a $2 expenditure one could purchase a first and a second unit of B, whose combined utility comes to 56 units, compared to realizing an additional 30 units of utility for the same expenditure should one have purchased the third unit of A. So, as a general rule, whenever one faces differently priced goods, marginal utility must be put on a per dollar expenditure basis in order to make comparable the additional utility derived. Our consumer will then end up buying 5 units of A and 6 of B. That is,

$$\frac{MU_A}{p_A} = \frac{MU_B}{p_B} \quad \text{or} \quad \frac{20}{2} = \frac{10}{1} \tag{4.2}$$

And since the income constraint can be represented by

$$Ap_A + Bp_B = Y \text{ (income)} \tag{4.3}$$

we have $5 \times 2 + 6 \times 1 = \$16$ with utility being maximized.

But the expenditure of one's entire income does not, of course, necessarily imply that one is doing so rationally. For example, say our consumer opts to spend $1 less on A to purchase one more unit of B, which means

Table 4.2

	Good A			Good B	
Quantity	MU	MU/p	Quantity	MU	MU/p
0			0		
1	40	20	1	30	30
2	35	17.5	2	26	26
3	30	15	3	22	22
4	25	12.5	4	18	18
5	20	10	5	14	14
6	15	7.5	6	10	10
7	10	5	7	6	6
8	5	2.5	8	2	2

that he gives up one-half of the fifth unit of A. Certainly on the basis of the utility calculation per se this is a wrong move; the consumer loses 10 units of utility to gain 6 units from acquiring a seventh unit of B—he has a net loss of 4 units of utility. And one will be purchasing less of the good whose marginal utility per dollar spent is higher. We find that

$$\frac{22.5}{2} > \frac{6}{1} \tag{4.4}$$

and

$$4.5 \times 2 + 7 \times 1 = \$16$$

There are other circumstances around which we can solve for a maximizing outcome. Suppose from the purchase combination of 5 of A and 6 of B, the consumer approaches these goods at a further time with a higher income level of $17. How would the extra dollar be spent? Based on our "behavior table" (Table 4.2) the additional income would go to good A, since it purchases one-half of a sixth unit, adding 7.5 units of satisfaction as compared to an increment of 6 utility units should our consumer act irrationally and decide to purchase one more of B. And what if income were to fall to $14? Then the decision is what to cut back and minimize the loss in total utility. The move would be to reduce the buying of A by 1 unit and relinquish 20 units of utility, rather than take the reduction in the form of reducing the buying of B by 2 units and thereby realizing a 24-unit reduction in utility. In the condition of reduced buying capability, one's position is maximized by minimizing the total utility loss from a smaller aggregate purchase.

We now want to go from the notion of utility calculation to the derivation of an individual's demand curve for a particular good. But before doing so, it is worthwhile to again bring into focus the underlying image. We find our representative consumer facing a familiar array of goods (commodities that one is accustomed to purchasing), with a given level of income and with what is usually described as an existing state of tastes or preferences for a particular good as compared to other products. What this latter condition is really saying is that there will be no sudden change in one's utility calculation resulting from outside influences; that the calculation stems from the consumer's own familiarity or experience, which forms the basis of the calculation regarding the worthwhileness of acquiring an additional unit of the product. A usual additional stipulation is that the price of closely related goods remains unchanged, again not wanting the utility calculation per dollar spent for the good in question to be altered by what happens to other goods. In discussions about the demand curve it may not be appreciated just how restrictive the *ceteris paribus* (other things being equal) conditions are as one explains the rational for what happens when the price of the good in question A changes.

We begin with the consumer in the maximizing (equilibrium) position

$$\frac{MU_{A1}}{p_{A1}} = \frac{MU_{B1}}{p_{B2}} \tag{4.5}$$

with the consumption of particular quantities of A and B. Now suppose that the price of A increases to p_{A2}. Should the response be to purchase the same quantity of A, then clearly the MU per dollar spent will fall. With income given, more dollars must now be spent on good A, necessitating that less of B must be consumed (again all income is to be spent on these two goods). But this decision will leave the consumer with a higher MU calculation for an additional quantity of B, calculating that

$$\frac{MU_{A1}}{p_{A2}} = \frac{MU_{B1}}{p_{B1}} \tag{4.6}$$

The consumer is no longer following a consumption pattern that is in line with the utility maximizing rule, and some reallocation of expenditures will follow.

Facing this decline in the marginal utility per dollar spent on A, less of A will be purchased, implying that more of B will be purchased (even though its price is unchanged), which, for the given prices of p_{A2} and p_{B1} will increase the marginal utility of A and lower it for B, thereby altering the utility per dollar spent ratios. This re-arrangement continues until the consumer is content with his purchase combination, that is, until satisfaction is maximized:

$$\frac{MU_{A2}}{p_{A2}} = \frac{MU_{B1}}{p_{B1}} \tag{4.7}$$

We see that what is happening above gives rise to a demand curve, as seen in Figure 4.2. We have derived two points on the consumer's demand curve per good A, and to derive more points we simply repeat the same rationale with other prices of A.

Once the demand curve is derived, whether one goes through this analysis or simply states its existence, there are other demand relationships that are part of the Principles course and that we would like to touch upon in relation to our measurable marginal utility approach. In particular, the reduced purchases of commodity A whose price has increased can be understood in terms of two effects: income and substitution.

From the latter view (substitution) the consumer is now substituting the relatively lower priced good B for the higher priced one. And from the former rationale (income) the higher price of A carries with it a fall in the consumer's real income. To purchase the same quantity of A requires a greater expenditure and hence a reduction in the quantity of B purchased, or in whatever combination is decided upon, the higher price of A has caused our consumer's real income to decrease, so that smaller amounts of A and B can be obtained with the same amount of nominal or money income. In general, a fall in real income results in a poorer individual with the tendency to purchase less of all goods.

Now an interesting question is which tendency will dominate, and in the Principles analysis, the emphasis is very much on the price substitutability impact. The real income effect, when it is talked about in relation to a change in demand or shift of the demand curve, is in terms of change in money income, allowing a greater amount of purchases of an existing or familiar combination of goods. It is normally not reckoned as a consequence of lower prices for the same money income. It is, though, understandable that the substitution effect would be emphasized since the consumer is presumed to purchase many different goods, so that there will not ordinarily be a large increase in real income should the price of a single good fall.

Yet the price emphasis puts the analysis within a very static (i.e., constrained) framework and to a great degree an unrealistic one. We know from

Figure 4.2

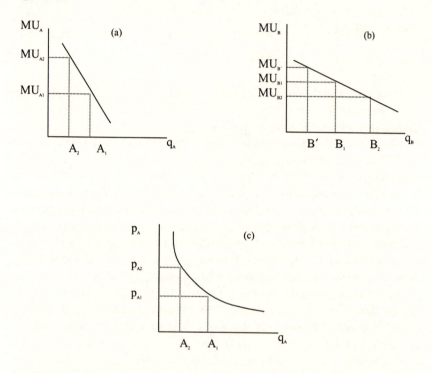

our discussion on pricing that consumer behavior, in practically all instances, is simply not the driving force behind price changes. We need to understand consumer expenditures as the means to constantly alter patterns of demand with the accompanying changes in capacity utilization that may or may not alter the markup price. The increase in demand that is normally reckoned in terms of an increase in money income and/or a change in tastes, opens to the consumer a whole array of new goods as one acquires different preferences in line with higher income levels. The orthodox emphasis on price-driven substitutability between familiar goods or even being able to increase one's purchases of such "baskets" misses much of what is involved in consumer behavior, especially when seen within a context of the secular growth of real income. This context will have our consumer acquire new needs and rearrange priorities (or desirability) among goods that one has been purchasing. The entire psychological (utility) relationship to a combination of familiar goods becomes unhinged (if indeed it was ever established) with factors such as social pressure and "what is new" being dominant in determining the pattern of demand. We return to these points when we begin to consider the heterodox approach to household demand; but now we want to set out the alternative ("modern") indifference-curve view of a utility-based understanding of consumer demand. We will then have before us the overall conventional treatment of this issue.

Consumer Choice—Indifference-Curve Analysis

It is suggested that this indifference (ordinal ranking) explanation is preferred because we can derive all of the conclusions of the marginal utility explanation without needing to assume the law of diminishing marginal utility, where preferences are reflected in a measurable (cardinal) utility framework that gives indication of consumer satisfaction; and the indifference explanation does so with regard to particular goods. We would reiterate that in the "older" marginalist theory, total utility to the consumer is viewed as the sum of the utilities derived from each good consumed, with the essential assertion that we are dealing with a cardinal measure, where it is possible to compare relative magnitudes of utility differences. In rejecting these restrictive assumptions, the indifference-curve analysis has been considered a superior explanation of the derivation of the demand curve. As one economist put it, "In a clash between opposing theories, the rules of the scientific game specify that, of two theories giving rise to the same conclusions, the superior theory is the one that involves the less restrictive assumptions. In scientific theory, this principle is known as Occam's razor (eliminate all unnecessary assumptions)."[3] And this has led to replacing the law of diminishing marginal utility as the explanatory tool in the theory of consumer behavior.

The alternative indifference explanation assumes the consumer to simply possess preferences over "baskets" of commodities involving combinations of different commodities, and to be able to assign a hierarchical (ordinal) ranking to these baskets; or the consumer can be said to be indifferent as between particular combinations of goods. The consumer is then making decisions involving sets of goods, so that the emphasis is on the substitution among goods in terms of preferences and in arriving at an optimum purchase of all goods. This differs from our previous analysis, where the consumer arrives at that optimum purchase of those, say, A and B commodities via the marginal calculating procedure of choosing commodity by commodity. Furthermore, one's preferences or rankings are exercised without reference to a calculated utility or satisfaction gain; in other words, the ranking is not seen as an indication of an "amount" of psychological satisfaction that one would come to possess over that of an alternative combination of goods. This brings us again to that notion of an ordinal ranking. We do assume that the consumer is consistently ranking bundles of goods in order of preference, and what we have been calling "utility" is the variable whose relative magnitude indicates the degree and direction of preference. But in an ordinal ranking the belief is that the relative magnitudes cannot be or are not calculated, that is, that utility cannot be assigned a cardinal measure (say like length or temperature). Certainly the consumer can state a preference direction for a combination of *A* and *B* over some other combination, because the former impacts a greater amount of utility than the latter, but what is not being stated is by how much one bundle is preferred to another. The utility notion in the derivation of the demand curve is then not abandoned in the indifference theory; different combinations of goods do impact different amounts of utility or satisfaction, and this calculation determines how baskets should be ranked—it reveals only the preference directions.

Consider Figure 4.3. Points *a*, *b*, *c*, and *d* represent different combinations or baskets of commodities *A* and *B*; and under the "laws of preference" we can say that the consumer is capable of ranking all four baskets and that such a preference ordering or ordinal ranking is assumed to be internally consistent. For example, as between bundles *c* and *b* the consumer can express a preference, and in doing so can make one (and only one) of the following statements: *b* is preferred to *c*, *c* is preferred to *b*, or *b* is indifferent to *c*. In the last situation the consumer is content to allow someone else to make the choice or the choice is made in some random blind fashion. Again we bear in mind that in this ordinal construction the numerical utility values assigned to *b* and *c* are irrelevant, except that should *b* have been preferred to *c* then the former would have been assigned a higher utility number. The internal consistency of the ranking appears in the sense that if *a* is preferred to *b* and *b* is preferred to *d*, then it is required that *a* be preferred to *d*. Furthermore, if *b* is indifferent to *c* and *c* is indifferent to *d*, then consistency requires that *b* be indifferent to *d*. It is fair to say that these laws of preferences are simply rules of rational behavior by the consumer, and the whole idea of utility is simply a reflection of the ordering of preferences.

Looking again at Figure 4.3 we note the four points, *a*, *b*, *c*, and *d*. Accepting the human trait that a larger bundle of goods is preferred to a smaller one, it is point *a* that is most preferred, point *d* that is least preferred, with *b* and *c* as intermediate—we can refer to them as points of indifference. The latter two points represent combinations of goods that are equally satisfying; indeed one can presume a set of such indifferent combinations, all imparting the same level of total utility. These bundle points would lie on an indifference curve such as *U* in Figure 4.3. And we reiterate that such a curve represents baskets or bundles of goods that the consumer treats as equivalent in terms of preference.

The state of consumer preference rankings can be set out on a field that maps an ordered set of indifference curves, each of which connects com-

Figure 4.3

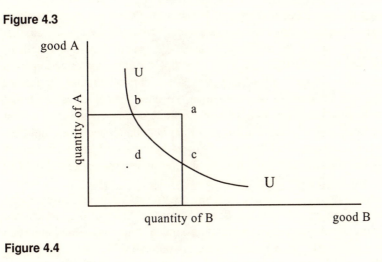

Figure 4.4

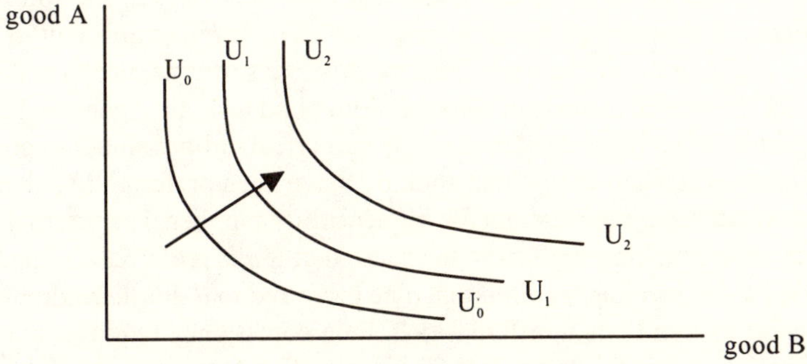

modity baskets that are indifferent to one another. This concept is seen in Figure 4.4. The ordered nature of the map reveals the direction of preference; each combination on U_1 is preferred to that on U_0, and baskets on U_2 are preferred to any basket on U_1. Now we need to clearly understand the characteristics of such a map, which will explicitly bring out the postulates underlying the conventional approach.

First of all, the curves slope downward to the right. This represents what is considered as the usual or normal case where, for the consumer's preference to remain unchanged between two combinations, one good must be given up and be compensated for by the addition of the other. But let us take a look at an abnormal situation where the indifference curve is horizontal. As shown in Figure 4.5, the individual is indifferent between baskets that contain the same amount of A but one contains a greater amount of B than the other. For such a condition we need to suppose that the consumer has reached

Figure 4.5

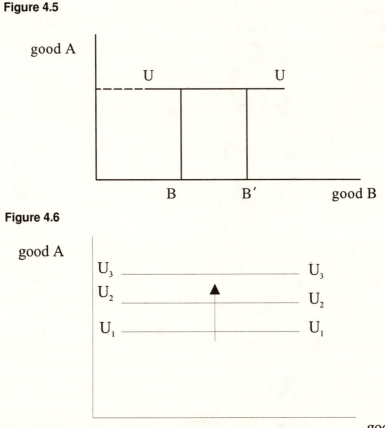

Figure 4.6

a state of satiation in the desire for good *A*, which does not, however, cause one to demand any less of it. Having more or less *B* does not require any compensations; indeed the individual's total utility is dependent on having acquired a particular level of good *A*. One could ask whether it is really abnormal to suppose that there may be some goods that one would not want to acquire more of in terms of a trade-off for other goods. We will come back to this to discuss the forces that could produce satiation.

One can shape an indifference map based on this unusual case as in Figure 4.6. The consumer is indifferent as to whether one has more or less of *B*; the aggregate level of utility is determined as a matter of the quantity of *A*. A commodity such as *B*, in this context, is at times referred to as a "neuter" since it neither adds nor detracts from utility.

But keeping with the standard approach, indifference curves not only slope downward to the right, but are also generally assumed convex to the point of

Figure 4.7

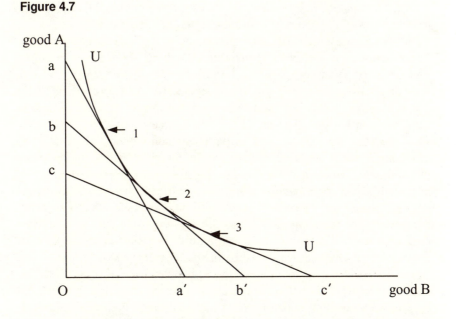

origin. We suppose that the degree of trade-off (or compensation along an indifference curve to maintain uniform satisfaction) is, in one respect, not uniform. While the consumer may be indifferent as between aggregate combinations of goods, there is no indifference as to how these aggregates are constituted. This brings up the notion of the marginal rate of substitution, which is defined as the amount of the *A* good that the consumer is willing to give up to acquire one additional unit of *B* and maintain the same level of satisfaction. Technically speaking, it is the slope of the indifference curve at a point that measures this marginal rate of substitution (MRS) because it shows the rate at that point (i.e., at the margin) at which the consumer will trade off one good for another. And we are at this point thinking of this compensation not in money terms, but in terms of units of one good for a unit of another good.

Figure 4.7 shows us what is occurring to this MRS along an indifference curve. The numerical value of the MRS can be determined by constructing a tangent to the indifference curve at that point. At point 1 the MRS is *−Oa/Oa′*; moving along the curve to point 2 we find a smaller MRS of *−Ob/Ob′* and so on. The tangents become flatter, and since the negative of the slope is the MRS, this indicates that the MRS diminishes as the individual acquires more of the *B* good.[4] What we are observing is the assumption of a law of diminishing marginal rate of substitution; more formally, "as the number of a commodity available to a consumer increases, the marginal rate of substitution of any other commodity for the commodity decreases."[5]

Yet this diminishing MRS is explainable on the basis of the same psychological rationale as is that for the cardinalist's diminishing marginal utility. The notion of declining substitution implies that one is reckoning the gain from an additional unit of B relative to the loss (in utility?) of parting with a unit of good A; and it is hard to believe that this kind of psychological calculation is not going on along an indifference curve. Should the consumer say that this basket with its particular combination of goods is as satisfying as some other basket with a different combination, it must mean that some calculation is at work, some mental process is involved, resulting in these unequal combinations of goods conferring equal amounts of satisfaction. I think that if we say that the ordinal approach poses a less stringent requirement for the consumer, we are simply supposing that the consumer does not overtly declare how much extra utility is gained or loss—but what is not said out loud may very well be internally calculated.

But be this as it may, let us go on to another characteristic of our indifference map, which is that of nonintersection of the curves. For if this were not so, we would, within the confines of traditional reasoning, observe a violation of those laws of preference or of rational behavior that we spoke of before; indeed, we would find that smaller quantities of goods would raise the level of satisfaction or that the same basket of goods would represent more than one level of satisfaction. We see what happens in Figure 4.8. Point a is a basket of goods on U_2 while that of c falls on U_1; thus the combination of goods described by c is preferable to that of a. But if baskets a and b are on the same U_2 curve, the consumer regards them as equivalent, and c and b are on the same U_1 curve the consumer treats them also equivalent; hence if a is equal to b and b is equal to c then this implies that the consumer regards a as equivalent to c, and that lesser quantities of A and B convey the same higher utility level as higher quantities. Yet this conclusion violates the principle that if c is preferred to a as it lies on a higher indifference curve. Since the assumption of the intersection of curves leads to this contradiction, the assumption must then be false.

The logic here seems clear enough. The individual is assumed to be able to rank all particular combinations of goods; a basket will convey either greater utility than some other one, or lesser utility, but the same combination cannot yield different levels of satisfaction at two points in time. Later we will want to question this seemingly illogical possibility.

Now that we have the foundation of this indifference–ordinal ranking approach, we move to arrive at the rule for utility maximization based on this, and then to derive the consumer demand curve. The construction of this

Figure 4.8

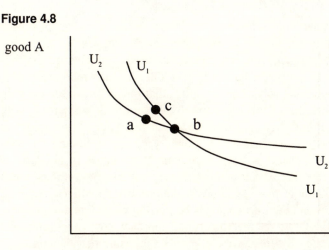

curve is merely a reflection of a consumer adjusting to an external event so as to maintain one's maximizing position, and the event is a change in the price of the good for which we want to derive the curve. Before the event occurs, the consumer has chosen a particular basket of goods that presumably mirrors the highest attainable level of utility, and the basic elements of this choice are obviously the individual's set of preferences as represented by an indifference map, the prices of the individual goods composing the basket, and the individual's money income. Before setting out the solution to this choice problem, it should be reiterated and emphasized that the solution here (and in the context of the marginal utility cardinal analysis as well) is based on what we can consider as "independence of preferences." Each consumer is concerned only with one's own consumption pattern; the utility or satisfaction derived from a particular purchase is attributable to the individual's own experience. In the solution to the choice problem the consumer is presumed not to be concerned or indeed influenced by what is going on elsewhere, that is, by the choices being made by other consumers. In Principles texts the student is shown an aggregate or market demand curve adjacent to individual demand curves and is told that points on the aggregate curve are found by summing horizontally the individual demand curves. The individual consumers behind the individual curves are considered to be in their own box, making their own decisions, and not at all being influenced by the behavior of the others. Certainly in an understanding of consumer demand this is one perception that we will want to question. But let us get back to the mainstream indifference model.

The consumer faces a host of combinations of goods that one may want to

Figure 4.9

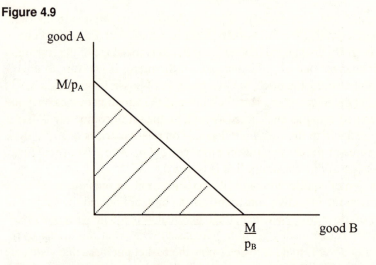

purchase and that we see as being reflected in the indifference map. What one would like to do is but one half the problem. The other and more telling half is what the consumer can do at the time of making the choice. The essence of the consumption choice is to narrow down the choices from all possible choices to those that are economically attainable. And what is attainable is dependent on the constraints facing the consumer—those being the prices of the goods and one's available income. Figure 4.9 illustrates such a budget constraint.

We set out the constraint as

$$Ap_A + Bp_B \leq M \tag{4.8}$$

telling us that the amount of spending on goods A and B cannot exceed the consumer's available income. The expenditure of less than one's full income generates the purchase of sets of baskets that lie within the dotted-lines area under the constraint line. The use of one's total available income (given prices) places one on the budget constraint line. This line evidences what is attainable (what the consumer can do), for it shows the set of combinations of A and B that can be purchased given the "objective" data of prices and income. The placement of the budget line is determined by finding the intercepts on the A and B axes. For example, if the consumer were to spend all income on good B, then the amount purchased would be given by M/p_B; likewise, if we were to set $B = 0$, we determine the good A budget intercept as M/p_A.

There are some features of this line that we should mention. An increase in money income with unchanged prices clearly shifts the line to the right, enlarging the available set of baskets. Clearly a change in the price of one of the goods, given unchanged money income, alters the slope of the constraint line as it changes one of the intercepts. Furthermore, if we were to double income and also double price, the available set of possible purchases would not change; the intercepts remain the same and the equation of the constraint line, of course, remains unchanged as well. So the set of commodity A and B baskets available to the consumer depends on relative prices (p_B/p_A) and on the real value or purchasing power of money $(M/p_B, M/p_A)$. We should note that the slope of our constraint line is $(-p_A/p_B)$.[6]

A position of equilibrium or utility maximization for our consumer is one where, given the objective constraints of the budget line and the subjective mapping of the indifference map, the individual will equate what one is able to do (those economically feasible purchases) with what one wants to do. And what one wants to do is to determine the basket purchase that yields the highest level of utility, that is, a purchase that places the consumer on the highest indifference curve within the set of attainable purchases. We are simply saying that when facing this choice of baskets composed of A and B goods, an individual will act in a manner consistent with one's preferences, which means choosing the basket that lies on the highest attainable indifference curve. This optimal solution is seen in Figure 4.10. Point H, which represents the optional solution, is one where the budget constraint is tangent to the indifference curve; it is a point where the marginal rate of substitution between the two goods is equal to the ratio of their prices. But let us again put this into clear focus. The MRS is the absolute value of the slope of the highest attainable indifference curve; it tells us the number of units of B that must be obtained (in terms of personal preference) to offset the giving up of a unit of A, while the curve of the ratio of the two prices conveys the number of units of B that can indeed be purchased as a result of not purchasing a unit of A. And at point H the consumer adjusts the consumption of A and B in such a way that the substitutability of B for A in terms of personal preference is equal to the substitutability between them in terms of market exchange.

Thus:

$$\frac{p_A}{p_B} = \text{MRS} = \frac{2}{1} \qquad\qquad (4.9)$$

Another way to appreciate point H as the optimum outcome is to see that from such a point it would not be possible to reallocate expenditures be-

Figure 4.10

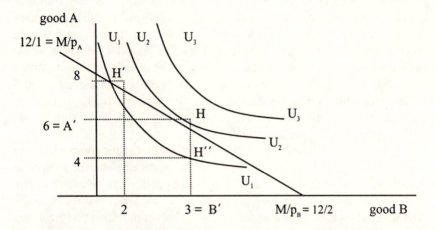

tween the goods so as to end up with a market basket on a higher indifference curve. Yet that is precisely what can be done if we start from a point such as H' where the slope of the indifference curve is greater than that of the budget line, that is,

$$\text{MRS} > \frac{p_A}{p_B} \tag{4.10}$$

Consider that at H', with an existing basket purchase in hand, the consumer would, on the basis subjective preference, be willing to forego the purchase of 4 units of A in order to acquire one additional unit of B; that is, a move on indifference curve U_1 from H' to H''. However, the consumer finds that one need only reduce the purchase of good A by two units to enable the acquisition of one more of B. Thus the consumer will surely alter his purchases to acquire the additional unit of B, for one ends up with foregoing a smaller amount of good A than what was internally (psychologically) deemed necessary. And the consumer comes away with a basket comprised of an increased amount of B and a smaller reduction in A than was thought required; the market basket at point H contains a greater combination of both goods than he psychological basket at point H''. The consumer's satisfaction has thereby increased, and in the move from H' to H one is thrust onto a higher indifference curve.

The equivalence of the marginal utility and indifference curve optional solutions is quite clear. Recalling the former approach, the solution is one where

$$\frac{MU_A}{p_A} = \frac{MU_B}{p_B}$$

(4.11)

And from the indifference curve approach the solution is

$$MRS_{AB} = \frac{p_A}{p_B}$$

(4.12)

In the move along the curve we find

$$\Delta A \times MU_A = \Delta B \times MU_B$$

so $$\frac{\Delta A}{\Delta B} = \frac{MU_B}{MU_A} = MRS_{AB}$$

(4.13)

then $$\frac{MU_B}{MU_A} = \frac{p_B}{p_A}$$

(4.14)

Implying $$\frac{MU_B}{p_B} = \frac{MU_A}{p_A}$$

(4.15)

We are now ready to confront the consumer with a change in relative prices and construct the demand curve. Suppose that the price of good B increases to \$3 per unit while the price of good A is unchanged at \$1 and money income remains at \$12. What will happen to that optimal market basket of goods?

The ratio of M/p_B will fall, and the budget constraint line will rotate about M/p_A toward smaller quantities of good B. As we see in Figure 4.11, the amount of good A that could be purchased if all income is spent on it is unchanged, but if all income is spent on B, only 4 units of B can be purchased. The original basket can no longer be purchased; thus the expenditure of available income will now command a smaller combination of A and B goods, conveying a smaller total level of satisfaction, and thereby positioning the consumer on a lower indifference curve. Because the higher price of B has changed the market ratio from $1B = 2A$ to $1B = 3A$, the consumer would be expected to adopt what we might say is a defensive strategy and

Figure 4.11

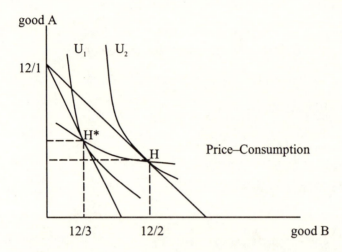

begin substituting the now more attractive relatively inexpensive good *A* for good *B*. Now if this were all that happened, as a general observation, we could say that an increase in the price of *B* would lower the quantity demanded of *B* and increase that of *A*. Well, what we can say with more certainty is that in practically all circumstances, as convention would have it, the quantity level added of *B* would go down; and since we are deriving a demand curve for the good whose price has changed, we connect points *H* and *H** to form a price–consumption line that describes the consumer's demand curve for *B* in relation to the price of *B*. Putting this more formally: The price–consumption curve describes the way in which the optional market basket of goods changes when the price of *B* is changed and everything else is held constant. A price–consumption curve describes the way the market basket shifts with changes in the relative price of the commodities.

But this is not all that may be happening as a result of this price change; there is a second effect that we need to consider. The increase in the price level and the resulting steeper constraint curve tells us that any attainable purchase will now involve a smaller combination of goods. It is as if the individual were to have a reduced level of money income with prices remaining unchanged. But what has happened here is that the money amount of income has not changed, but because good *B* is more expensive, the consumer has become poorer in terms of purchasing power. Now if the consumer does indeed translate the higher price as an "as if" reduction in money income, then the shift to a lower indifference curve and lower realized level of satisfaction may very well reflect a basket containing a smaller amount of both goods.

Figure 4.12

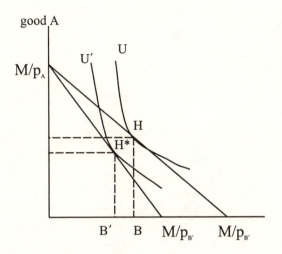

We need to reckon with two effects on the quantities demanded of *A* and *B* due to the higher price of *B*. One is the force operating in the direction of substituting *A* for *B* as the latter becomes relatively more expensive, and the other is the force operating to cause a decline in the purchase of both goods through a decline in the purchasing power of money income. The first force, shown in Figure 4.11, is considered the substitution effect, and the second is labeled the income effect. Figure 4.12 shows this income effect. In the move from *H* to *H** in Figure 4.11, both goods are portrayed as normal goods, that is, goods whose consumption is positively associated with changes in real income. But in the usual introductory explanation, the "normal" or "inferior" goods are ones whose consumption is positively or negatively associated with changes in money income when relative prices are held constant.

Now let us portray the workings of both effects on a single diagram to make matters more vivid, and we see the results as no change in money income. Thereafter we will portray the effect of income changes when prices are held constant and money income is changing. All of these become important for us, and we come back to them in later discussions as we come to grips with consumer behavior within the realistic context of an expanding economy over time (though not necessarily at a constant rate). In such a context, where we abandon the Principles text's usual static framework, both money income and prices are increasing, and these changes result in rising levels of real income.

In Figure 4.13 we see the income and substitution effects when good *B*, whose price is changing, is a normal good. Similar to what occurred in

Figure 4.13

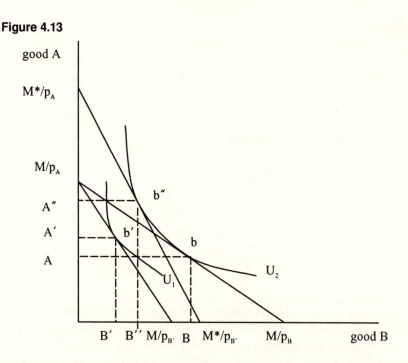

Figure 4.12, the increase in the price of *B* rotates the budget-constraint line, with the consumer maximizing satisfaction at *b'* on the lower indifference curve (of course, real purchasing power has fallen, which we would presume would reduce one's happiness). But if we would want to maintain the consumer's real income so that a position is maintained on U_2 and the basket purchased does not convey less happiness in the face of a price increase, the consumer would need to receive a money income subsidy. Now what this does is to shift the budget line upward, based on the higher level of income M^* and confronting the same set of prices p_A, p_B. We are asking the consumer to designate what would be purchased with relative prices changing but with the same real income. And the response is a move from *b'* to *b"*, resulting in a basket yielding the same level of satisfaction as the purchase that occurred before the increase in the price of good *B*. But note that the basket purchase at *b"* results in a degree of substitution for the higher priced commodity. Clearly we would consider the change in these basket combinations as the substitution effect—being driven only by the change in relative prices.

Now consider that the subsidy is removed, so that the change in prices translates into a poorer consumer in terms of reduced purchasing power; we would then find a move from *b"* to *b'* resulting in a basket purchase with smaller quantities of both goods. Clearly this would be the same type of

Figure 4.14

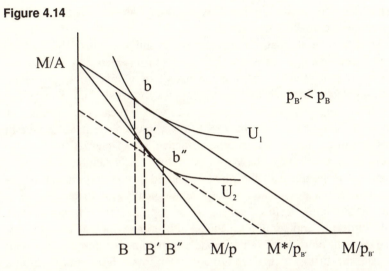

response we would expect if the consumer were to suffer a reduction in money income with no change in relative prices. Thus the move from b'' to b' would be considered the income effect—being driven by changes in real income. If we had begun our discussion with the b' basket purchase and increased the level of money income for existing prices $p_{A'}$ and $p_{B'}$, we would move from b' to b'' and trace an income–consumption curve as a result of parallel shifts of the budget constraint line.

Getting back to Figure 4.13, we note the reinforcing results of the income and substitution effects—both working to reduce the purchase of B. This gives support to the demand-curve construction and to the emphasis placed in introductory economics courses on understanding that consumer behavior is essentially being determined by a response to price changes. Of course, this takes for granted that, overwhelmingly, goods are normal and price flexibility is the ruling characteristic of the economy (this latter assumption was very much put into doubt as one recalls our analysis of pricing in chapter 3).

Yet a change in relative prices can lead to results that differ from what we would expect along the demand curve. What if we had a good that is considered inferior, and sufficiently lesser, so that the income effect is large enough to cancel the substitution effect. We see this in Figure 4.14 and presume that prices are decreasing simply to present a different view. As we note the move from b' to b'' is overcome by the move from b' to b; the real income effect of the price decline in terms of making the consumer feel wealthier is more influential on the quantity of B purchased than the decline in its price. What we have here is what is known as the Giffen case, where the increase in real income now provides the affordability to purchase more of good A; indeed, the consumer is replacing the good whose price has decreased, giving an upward sloping demand curve for B.

We want to reiterate that in the construction and analysis of the demand curve in Principles courses, there is usually the unstated assumption that there is no income effect so that it is the change in relative prices that is the determining factor in the quantity demanded of a good. And if one does bring in an income influence, it is usually from, so to speak, the "outside" as a result of a change in money income. But we now realize that a change in purchasing power, that is, that income influence, is as "internal" to the buying decision as is the set of relative prices; and we really cannot, as a general rule, say that if we decrease the price of a good the observed quantity demanded will increase. The internally (psychologically) calculated change in real income stemming from a change in relative prices may shift goods from normal to inferior; and certainly if the level of money income changes, we would expect the consumer to change one's accustomed preferences between goods. And this brings up the need to understand what is at work to make a good inferior or to drive the consumer to a position of satiation with regard to the "want" of a good. Is this explainable in terms of what we referred to as independence of preferences, or is there a degree of interdependence among consumers, or a societal effect, that impacts the preference ranking of any single consumer? We hint thus at further discussions when we say that this will lead to a consideration of the difference between needs and wants.

Some Critical Observations

We now have in place the essence of the mainstream theory of consumer choice; and with this as background we open some critical discussion of this seemly very logical construction, which will bring us back to some observations made in the introductory remarks to this chapter. Furthermore, in response to our remarks, we will look briefly at yet another approach to consumer demand that emphasizes the choices themselves, that is, the observed behavior of the consumer, rather than focusing on the structure of a consumer's preference and how that influences one's choices.

Is there an adequate theoretical justification or, let us say, is there in general an observable behavior pattern that would support a utilitarian explanation of consumer behavior and a theory of demand? Before tackling this, it would be helpful to briefly examine some history of economic thought. This concept of utility in economics goes back at least as far as Jeremy Bentham (1748–1832), an English economist-philosopher and social reformer who developed a utilitarian school of ethics. This school represented a comprehensive system of social science embodying a uniform method of analyses that gave rise to a long list of social legislation and reform. "Bentham had proposed birth control, and Benthamites later advocated a long list of reforms, including adult suffrage (including women), prison reform, free speech and free press, civil service, and legalization of unions."[7] And the operational bases of these reforms, of this system of social ethics, is that of a society able to construct a quantitative measurement of the pleasures and pains associated with its various actions as felt by individual citizens. The governing body of the society is called upon to be aware of the "felicific calculus" (the utility calculation) associated with its actions; as a result, laws could be created that would result in the greatest amount of happiness for the greatest number of people.

All individuals were presumed to equally calculate the "pleasure" and "pain" associated with a particular social action; thus by the assumption that all individuals count equally and that a given action is associated with identical experiences by everyone, Bentham applied the idea of a felicific calculus to society as a whole. Schumpeter explains this notion as follows:

> The pleasure and pain of each individual are assumed to be measurable quantities capable of being added into a quantity called individual happiness (felicita). These individual happinesses are again summed up into a social total, all being weighed equally—everyone to count for one, nobody to count for more than one. Finally that social total is substituted for, or identified with the common good or welfare of society.[8]

So what we have is a guide for social policy. Bentham's point was that conduct (essentially government action) should be judged morally according to its effects on the balance of human happiness. Utilitarianism was then the philosophical basis for a group of people that looked to make social reform an exact science by designing laws that would lead to the greatest good for the greatest number (the normative principle of utilitarianism).

Now whether this notion of measurability of utility (in this context being the difference between the societal pleasure enjoyed and pain suffered) is actually viable may be greatly beside the essential principle of action that utilitarians were promulgating. That positive aggregate gain (utility) should be the guide for public policy; as decision makers try to gauge this, they should keep in mind that the citizenry are be treated equally as the displeasure that may be voiced by a particular group should not overweigh the gain that would accrue to the many. Perhaps we might all agree that it is very laudable that the guide for public policy should be one that results in the greatest good for most people.

We have gone through this brief digression because we have, I would say, another example of an idea or a principle taken out of its original context, where it may have served admirably, to be used as an explanatory mechanism within a different context for a different purpose. And we will propose (similar to one discussion of the law of diminishing returns) that such a transformed use of the utilitarian principle was a misapplication. It is one thing to draw up a list of proposals with the intention of, say, addressing society's ills, and attempting to calculate (or judge) which constituencies gain increased happiness (utility) and which may realize some pain (suffer a cost and disutility). It is quite another to relate such a calculation (an aggregate rationale) to an individual consumer who is thereby seen as balancing small changes in utility and disutility as one alters the combination of purchases in order to arrive at a balanced point of maximization of happiness. The individual is conceived of as behaving in a thoughtful, deliberate manner and weighing the pros and cons of each item when facing an array of goods; however, this psychological basis for the utilitarian approach to consumer behavior has been criticized for quite some time and, indeed, is now seen to be hopelessly discredited. Consider the following critique:

> Marginal-utility theory has usually been formulated in hedonistic terms. . . . Hedonism is hopelessly discredited by modern psychology. . . . Deliberations, reasoned choice, plays but a minor part in the affairs of men. Habit, not calculation, governs the greater part of all our acts. . . . The habits of thought which count for most in shaping choice are not the result of provision (i.e., the act or power of foreseeing), but are of the nature of conventions uncritically accepted by virtue of membership in a particular group. . . . Calculation is difficult work. It is much easier to act on a suggestion than to weigh alternatives.[9]

This is clearly an attack on the notion of the individual engaging in deliberate utility calculations based on one's own mental processes and emotional states, that is, what we referred to previously as independence of preferences. James Duesenberry comments on existing theory as follows:

> For a long time it has been assumed that tastes can be regarded as part of the data in economics. This does not mean that tastes are constant in time. But it does mean that the parameters of the preference system are substantially independent of the other economic variables. In particular it usually implies that the preferences of each individual are independent of the actual purchases of others. Otherwise it would be impossible to obtain aggregate demand curves by the simple addition of individual demands.[10]

Duesenberry goes further to point out that: "There is little observational warrant for the independence of different individual preferences, yet it is implicit in most economic theory. The assumption has slipped in during the course of the historical development of consumer behavior theory."[11]

This slippage has, of course, taken hold to form the utility scaffolding to construct the demand curve that in turn is used to formulate a theory of value. Recall our discussion of pricing in the previous chapter, where we showed that save for very particular circumstances the model of a market-determined (demand–supply) price is illusionary. But this too has slipped in to become part of economic lore; however, by putting our understanding of consumer behavior and demand on a realistic footing, we add a supportive pillar to our analyses of pricing.

Orthodoxy's response to this psychological critique of consumer behavior has been, in one regard, to claim that no attempt is made to explain the bases of choice; that the concern is only with the fact of choice. But this leaves one with the observation that consumers purchase a good because they want it, which in and of itself explains nothing, for what we would like to know is the basis for their wanting it. If we say that it is a utility calculation, then the question is how is utility to be interpreted or, better yet, gauged? If it is to be interpreted hedonistically (i.e., the pleasure–pain calculation) then such a interpretation of behavior has been generally taken to be invalid. If it is not this, then the conventional utility explanation of demand is in reality no explanation—all we are left with is an observation of human conduct. The following from Landieth and Colander is very much to the point:

> First we assume that consumers are free to purchase any goods consistent with their incomes and preferences. Since we have no way of determining preferences except as revealed by actual purchases, it follows that what is actually purchased must be preferred. And since the consumer is assumed to be maximizing, purchase equals maximizing. Such a tautological theory tells us nothing about consumer behavior.[12]

The tautological reasoning (the same notion repeated in different words, implying a circularity of reasoning) is seen by the approach that consumer behavior is explained in terms of preferences that are in turn defined only by behavior. Or by reasoning that a consumer acts in accordance to what is deemed best, and what is deemed best is evident by how the consumer acts. But what are the forces that determine what is deemed best? It would then appear that the conventional utility-based models that we elaborated upon have presented us with a rationale for a theory of demand but have left us without a theory of consumer behavior—it tells us nothing about the motivational forces behind the behavior upon which the demand curve is supposedly based.

Students should not come away from their assignments on consumer demand-curve constructions feeling that—nor should professors imply that as a result of those supposed complementary utility explanations—there is in hand an understanding of household consumer behavior. But this is generally just what is promulgated; and I would think all the more so after having gone through the so-often referred to as advanced or modern indifference curve—the budget line approach. So it is worthwhile to offer some remarks about that model, which the reader, at this point in the chapter, is quite familiar with.

As we pointed out in our earlier analysis, the indifference map approach to consumer behavior does not really solve the problem of the earlier cardinal measurement—diminishing marginal utility framework. It does contain many of the inherent assumptions of the cardinal measurement. But it should also be emphasized that the concept of an indifference curve is purely a mental construction; there is no way of empirically measuring indifference or constructing indifference curves. A utility map has been assumed to exist as a natural phenomenon that need not be proven; it is an introspective notion, and the simple reference to introspection cannot be accepted as a scientific demonstration of existence. This is akin to the reasoning that introspection cannot be accepted as a scientific demonstration of the existence of a soul, as much as we would like to believe in its presence. As Roncoglia succinctly puts it:

> The contention that "utility maps" are simply imaginary constructions is confirmed by the fact that they cannot be identified independently of the observations of the behavior of the consumer. But if the utility maps are derived from consumer demands it would be circular reasoning to then state that the demand curve can be derived from the utility maps.[13]

We would therefore conclude that a utility-based theory of consumer behavior, that is, of consumption, is incapable of serving as an explanation of the formation of prices because it is incapable of providing an adequate basis for the demand function. The whole utilitarian theory of demand, be it in its cardinal or indifference-curve guise, must be put into the category of pseudoexplanation. This important point does bear repeating: If conventional analyses cannot provide an effective explanation of the quantity demanded in a market, then as a consequence it (i.e., the neoclassical model) cannot provide a satisfactory realistic basis for a theory of pricing. We arrived at a similar conclusion in our chapter on pricing, though by a different route; the reader recalls that we eschewed the supply-and-demand mechanics for a whole different apparatus.

A Behavioral Approach

In response to this critique there has emerged a revision of demand theory that abandons any assumptions about the psychological motivation inherent in the utility approach, and deduces the downward sloping demand curve by observing the choices or preferences revealed by consumer behavior itself. We look at this revealed preference theory of demand to see whether anything is really gained by focusing on the choices themselves as against focusing on the implications of utility maximization for the choices involved.

What appears very positive about this revealed approach is that it can construct a rationale for the law of demand without needing to talk about marginal rates of substitution, indifference curves, or higher or lower levels of satisfaction or well-offness. The theory allows the construction of a curve similar in configuration and akin to an indifference curve without any reference to levels of utility. The major developer of revealed preference theory was Paul Samuelson, who set out to demonstrate what he considered as the fundamental theorem in consumption theory. He observed that most goods are normal goods and therefore exhibit positive income elasticity (this is an empirically testable proposition); accepting this, and making use of hypothetical changes in the level of money income, he showed the operation of the theorem that: "If demand increases when income increases, then the quantity demanded will decrease when price increases. In other words, goods that have positive income elasticity will necessarily have negative price elasticity."[14] Since most goods are taken as normal goods as a result of the individual consumer's own buying experience (at least in orthodox thinking), then what we have is a theorem that generally supports or gives corroboration for the law of demand and a downward sloping demand curve.

The theory makes some easily acceptable assumptions about consumer behavior in support of a rather simple idea. And that is that one will decide to purchase a particular basket because one has preference for it over some other collection or because it is less expensive when compared to another collection. Say that one purchases basket *a* rather than *b*; one could, it would seem, say that there is a revealed preference for *a*. Yet not necessarily so; it may be that *b* is preferred but that one simply cannot afford to make that purchase. We obviously need some price information, that is, a budget constraint line, before making statements about preferences from observed behavior.

And this would have us look at a familiar diagram, Figure 4.15 with a budget line pp and points representing baskets of *A* and *B* goods. We note that basket *a* is equally as expensive as *b*; now should one choose *a*, then it is revealed preferred to *b* and to all other combinations on pp. Basket *c* is revealed inferior to *a* for it represents a less expensive combination; that it is not

Figure 4.15

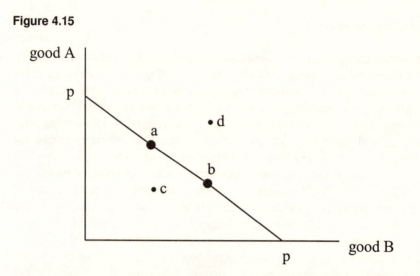

purchased reveals the assumption that the desire is to obtain the maximum combination of goods. Clearly, a point like *d* being more expensive and containing a greater combination of goods cannot be revealed inferior to point *a*.

With these considerations in mind we can look at those assumptions supporting this revealed preference approach. The first is that the consumer should behave consistently and reveal what is called the transitivity property in the ranking of preferences. In the latter sense we mean that if one prefers *a* to *b* and *b* to *c*, then it is required that the individual also reveal a preference of *a* to *c*. Furthermore, if *a* is revealed indifferent to *b* and *b* is indifferent to *c*, then transivity requires *a* to be indifferent to *c*. Additionally, to emphasize the consistency property, it is assumed that if there are a number of circumstances in which the same set of choices are available and if the consumer selects one and rejects the others in any one circumstance, he will do the same for all other circumstances. We would not find *a* preferred to *b* and then find *b* revealed preferred to *a*. The second and third assumptions are that the consumer will choose only one collection of goods in a budget constraint; in other words, given any particular basket of goods, there exists a budget constraint line that will induce its purchase. And third, the consumer will always prefer more to less.

Now let us see how all this works out. Figure 4.16 presents a consumer's budget distribution between a normal good *B* on the horizontal axis and money income (*M*) on the vertical axis. Assume an initial circumstance represented by the constraint Mp_1. The individual can possess any combination of money and good *B* on the constraint, ranging from purchasing no *B* at the

Figure 4.16

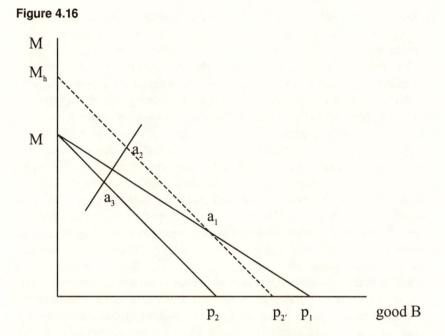

intercept with the vertical axis to spending all income on *B* at the intercept with the horizontal axis purchasing OP_1 of good *B*. Again, we bear in mind that the individual is free to choose any combination on or within the budget constraint; and in the freedom to select whichever one most prefers, let us suppose that combination a_1 is chosen. And using the language of this discussion, we see the combination a_1 as being revealed preferred to all others; given the consistency assumption we must suppose that the consumer will choose the combination a_1 if given the same set of choices in the future.

Now suppose the price of good *B* increases from p_1 to p_2, confronting the consumer with a new budget constraint Mp_2. How does the consumer respond? Where will the individual go on the new budget constraint? In order to understand the move, let us presume a hypothetical increase in money income large enough to compensate for the higher price, thereby enabling the purchase of the original basket a_1 at the new price p_2. This leads to our hypothetical constraint line $M_h p'_2$. Notice that our hypothetical line has a slope governed by the higher price p_2 and that it intersects the original purchase quantity at a.

Now all points on our hypothetical budget line are, of course, attainable, but some of these options were not attainable in the original circumstance of Mp_1. We are referring to the segment $M_h a_1$, representing options that lie outside and to the right of the original constraint. But as we can see, there are options along the $M_h p_{2'}$ constraint that were available to the consumer in the original circumstance; those lying on the segment $a_1 p_{2'}$ to the left and within the Mp_1 area.

The original condition evidenced a revealed preference for a_1, thereby revealing a rejection for those combinations along segment $a_1 p_{2'}$, which were at that time concurrently available. Now maintaining our consistency assumption, we can certainly presume that our consumer will again reject those options in the new circumstance of budget line $M_h p_2$ since he is still able to obtain the preferred combination a_1. As we said, if in a particular circumstance, from an existing set of choices, the consumer reveals a preference for one and rejects all others, then in a different circumstance, for the same set of choices available, the individual will reveal the same preference as in the original circumstance. Then in reaction to the hypothetical budget constraint the individual will continue consuming a_1—what was rejected in the original constraint is rejected now. But it is also possible for the consumer to reveal a preference or a point along the segment $M_h a_1$ since these options were not available in the original circumstance and hence could not have been rejected.

Let us then presume that in response to this hypothetical constraint the consumer moves to a combination such as a_2. Again let us set the framework. In an original circumstance of constraint Mp_1 the consumer reveals a preference for a_1. Now the circumstance has changed, with the price level increasing to p_2 and a constraint of Mp_2 confronting the consumer with a different set of options. But now we suppose a change in money income just enough to compensate for the real-income effect of the price change, and we will see what choice is revealed in the face of this higher price but with no change in real income. The setting of the hypothetical budget constraint is to determine what the consumer would do when faced with a higher price of B that does not carry any income effect. And we note a revealed substitution effect in altering basket purchases from a_1 to a_2.

But now let us engage the income effect by removing the hypothetical increase in money income at the higher price p_2, thrusting the consumer back onto the constraint Mp_2. What will the consumer do in the face of a reduction in money income that carries a reduction in real income? Assuming that B is a normal good, that is, having positive income elasticity, the reduction in income will result in a reduction in the quantity of B purchased along an income consumption line moving from a_2 to a_3. Of course, combination a_3 must of necessity be to the left and below a_2 because it is on constraint Mp_2, which lies parallel and below $M_h p_{2'}$. And because the quantity of B at a_3 is less than at a_2, which in turn is less than at a_1, then the quantity of B at a_3 is less than that at a_1.

Hence, if B is a normal good, an increase in the price must result in a decrease in its quantity demanded. We have extracted the law of demand from the observation of behavior without having to fall back on a utilitarian and/or indifference analysis. This approach does give us definite pieces of information about consumer preferences from the observation of behavior. By comparing preferences revealed under different conditions, that is, in different price–income situations, a preference scale can be drawn up leading to the demand-curve construction. And this without any assumptions about psychological motivation and the concept of utility; it is a theory that is completely behavioristic in nature. We have, one could say, a theory of demand without a theory of consumer behavior.

Where Convention Leaves Us

Be this as it may, the question is whether revealed preference moves us any further along in providing an explanation of the quantity demanded. One would, it would seem, need to respond negatively. To reiterate a point: What we have is a description of observations but no theory explaining these observations, other than to say that if preferences remain unchanged over the period of observation, and if the individual is rational (evidences consistency), then the choices that are observed will correspond to one's preferences. As Roncoglia puts the matter:

> [J]ettisoning the original utilitarian grounding of demand theory the theory of revealed preference shows even more clearly the tautological character of the objective theory of demand. In fact, a demand function constructed by observing the market behavior of consumers cannot furnish a criterion for the explanation of such behavior. In other words, this is not a theory, but a simple description of the state of the world.[15]

All that has happened is that we have substituted "preferences" for the term "utility map" to identify the cause of the behavior of the consumer. But if utility and preferences are causes that are deduced from consumer demand behavior, then how can they serve to explain that very behavior? There is a clear circularity of reasoning here, as the cause is deduced from the very phenomenon (demand) that it is supposed to explain. There are other critiques that can be brought to bear on the revealed preference approach, though we do not consider them. We should mention, however, a conclusion by Hicks, who after some analysis states, "I feel obliged to conclude from this that there is in practice no direct test of the preference hypothesis."[16]

It is then important for the student and professor to see that we have no theoretical foundation for the demand-curve message, and as such we may have a descriptive curve from which we can draw no explanatory power. But this has to cause us to question the emphasis that has been placed on the ordering of goods in response to price variations. Perhaps we should relegate to minor importance the prevailing notion that to understand consumer behavior is, in general, to see consumers ordering goods on the basis of price-driven substitutability, that is, on changes in relative prices. Well, we propose exactly that, and we will therefore need to look elsewhere for a realistic explanation of consumer demand.

A Different Reasoning

What is needed is an objective standard by which one can establish an ordering of goods that is derived apart from the behavior observations themselves. To get at this, we need to reckon household spending not as an act of simply acquiring that general amalgam labeled consumer goods, but as an act of fulfilling different needs. Put the matter this way: Consumers do not demand commodities as such, what they demand is the fulfillment capability that can be derived from those goods. This reference to needs then reflects the being of a set of preferences that may be justified as a natural fact or, in modern society, is all the more likely to be seen as a result of a learning experience. What we call a need is in all likelihood a learned or acquired want. In taking this tack, we escape the circular reasoning criticism; for in principle, needs and the resulting preferences for particular goods can be identified and ordered independently or ahead of their manifestation as demand for goods. As Roncaglia tells us, "By taking the needs as the given data of the problem, the demand functions for commodities can then be derived from them."[17]

We then suppose that our consumer possesses a multiplicity of needs that give rise to a set of preferences; the satisfaction of these needs results from the purchase of particular types of goods. It is perhaps more revealing to talk in terms of the purchase of the "characteristics" (real and psychological) that can be derived from these goods. But the satisfaction of preferences does not reflect a helter-skelter approach to purchasing; there is a definite order of priority in consumer needs and therefore among groups of goods and services. It is an important connection to note that this order will manifest itself as real income rises. So we suppose a hierarchy of needs, where some are more basic than others, which implies that they are fulfilled on a priority basis. All needs and, importantly, the goods reflective of their satisfaction are not equal.

The Framework

Let us consider the following framework. Imagine a stacking of baskets, each containing goods that fulfill particular needs. The basket placed first in one's consideration, at the base of the pyramid if you will, fulfills the most essential physiological need of essential nutritional demands. A second basket, ranked somewhat below the first and therefore placed on top of the first basket, might be one composed of clothing, and a third, placed still higher, could very well consist of shelter and medical fulfillments. A fourth might be composed of transportation needs, the fulfillment of which is required to move the consumer to and from the workplace. So we are placing baskets of goods at successively higher levels; and beyond some placement level the characteristics of the goods are less and less related to the fulfillment of physiological or necessary needs, and become more a reflection of the gratification of social needs, or perhaps we should refer to them as wants.

A consumer comes into a "market space" with an existing price and a level of disposable income. What happens when the consumer confronts not goods as such but goods that are reckoned to fulfill particular needs and wants? To help us along here, we can imagine these baskets stacked like sandbags on a levee, with the rising water level representing levels of income. The rationality of behavior is that if we imagine starting from the basket at the base, the goods and services at each level of basket will not be consumed until the level of income (the water level) rises sufficiently to absorb the goods (to inundate the basket). The term used here is that the hierarchy of baskets is lexicographically ordered; that is, that particular goods and services are called in after others have been consumed and others will be called in after these have been consumed. The consumer will not opt for goods, say, from stack number 5 until fulfillment has been achieved from the characteristics of the goods in baskets one through four. Should the cost of a basket change substantially as a share of one's income, then the demand adjustment is made through the budget constraint line, that is, the change in the composition of purchases is based upon the income rather than the conventional substitution effect. In the face of an increase in the price of, say, the fourth stacked basket, the consumer response is to reduce the quantities purchased of the higher placed baskets in order to be able to maintain the fulfillment gain from the higher priority goods. An increase in the price of a particular basket will reduce the consumption of lower priority goods; it will not in general cause a reduction in the purchase of the goods whose price has gone up. It is the consumer's behavior pattern to try and maintain in physical terms the budget share of those high priority goods.

Thus for a given water level that immediately inundates and reveals the lowest priority basket, an increase in the price of, say, a middle-stacked basket, is immediately reckoned as a reduction in the water level (income) itself sufficient to dry up an amount of the higher placed baskets so as to allow the continued purchase of that middle-stacked basket. Let us reiterate: The consumer should not be regarded as purchasing less of that middle (high priority) placed basket; there is no substitution effect here, the consumer is not substituting lower for higher regarded goods. And this comes back to our basic point: The consumer does not purchase commodities as a general concept, but commodities that are particularized by the consumer in fulfillment of biological and, more and more, socially determined needs.

Let us look at this point of view the other way. Suppose the cost of the fourth stacked basket declines; we will not find the assumed response. We will not find a decline in the purchases of the basket stacked third and lower; consumers do not substitute lower priced–lower ranked goods for higher priced–higher regarded goods. Indeed, the price decline will propel the consumer toward increasing the basket stacking by reaching out toward different goods that now take on a priority status. But in proposing this, we need to consider the movement of baskets within the hierarchal positioning.

Certainly an increase in the level of income will bring with it a higher stacking of baskets and a fuller basket at each level. Yet as incomes increase, the consumption of what was regarded as high-priority goods in the fulfillment of basic needs is, in the main, taken for granted—we should assume basic needs are provided for as a given. What has taken on a greater priority is the fulfillment of wants, which seem to expand almost without limit as higher income levels permit exposure to and consumption of new commodities. Thus a decline in the price of a need-considered good would as a general rule of behavior propel the consumer forward toward different and want-considered goods that now take on a high-priority status. We propose that higher income (whether through the income effect or via higher levels of money income) will serve as the means to form new experiences, and not bring about the greater purchase of goods that one is familiar with. And with these experiences embedded, we should find wants "hardened" into need-fulfillment goods; needs are then constantly being created. It is as if with higher levels of income (the higher water level) our basket stackings reverse themselves. The higher-stacked low-priority baskets now revert to low positions, transforming them into high-priority commodities, with those previous high-priority "sustaining of life" goods simply pushed out of the main consideration (or out of its previous central position) in the pattern of consumer expenditures.

We would then also propose that in a climate of declining income (and especially if it has been doing so for a period of time) the baskets would reshuffle themselves in a reverse manner with those baskets of essential-need goods coming back to center stage.

But what of the Principles of Economics approach concerning the price-substitution effect that, as we stated previously, we would relegate to minor importance—certainly after our critique of a utility-based understanding of demand? It would behoove us to offer an additional rationale for our heterodox point of view that the importance given in the introductory course to the substitution effect and the associated "tools" of price-elasticity and cross-elasticity is much of an exaggeration. These notions play a very modest role in understanding consumer behavior.

To reiterate, the higher the level of income the higher the pyramid of needs and the fuller the baskets at each level of stacking. We could then suppose that traditional demand theory would apply within each basket, with the consumer viewing different goods as fulfilling the same need and acting to minimize expenditures for the basket. But this runs up against some realities.

While we may designate a particular basket category in fulfillment of a broad need such as shelter or housing, there is in reality a host of subneeds or minibaskets within that broad category that are themselves lexicographically ordered. Within the shelter basket there is the subbasket of beds and bedding, perhaps followed by seating furniture, then followed by kitchen appliances and cookware, and so forth. These minibaskets are populated with goods that have different characteristics; we are not going to see the price-substitution effect here because we are dealing with goods that cannot compensate one for another. And we are saying this within a single basket category of need. The reality of consumer expenditures is that overwhelmingly one is dealing with a hierarchy of nonsubstitutable minibaskets in the fulfillment of an overall category of need.

Yet even within the minibasket itself, one does not contemplate an array of goods that is viewed as possessing identical characteristics, as if one faces them for the very first time and knows nothing about them other than their prices. Clearly this is basic to the traditional reliance on the price-substitution effect.

Consumers establish a history, or have accumulated experience with goods in that minibasket; expenditures are therefore normally directed toward goods that are familiar—they are, as Lavoie states, of a repetitive nature.

> That is, they depend on past behavior, the habits which have been incorporated in the consumer behavior. These habits may come from past family behavior, that is, the behavior of parents, or from cultural behavior, or from the visible behavior of friends, neighbors or colleagues at work. They may also have been acquired through persuasion, that of publicity and advertising.[18]

One can argue that it would be quite rational for the consumer not to engage in time-consuming acts of perusing and comparing the different prices of familiar goods but to follow an established buying routine. Quite possibly if one were to encounter a new product, its price would play a heightened role in a possible substitution effect, but this rarity cannot serve as an overall explanation of consumer actions.

There is evidence to support our point of view. The price elasticities of such basic items as clothing and housing are very small, being 0.49 and 0.01 respectively. And for a group of diverse items such as medical care, gasoline, legal services, eggs, and telephone service, we have numbers ranging from a low of 0.1 (eggs) to a high of 0.37 (legal services). Certainly we see very small substitution effects. Now Principles texts offer up the usual explanations in terms of the cost of the good as a proportion of income, whether the good can be substituted for (generally, as we pointed out, it cannot be); though at times one finds a butter–margarine example as a substitutable case. But we would argue that in the modern world these are, overall, not considered as perfectly substitutable in the light of medical findings and particular cooking needs. As well, different elasticities are explained in terms of whether the good is necessity or luxury (presumably the counterpart to needs and wants). Yet this explanation only reflects the static nature of the argument. In an economically changing world where incomes are increasing over time, what is a luxury at one point in time quickly becomes a necessity at another. Even for such a presumed luxury item as foreign travel, the elasticity coefficient is approximately unity.

We would conclude that the conventional rationale to account for a small price substitution effect misses the basic point, which is that in the main, consumer expenditures are for goods that have different characteristics, fulfilling different needs and cannot be substituted one for another. Thus the fundamental point that variations in their relative prices will evidence no change in consumer behavior, or very small ones. There is a study that points out that with eighty categories of consumer goods, expenditures are mainly determined by habits and income effects, while that price-substitution effect plays a most modest role.[19]

Different Diagrams and Different Rules

Now that we have a realistic framework in place we want to diagram this nonprice emphasis, and also draw some different "rules" underpinning an understanding of the consumer.

It is the level of real income that is the relevant and critical variable; in the main, a change in the price level is responded to via its effect on real income. Recall our basket-stacking–levee image, where it is the level of real income that determines the height of the levee and the fullness of the basket in relation to habit and convention. The connection between the proportion of one's income spent on the various goods composing the different baskets (thereby satisfying different needs) and the change in the level of real income can be depicted via Engel curves.

The first empirical observation on changes in the pattern of consumer expenditures in response to increases in income comes from a study by Ernst Engel in the mid-1850s. He studied the pattern of spending by workers in the German kingdom of Saxony and concluded that the proportion of income spent on food declines as income increases—a conclusion that become known as Engel's law. But for our purposes it is the more general formulation of the law, as discussed by Pasinetti, that is essential; namely, "that the proportion of income spent on any type good changes as per capita income increases."[20] This broader statement has been confirmed by many econometric studies concerned with empirical work on demand.

The reader will recall the analyses of income-elasticity of demand in the Principles course, with emphasis placed on the coefficient of elasticity sign being either positive or negative. In the latter instance the explanation customarily rests on the "inferiority" of the commodity, implying a commodity that one would purchase at very low (poverty) levels of income; at higher levels of income the good is totally eschewed in favor of goods fulfilling the same need but in a more "satisfactory" manner. The positive coefficient sign conveys to the student that beyond same threshold level of income all goods that the consumer has experience with are supposedly noninferior; and as income increases purchases will increase in accustomed proportion to income. Inferiority or noninferiority of goods would seem then to have everything to do with income levels. Now while this connection does exist, the emphasis given to it is much exaggerated; it is a relatively minor element. Goods may quickly become inferior for any level of income due to changes in convention and, perhaps more important, due to changes in the demand pattern of other consumers with whom a particular consumer relates. As one study cited in Lavoie concludes: "The consumption pattern of individual households is thus influenced by the demand structure of households with similar incomes or similar types of jobs, as it has been empirically shown."[21]

In Figure 4.17 we portray an Engel curve for a good or a particular basket of goods satisfying a given need. The way the curve is drawn, we are clearly considering goods that go beyond the fulfillment of the basic material and physiological needs, as expenditures begin at some intermediate level of income. Akin to our levee image, this basket (this need) does not come into play until all previous baskets have been submerged; that is, until the consumer has surpassed a threshold income level. It is this ordering of fulfillment (we elaborated on this previously) that gives rise to our first rule or

Figure 4.17

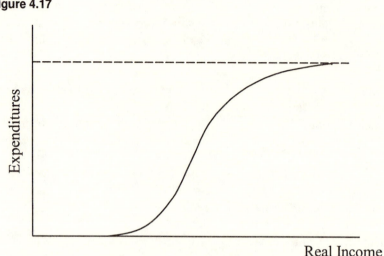

principle, which we refer to as nonindependence of purchases or, in the conventional way, the nonindependence of derived utility.

Consumer behavior demonstrates that there are inescapable irreversibilities in the process of consumption. What this is telling us is that the utility derived from the consumption of a commodity depends on other commodities having already been consumed, which is saying that it depends on the level of real income. Here we have a connection that is, of course, different from that put forth in the Principles course, where the student is given to understand that absolute levels of utility depend upon the levels of consumption of the good that has taken place. This orthodoxy is largely a misunderstanding. What is crucial is that the utility derived from the consumption levels of different goods depends on the order in which the various goods have been consumed. We are by no means suggesting that consumer behavior should be reckoned via a utility function (considering our critical analysis of the mainstream approach); but if one were to insist on this, then as Pasinetti says, the "function may turn out to have very different shapes indeed in correspondence to each good and service, according to whether and how other goods and services have been consumed."[22] And the essential point is that the pattern of consumption of other goods and services is, in reality, not a result of equating marginal utilities, but has everything to do with the level of income and social convention.

Looking at our Engel curve, we see that a given level of real income infers a particular pattern of consumption expenditures (a certain number of baskets have been submerged) and an increase in income propels the consumer toward a different pattern, reducing the expenditure proportion of income on existing baskets. And very much to the point here is that some types of goods will quickly be moved to the level of satiation—to the top of the curve—where expenditures for them may be reduced. As incomes increase, successive additions of the same need-satisfying good may quickly yield a negative marginal satisfaction, but not as a function of the amount of the good one is already purchasing. It is greatly due to a behavior pattern whereby consumers rapidly find other goods that now become necessities.

And this brings us to our second rule, which is nonindependence of consumer choice. For what becomes a want and/or a necessity for a consumer at a given level of income is greatly determined by the demand pattern of other consumers with which the individual relates. Thus another observation from Lavoie: "A household's pattern of consumption reflects the lifestyle of other households that constitute its social reference group."[23] This kind of connection will very quickly bring particular goods to a state of obsolescence (or in conventional terms to a state of zero or negative marginal utility) and cause them to be discarded. This approach to making choices and constructing a demand pattern in the face of the reality that consumers do care about what other consumers are doing, and where all consumers are subject to the onslaught of modern marketing techniques, is certainly in opposition to the standard Principles approach, which talks of consumers making independent choices within a framework of utility calculations.

The presence of rising income levels allows consumers to be always "visiting" previously unattainable baskets and, by observing how other households behave, to learn how to spend their higher income and form different demand patterns. In a very real way consumers are always discovering their preferences via a leaving process, as a result of observation and imitation. Preferences are not innate; they are the result of learned social behavior and are not given or ordered by some natural law. As Pasinetti says, "Thus consumers' demands become dependent less and less on their instincts and more and more on their knowledge. This means that each consumer is increasingly bound to carry out a preliminary process of discovering his preferences before he (or she) can express them."[24] The reality that preferences are mainly driven by external social factors rather than by some internal rational mechanism will give rise to rapid demand shifts, and all the more so in response to changes in income. In Figure 4.18 we employ an Engel curve to illustrate the expenditures on goods that rapidly "fall away" as real income increases.

All that we have been saying gives us a way to highlight the difference between our approach and that of traditional consumer analysis both from a basis of a "change in the amount demanded" and a "change in demand"—to use the standard Principles vernacular. The former, of course, imbues the

Figure 4.18

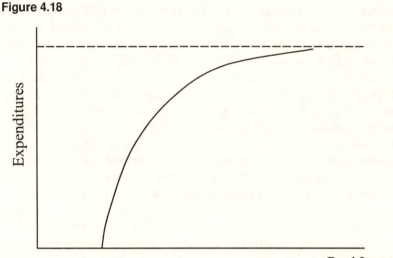

Real Income

student with the idea that the essential element of consumer behavior is that of price substitutability (the degree of which is reflected in the elasticity calculation). And that as long as prices are positive (we can think of a linear demand curve along which we read prices that are declining from some high level) there will be a corresponding amount demanded. Expenditures would approach a zero level—consumers reach a point of satiation—when the price level approaches zero. Thus as long as prices are positive, then the particular good can serve as a replacement good (and all goods are treated the same way along their respective demand curves); this is a reflection of the conventional approach that the "amount demanded" is for goods in the general, where these goods are for all practical purposes treated as identical or very highly substitutable (this is usually not overtly stated).

Now our analysis about this asks the student to abandon this unreality, for as we have talked about in different ways, the consumer does not purchase goods as such, but the characteristic of goods in fulfilling particular ordered needs. So that as a general observation, needs and the goods inherent in them cannot be substituted for one another. Thus at an income level and for some positive price some goods may not be purchased at all, but not for the reasons normally given by conventional price analysis. Thus we maintain, contrary to orthodox thinking, that everything does not have a price. We consider this our third rule.

Regarding the "change in demand," the conventional approach would bring goods to satiation as a response to continuous increases in income, that is, if incomes are infinite. In this context all goods are taken to be familiar goods;

no new "needs" are assumed to arise, as consumers are presumed to make no "discoveries" as income increases. However, we are now aware that goods become inferior not primarily in relation to changing levels of income, but can become so for a given income level. It is a hallmark of a dynamic consumer world that familiar goods can be quickly brought to satiation or even a negative purchase position. And this has little to do with the conventional wisdom concerning an "inferior good." We consider this piece of reality as our fourth rule of understanding consumer behavior.

It is with these heterodox rules and associated Engel curves that we conclude these discussions concerning consumer behavior and the demand-curve construction, having proposed a case for an alternative understanding, if not an outright jettisoning, of conventional consumer-demand theory.

Notes

1. Luigi L. Pasinetti, *Structural Change and Economic Growth* (Cambridge, UK: Cambridge University Press, 1981), p. 76.
2. James P. Quirk, *Intermediate Microeconomics* (Chicago: SRA, 1983), p. 73.
3. Ibid., p. 76.
4. Along an indifference curve, total utility for combinations A and B is constant. So:

$$0 = dU = \frac{dU}{dB} \cdot dB + \frac{dU}{dA} \cdot dA \quad 0 = dU = \frac{dU}{dB} \cdot dB + \frac{dU}{dA} \cdot dA$$

The slope of the indifference curve is

$$-\frac{dU}{dB} \cdot dB = \frac{dU}{dA} \cdot dA$$

then:

$$\frac{dA}{dB} = \frac{-\dfrac{dU}{dB}}{\dfrac{dU}{dA}}$$

5. Quirk, *Intermediate Microeconomics*, p. 83.
6. Given $Ap_A + Bp_B = M$, we may solve for B. Thus:

$$Bp_B = M - Ap_A$$

$$B = \frac{M}{p_B} \cdot \frac{p_A}{p_B}(A)$$

The slope of the line is:

$$-\frac{p_A}{p_B}$$

7. H. Landieth and David Colander, *History of Economic Theory* (Boston: Houghton Mifflin, 1989), p. 143.

8. Joseph A. Schumpeter, *History of Economic Analysis* (New York: Oxford University Press, 1955), p. 131.

9. Marc Lavoie, *Foundations of Post-Keynesian Economic Analysis* (Aldershot, UK: Edward Elgar, 1992), p. 61.

10. James S. Duesenberry, *Income, Saving, and the Theory of Consumer Behavior* (Cambridge: Harvard University Press, 1952), p. 13.

11. Ibid.

12. Landieth and Colander, *History of Economic Theory*, p. 329.

13. Alessandro Roncoglia, *Sraffa and the Theory of Prices* (New York: John Wiley, 1978), p. 107.

14. R.K Army, *Price Theory* (Englewood Cliffs, NJ: Prentice Hall, 1977), p. 112.

15. Roncoglia, *Sraffa*, p. 108.

16. J.R. Hicks, *A Revision of Demand Theory*, chap. 7 (London: Oxford University Press, 1956). For a commentary on Hicks see Stanley Bober, *Recent Developments in Non-Neoclassical Economics*, chap. 3 (Brookfield, VT, and Aldershot, UK: Ashgate, 1997).

17. Roncoglia, *Straffa*, p. 67.

18. Marc Lavoie, *Foundations*, p. 67.

19. See the analysis in Lavoie, *Foundations*, p. 86.

20. Pasinetti, *Structural Change*, p. 70.

21. Study cited in Lavoie, *Foundations*, p. 73.

22. Pasinetti, *Structural Change*, p. 72.

23. Lavoie, *Foundations*, p. 73.

24. Pasinetti, *Structural Change*, p. 75.

5

The Determination
of Income Distribution

The Conventional Approach

Preliminary Observations

Beginning students come to an awareness of the distribution of the output usually within a general discussion of the operations of the market system (reflective of those independently situated supply and demand curves), in the solution of those so-called fundamental questions that, indeed, every functioning economy must address. Specifically, the relation between the answer to the "how" question (which is, how is production to be organized by the operating firms, that is, what combination of capital and labor, what technology, will each firm employ?) and the answer to the "for whom" question, which is, as Samuelson and Nordhaus put it, "Who gets to eat the fruit of the economy's efforts?"[1] That is to say, who gets the income from production, how much goes to compensate the owners of capital, and how much goes to compensate workers?

The usual application informs the student that privately owned enterprises make the overwhelming number of decisions concerning production in terms of what is to be produced and in what quantities, and, important for our discussion, how production is to be carried on, while individual households make the decision regarding how to spend the income earned from property and labor generated by the ownership of these resources or inputs which they commit to the productive process via selling them at a price to the enterprise. Thus prices of these inputs play a leading role in determining the size of each household's income, thereby determining its claim against the output of the society.

Now let us assume that an enterprise confronts the possibility of producing a unit of output with more than a single technique; that is, it is able to choose from among different particular combinations of labor and capital inputs. With existing prices of these inputs (presumably determined within the competitive market apparatus) the firm will choose the least costly combination of these inputs; it will, let us say, want to use the most efficient technique because, for the given output price, it yields the greatest profit. And "most efficient" implies obtaining a level of production with the smallest input cost.

Then the decision entered into by firms regarding their technique of production will feed back to households in the form of different levels of earned income, as each household possesses and "sells" different quantities of those "capital" and labor inputs. The point is that households trade the services of those productive inputs that they possess in specific factor markets, which determines their prices, which then become costs to the producing units. The latter, to reiterate, then considers these costs in conjunction with the particular technical requirements needed of these inputs to determine what combination of capital and labor inputs to employ. And this gives rise to differences in earned income across the population, which can be aggregated into an overall income distribution picture with regard to the earnings of labor and that of capital.

We are going to consider the basic mechanics involved for such a market-determined income distribution in order to have a clear base from which to mount a critique of this conventional approach and propose an alternative understanding, similar to the way we handled consumer-demand theory.

The essential point then for the orthodox explanation is that the distribution of income is determined by the price at which the household (or each individual) can sell, in the competitive marketplace, the services of the factors of production which it possesses. The whole matter of distribution is simply a facet of price theory; that is, one derives a theory of distribution as incidental to the pricing mechanics, in that distribution is determined by conditions of exchange. There is no need then for a particular analysis or understanding of the "reward" to each factor of production; one need not relate or justify the payment to an input as stemming from its particular role in the production process and as an outgrowth of the social and technical relationships between people who reside behind the faceless term of "inputs" or "factors." In conventional theory the distribution of the output does not relate to the existence of social classes in society with an inherent conflict between them that is grounded in a historical context. Indeed, since all factor incomes are seen to flow from the same explanatory pricing principle, it is but a short step to consider the relationship between those whose income is composed of the reward to capital (interest and profits) and those whose income is composed of the reward to labor (wages) as an essentially harmonious one. Each makes a distinct contribution to production and receives an appropriate market-determined reward. Of course, households may receive more than one classification of income, but as we will be looking at the mechanics of the distribution to each input, it may be clearer to think of the income from capital and that from labor accruing to different households—designating the former as capitalists and the latter as workers. And what is taken as underlying this pricing approach is, to reiterate, the cooperative spirit of these different households. If there is an antagonism between them (e.g., a worker strike) it is merely a form of competing with one another as to who should get more of the value that they conceive of having jointly created. There is, one might say, a double harmony between the labor and capital inputs; they cooperate in the act of production, and in distribution their struggle is merely the manifestation of an underlying community of interest to bring about a higher level of output.

Yet, as we hinted, there is a different approach to understanding what lies behind income distribution that we will want to get at. It is one in which there is no shared understanding of an objective rationale for distributional differences, where distribution is at the center of conflicting claims inherent in the act of negotiation between capital and labor, and where such bargaining may take the form of active demonstrations of economic power (sometimes quite violent) based on class interests. In this nonorthodox view of the economy, distribution does not result from the meshing of "nondescript" (malleable) factors of production in a framework of some objective productivity calculation, but from the relationship between distinct social-economic classes that is inherently one of conflict, and within a productive process that to a large extent mirrors class economic power. We will argue in this alternative approach that in the real world there is no "natural" solution that implies optimality in establishing values for the distributive variables, that is, wages and the rate of profit; on the contrary, it is the power struggle between capital and labor that is basic in the determination of relative income shares. However, before getting involved with heterodox reasoning, we will set out the conventional analysis of distribution.

Distribution and Marginal Productivity—The Wage Rate

The theory of income distribution is considered to be a special case of the theory of prices; hence the employment and pricing of economic resources (that is, the productive inputs of capital and labor) are based on the operations of the supply and demand curves constructed for the particular resource in question. And we illustrate this mechanism with respect to the determination of the wage of labor.

The key element in the distribution of income (here, the earnings to labor) is found in the marginal productivity theory of the firm as the force behind the demand curve for labor; as we will see, the demand for labor is derived from its contribution to output at the margin of output, that is, from its marginal productivity. This productivity approach embodies what can be considered as the principle of variable-proportions production, which implies two assumptions about production. One is that a variable input can be combined in different proportions with a fixed input to produce various quantities of output; as the amount of one input is changed while the other is kept constant, the input ratio changes with particular affects on the variations in output. Secondly, it implies that a particular level of output can be produced by combining inputs in different proportions when both inputs are variable. In this latter situation the firm will not only determine the level of output but will simultaneously decide on the optimal (least-cost) proportions in which to combine inputs. Both of these notions of variability play a role in the usual income distribution story. The reader will recognize that we are talking about production mechanics (the law of diminishing returns and variability of input ratios) whose abandonment we urged in our discussion of costs in chapter 2. There we also had some discussion of income shares, essentially in relation to rent. The principles of variability are being used here within the context of an explanation of distribution shares generally; as we proceed in this chapter we will again urge that they be put aside if we are to gain a realistic understanding of this distribution issue. But let us now follow the conventional path.

The notion that the quantity of output is a function of, or depends upon, the quantities of the various inputs used is, in technical language, described by a production function that Ferguson defined as "a schedule (or table or mathematical equation) showing the maximum amount of output that can be produced from any specified set of inputs, given the existing 'state of the art.' In short the production function is a catalogue of output possibilities."[2]

In general terms we write the function as

$$Y = F(K, L) \tag{5.1}$$

stating that the amount of output (Y) is a function of the amount of labor (L) and the amount of capital (K). We do stress the point that for any given combination of capital and labor employed, the maximum amount of output that can be produced depends on the state of technical knowledge inherent in the unit of capital as well as it depends on the capability of the labor input. Certainly if one invents a better way to produce a good, the result will be more output from the same combination of labor and capital.

Now the variable-proportion that we are concerned with describes a function as

$$Y = F(\overline{K}, L) \tag{5.2}$$

(where the bar over the variable means that
it is fixed at some level)

The reader will recall from the analysis in the cost chapter that this type of function will yield diminishing returns as reflected in the diminishing marginal product of labor (MPL). That is, holding the amount of one input fixed, the marginal product of labor decreases as the amount of the labor input increases in conjunction with the fixed input. We illustrate this productivity outcome with Table 5.1 where we suppose eight tracts of land, each containing five acres, with the same fixed amount of machinery on each tract. These tracts are our fixed input (like the K in the production function of Equation 5.2). The first tract is worked by one man (one unit of labor); the second tract is worked by 2 units of labor, and so on until the eighth tract is worked by 8 units of labor. Diminishing returns is seen by the fall in the marginal product as the number of units of labor increases, which shows up on land tract 4. However, before going on, the reader is at this point asked to adopt a certain mind-set. Principles texts invariably illustrate this law of diminishing returns with reference to agricultural output, and then, as if it were a natural consequence, will generalize its application to all types of production.

Recalling our discussion in chapter 2, we argued that to use the law in an explanation of pricing of output in terms of the supply-curve construction is, in the very least, a misapplication; what is as serious is to presume its applicability across the board in all sectors. As we shall see, orthodoxy applies this law again, this time in an explanation of this pricing of inputs via the construction of the factor demand curve. We will work all this out, so the reader is asked for the moment to suspend our criticism concerning the generalized use of this law. With this said, we return to Table 5.1, where we see diminishing returns at the point where for the same increase in the labor input we obtain a smaller increase in output or, if one wanted to achieve the same increase in output, we would need to increase the variable input by greater amounts.

Thus we can portray what happens to the amount of output as we vary the amount of labor via Figure 5.1, which is a visualization of the production function of Equation 5.2. The figure shows that the marginal product of labor is the slope of the production function; as the amount of the labor input increases, the function becomes flatter, indicating diminishing marginal product.

At times this portrayal is on a per-unit-of-input basis, so that the production function relates output per unit of labor ($Q/L = q$) as a function of the labor-to-capital ratio ($L/K = l$). Table 5.2 gives us the numbers from this view. Output per unit of labor increases diminishingly as the labor-to-capital ratio increases. We see the production function expressed this way in Figure 5.2.

Figure 5.1

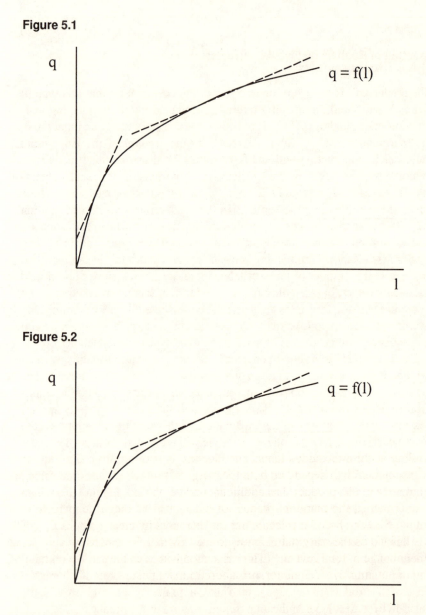

Figure 5.2

The next step is to go from the marginal product of labor to the labor demand curve. The decision as to whether to increase the hiring of labor will depend on how this affects profits. The firm will employ additional labor inputs because of the increase in production and revenue that it expects to realize, and it will compare this gain to the additional cost of the higher wage

Table 5.1

Output of Bushels on Five-Acre Tracts of Land

Tract number	Units of labor	Total output	Marginal output of labor
1	1	10	
2	2	24	14
3	3	39	15
4	4	52	13
5	5	61	9
6	6	64	3
7	7	65	1
8	8	64	−1

Table 5.2

Tract number	Units of labor	l	k	q
0				
1	1	0.2	5	10
2	2	0.4	2.5	12
3	3	0.6	1.66	13
4	4	0.8	1.25	13
5	5	1	1.00	12.2
6	6	1.2	0.83	10.6
7	7	1.4	0.71	9.3
8	8	1.6	0.62	8

bill to acquire the added labor. The increase in revenue from the additional employment will depend on both the marginal product of labor and the market price of this product. The additional unit of labor input produces what we described as the marginal-product-of-labor units of output, of which each unit sells for a p-dollar price; hence the increased revenue is $p \cdot$ MPL, which is labeled as the marginal revenue product (MRP). This MRP is defined as the change in total revenue (TR) associated with a change in the amount of an input employed. Thus for our labor input we designate:

$$MRP_L = \Delta TR / \Delta L \qquad (5.3)$$

To compute marginal revenue product, we first change the amount of a given input and employ it in the production process to obtain a change in output, and then sell the output on the market.

The firm will be making decisions about inputs in such a way as to maximize profits (as the conventional story goes), so that it will be relating this MRP to the extra cost involved in bringing it into being, which is the going wage of labor (*W*). And profits will be increasing as additional units of labor are employed as long as

$$p \cdot \text{MPL} > W$$
or
$$\text{MRP} > W$$
(5.4)

A demand schedule for labor will describe the price per unit of labor (the wage) that the firm is willing to offer for different quantities of this input. And from Equation 5.4 we can see that this price will depend on the selling price of the good that labor can produce and on the existing technology that prescribes the productivity of the labor input. Table 5.3 gives us these two pieces of information from which we construct the derived demand schedule for labor; we use the term "derived" to emphasize the point that the labor input (and inputs in general) does not have a value (command a wage) for "something" in and of itself; the value that it has (as reflected in its wage-price) is derived from the price of the goods that the labor input is, so to speak, converted into.

In Table 5.3 we use the variable labor input and fixed-acreage–capital factor with different productivity numbers and the necessary additional information to construct our labor-demand schedule. The agricultural firm is assumed to operate in a purely competitive environment (the usual Principles approach) so that it is a price-taker with regard to its product price (as the reader will recall); as well, it is a taker with regard to the wage per unit of labor hired—it is simply too small to affect the wage rate by changes in its labor input. Thus similarly to the demand curve for its output, it faces a perfectly elastic supply curve of labor at the level of the market wage. The problem is to determine the firm demand curve for labor given the technology and the market price of the output produced. The firm is able to sell its output for $5 per unit, and we put its horizontal wage line at a $20 level.

When the first unit of labor is employed, the increase in the firm's revenue is $50 for an increase in costs of $20, resulting in a $30 profit. Hiring a second unit leads to a further increase in revenue of $45 for an additional cost of $60, increasing profits by $35 and resulting in total profits rising to $55, and so forth. Hence, for a given wage of $20, the firm will continue to employ additional labor up to the point where the MRP (its addition to income) is equal to the marginal input cost (the wage rate of $20). In this example the firm will employ no more than 7 units of labor, for with the seventh unit profits are maximized at $105. The employment of an eighth unit of labor increases costs in excess of the increment to revenue, reducing the level of profits to $100. But this eighth unit would be employed if the wage were to fall to $15 or less; so we would say that the firm would not be willing to pay more than $15 per unit of labor for an employment of 8 units of labor (given the technology, which, to reiterate, reveals itself in columns 1, 2, and 3 of Table 5.3).

The marginal revenue product schedule represents the derived demand schedule for labor, indicating the level of employment the firm would engage at different money wage rates. We see this in Figure 5.3. At the profit-maximizing input of 7 units of labor we have the equality of:

$$p \cdot \text{MPP} \equiv \text{MRP} = W$$

or $$(5.5)$$

$$W/p = \text{MPP} \equiv \Delta Q / \Delta L$$

With the understanding that the MRP is the individual firm demand curve for labor, we can see from Figure 5.3 that at a wage above $\overline{W}$ (i.e., at a higher real wage) the firm would reduce the level of employment to equate the value of the marginal product to the higher given wage rate. Similarly at a wage below $\overline{W}$ (i.e., at a lower real wage) the firm would increase employment.

These points along the MRP curve, to say again, denote the wage that the firm would offer for different levels of employment, determined by the marginal product of the last worker employed. And conventional theory would obtain the aggregate demand for labor by adding together the derived demands for labor at, say, $W = 20$ for all firms. And assuming that the wage that the firm is willing to offer is the market wage, we have the marginal productivity principle determining wages. Then the marginal product of labor can be read by the slope of a tangent drawn to a point on the production function in Figure 5.2, which relates output per unit of labor to the increase in the labor-to-capital ratio. And as we can see, the function becomes flatter, indicating diminishing marginal product.

However, a more complete understanding of this productivity-related explanation of the compensation of labor should also involve some analysis of the supply curve of labor. Let us see how the orthodoxy handles this. A basic assumption is that work represents a sacrifice for which the worker must be compensated. And what is being sacrificed is hours of leisure for which the compensation is the purchasing power of earnings. The individual's well-being is related to a mix of these two considerations. It is argued that given the money wage that workers can command and the existing price level, workers will find combinations of leisure time and real income that are attainable, while some others are not. As Eichner says, "Each worker will

Table 5.3

Units of labor	Total output	Marginal output	Total revenue	MRP
0	0			
1	10	10	50	50
2	19	9	95	45
3	27	8	135	40
4	34	7	170	35
5	40	6	200	30
6	45	5	225	25
7	49	4	245	20
8	52	3	260	15

then choose to supply that number of hours of labor which maximizes his or her well-being. The individual's labor supply decision thus depends on money wages and the price level."[3] The reader will note a similarity of thinking here: In our analysis of consumption, we encountered the labor unit as a consumer that is conventionally seen to be governed by the utility calculus to maximize satisfaction for a particular combination of purchases. Now we encounter the individual as a seller of labor services, seeking to achieve maximum well-being for a particular choice of real income and leisure. We employ the indifference curve analysis to bring this out and thereby determine the supply of hours of work offered by a unit of labor.

We are dealing here with a choice problem; as in the customary approach, the individual is assumed to have preferences between the goods involved (here real income and leisure) that can be summarized in the form of an indifference map. Figure 5.4 shows such a map, with hours of leisure on the horizontal axis and the purchase of other goods as given by real income on the vertical axis.

Figure 5.3

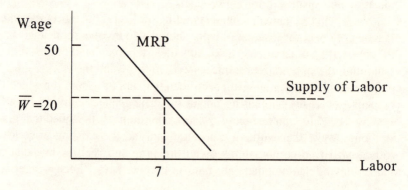

Figure 5.4

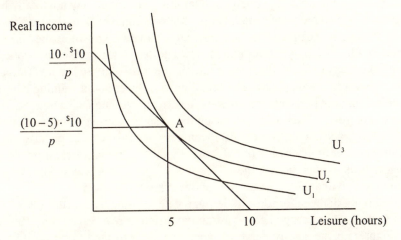

Let us assume that the maximum time available for work is ten hours at a wage rate (W) of $10 per hour, with p the price of those other goals. This information gives us the individual's budget constraint line: Should the individual opt to accept none of the available hours, then one acquires ten hours of leisure (but no income, as we presume that income is derived solely from working); however, should one partake of all available working time, then one earns a maximum real income of $100/p$, but at a cost of having no leisure. The wage rate is the opportunity cost of leisure with the slope of the budget line being that of the real wage rate ($-W/p$).

Given the individual's preferences and constraint line, the optimum combination of work and leisure is at point A, imparting the maximum well-being. The reader will immediately recognize the similarity of reasoning for our labor unit as a consumer in the utilization of the indifference approach to arrive at an optimum level of utility. Within Figure 5.4 we have that the marginal rate of substitution between leisure and income is equal to the hourly real wage. That is, the value of an extra hour of leisure is exactly equal to the opportunity cost of acquiring it; that is, the $10 that the individual would have earned had one worked that extra hour. If point A represents five hours of leisure, the individual's daily income will be $[(10 - 5) \cdot \$10] / p$.

We can generate a supply curve of labor, plotting the relationship between hours worked and the wage rate, by altering the slope of the constraint line by increasing the real wage via an increase in the money wage, as seen in Figure 5.5. The benefits of higher wages is taken in the form of reduced leisure hours as the wage rate rises from W to W'', leading to higher real income levels. This results in the conventionally shaped supply curve where continued increases in the price of the input produces increases in the amount offered as in Figure 5.5b). But a hint that this labor input may not totally be treatable as a commodity generally (and we will come back to this) is that a higher wage rate can lead to the paradoxical situation known as the "backward bending" supply curve; that is, as wages continue to rise, the worker may take the benefit of higher wage rates in the form of more leisure. Thus at a higher wage one may decide to actually work fewer hours; earning a high income may not persuade one to want to earn an ever higher income, as we see in Figure 5.6. Then why not reason the other very possible outcome that at a lower wage and decreased real income one would likely be persuaded to offer a greater number of hours of work; that the "affordability" of hours of leisure falls as income declines. This would result in a negatively sloped supply curve like the upper portion of our curve in Figure 5.6.

Thinking of the labor force in the aggregate of being of a uniform type (to get at the basic message here) confronting different real wage rates, we see in Figure 5.6 the supply curve of labor that we will take to be positively sloped. We now have the conventional approach of a market-determined explanation of wages where both aggregate labor demand and supply are functions of the real wage rate. And this leads to the orthodox macro conclusion based on these micro foundations, that in the absence of rigid money wages, supply and demand in the labor market would simultaneously determine the level of employment and real wages. The overall picture is seen in Figure 5.7, where the demand and supply curves are placed in a money wage (W)–aggregate employment (N) space. However, as profit-maximizing firms are concerned with the real wage they pay labor, that is, the price of the input relative to the price of the output, the price level enters Figure 5.7 as the shift variable of the curves. An increase in the price level results in an increase in demand (as well as a reverse shift in supply), which will increase the money wage; whether it changes the real wage and employment levels or not, is one of the matters we will consider at a later point. The shift function of the price level means we can designate the demand curve for labor as

$$W = p \cdot f(N)$$

where (5.6)

$$\Delta Y / \Delta N = f(N)$$

We now have the mechanics of a market-determined explanation for the compensation of labor. And it is the orthodox viewpoint that this design is applicable to the pricing of factors of production generally. Thus in Principles texts, when showing the profit-maximizing combination of inputs (i.e., the least-cost rule), the assertion is that the firm should employ inputs to the point where:

Figure 5.5

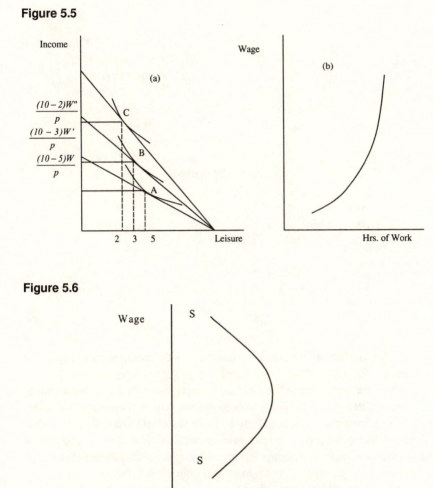

Figure 5.6

$$MPLabor \cdot p = \text{price of labor} = W$$
$$MPLand \cdot p = \text{price of land} = R_e \text{ (rent)}$$
$$MPCapital \cdot p = \text{price of capital} = R \text{ (rental price)}$$
or
$$MPL \cdot p/W = MPLand \cdot p/R_e = MP \text{ of Capital} \cdot p/R$$

(5.7)

The least-cost rule tells us that profits are maximized when the marginal product per dollar is equalized for all inputs. The reader will surely recog-

Figure 5.7

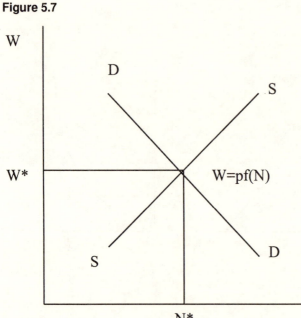

nize the similarity of reasoning to the utility-maximizing rule governing consumer behavior.

It is questionable whether we should accept this orthodox explanation of the distribution of income in its various forms, which relies on equilibrium prices as determined by the marginal disutility or sacrifice associated with the use of an input service. An essential element of all this is the notion that the reward or payment to an input is the result of an exchange process within markets that are guided by marginalist considerations.

This conventional approach has been subjected to trenchant criticism at its basic analytical structure (its microeconomic base) and on the generality of its approach. Even if we were to accept the conventional supply-and-demand framework for the explanation of wages (and this is a big if), it is doubtful that this can be carried over—with any degree of realism—to an explanation of the amount of capital employed and the associated level of income earned.

It is with respect to the determination of the rate of profit that the conventional and heterodox reasonings (our alternative approach) are, I would say, most vividly contrasted. In an understanding of the profit rate, we will first set out the orthodox reasoning, so that here as well, we have the standard approach before us to which we will juxtapose an alternative reasoning.

Distribution and Marginal Productivity—The Profit Rate

The simplest approach is to suppose that the firm rents its capital goods,—its machines, trucks, and so forth—with the term "rentals" referring to payments for the temporary use of these items of capital. A basic decision is whether or not to rent and bring into the production process an additional unit of capital, which is, of course, identical to the decision as to whether to hire an additional worker. And the orthodox guide is the same in both circumstances: The firm will rent an additional item of capital as long as the rental rate is less than the marginal revenue product generated by the rented piece of equipment.

Again we are dealing with a one-variable input case and its effect on production levels. Thus:

$$Y = F(K, \bar{L}) \tag{5.8}$$

with the marginal product of capital (MPK) being

$$\text{MPK} = F(K+1, \bar{L}) - F(K, \bar{L}) \tag{5.9}$$

The increase in profits (P) attributable to an additional rental is

$$\Delta P = \Delta \text{Revenue} - \Delta \text{Cost}$$
$$= p \cdot \text{MPK} - R \tag{5.10}$$

Assuming the competitive environment, both the rental payment (R) of the capital item and the selling price of the related increase in production are independent of the level of production. Thus the firm will rent additional pieces of capital up to the level where profits no longer increase, that is,

$$p \cdot \text{MPK} = R$$

or $\tag{5.11}$

$\text{MPK} = R/p$

Where the MPK falls to equal the real rental price.

In this context of a capital input, what is the terminology to designate the earnings to this input; that is, what is it that the firm is realizing as a result of "owning" and utilizing a piece of equipment? Consider a rental price (cost) of \$3,500 and say that after calculating the expenses of its operation (insurance and maintenance) there is a realization of a net income of \$4,375. We designate this net earning as a rate of return (expressed as a percentage) on the cost of the equipment. Thus:

$$4,375 / 3,500 = 1.25 \tag{5.12}$$

where this return of 25 percent above costs is usually expressed as a percentage per time period of the rental—say as a percentage per year. So that the increase in profits (the ΔP in equation 5.10) is a return on capital investment and has the dimension of dollar of earnings per year per dollar invested—in this case per dollar invested as a rental payment. Then:

$$\Delta P = 4,375\text{--}3,500 = 875 \tag{5.13}$$

with the rate of profit or rate of return per dollar cost of capital expressed as

$$875 / 3,500 = .25 \tag{5.14}$$

In a manner similar to our labor demand curve, we can then depict a demand schedule for the capital input in Figure 5.8. The firm will increase its use of machines (given the rental cost) as long as it realizes a positive rate of return (i.e., a rate of profit). Of course, this positive return will be diminishing, carried down by the declining marginal productivity. The profit-maximizing capital input is at K^*, for to go beyond this results in a negative rate of return.

We do bear in mind that this rate of return is included in the aggregate notion of profits; that is, profits are considered as a residual income equal to total revenue minus total costs. In the condition of our one variable input, all input costs other than capital costs are not changing, so that it is the change in the rate of return on capital that is the determining element of profit levels.

While rental capital markets are common, they are certainly not the only way that firms obtain capital equipment. Firms also purchase capital, for example, machines, buildings, and so forth, which is expected to be in use for several years and which will yield a future stream of income over the economic lifetime of the particular piece of equipment. That is, the firm is estimating the annual marginal revenue product generated by the capital over its operating lifetime, assuming that the purchase price is given data, so that the cost is not a function of how many machines the firm purchases. Then the decision as to whether or not to purchase an additional unit of capital depends on the comparison of two values: the existing purchase price and the estimated stream of MRP that is generated over the several years of its use.

This comparison will answer the question as to whether it is worthwhile to spend the cost-price of this piece of capital as a means to generate future

Figure 5.8

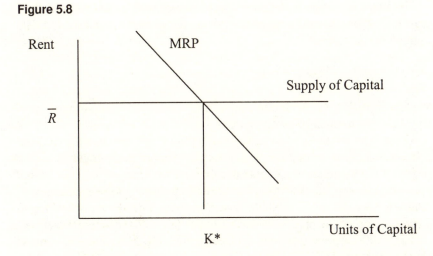

income. Indeed, what is the way to arrive at a fair price to pay for this income stream that will then be compared to the income's actual price, that is, the cost of capital? The price that the firm would be willing to offer for capital is reflective of the calculation of the present value of that future income, namely, the value today—at the time of decision—of the entire stream of future income. And the present value of a unit of capital is the sum of money that would need to be invested today, at the current rate of interest, to generate that capital's future stream of receipts. The decision maker in determining present value is alert for the possibility of a less costly way to generate that income.

Before we have illustrations of calculating present value, we want to clarify the usage of our term rent-payment. In the present discussion, as we said, the firm is not renting the equipment; it is either using borrowed funds for which it engenders, say, monthly interest payment, or it purchases from its own funds. These monies of its own could have been used alternatively in some investment instrument to generate a stream of interest payments. The interest payment on the borrowed funds is similar to a rental payment; and the monthly interest income lost as a result of using internal funds to purchase the capital can be considered as the opportunity-cost of this investment, and is also akin to a rental payment. We would consider both of these interests (we can see them as "prices") as the implicit rental price of purchasing the unit of capital. There is an additional component of this implicit price consisting of the wearing-down or depreciation over time of the equipment of a dollar value per year. So it costs the firm a dollar amount each year, which, so to speak, it puts aside to generate the replacement funds at the end of a number of years.

For example, suppose the machine purchase price of $100,000 and an existing interest rate of 5 percent with an annual depreciation of $3,000. The implicit rental price is

$$100,000 \,(.05) + 3,000 = 8,000 \tag{5.15}$$

We take note that it is the interest rate that essentially determines the "internal" or implicit rental price of capital.

We now set out the present value formulation that does contain an interest rate variable. First a quite simple illustration. Suppose an individual has an opportunity to purchase an asset that is expected to increase in value, so that upon its sale, say one year from the time of purchase, the buyer expects to realize a sales value of $100,000. How much would the buyer be willing to pay today for that asset; that is, what is the present value or present worth of that $100,000 income one year into the future? The determination is made via the formula

$$V = R \,/\, (1 + i)$$

Where

i = rate of interest
R = future receipts
V = present value

$$\tag{5.16}$$

Assuming an interest rate of 10 percent, then:

$$V = 100,000 \,/\, 1.10 = 90,909 \tag{5.17}$$

The seller (knowing that the buyer makes this calculation) will offer the asset at a price of $90,909. A buyer will not pay in excess of the worth of the asset, its present value, for that present value sum is all that one would have to "invest" alternatively (at 10 percent) to generate the expected revenue of $100,000.

This present value (V) formulation can be seen as resulting from a different question: What will the future income be in one year if one were to invest say $100 into an account that pays an interest rate of 9 percent per year? Or one can ask what the future income will be if that money were invested, say, for two years. The realization at the end of one year is

$$100 \,(1 + .09) = 109 \tag{5.18}$$

and at the end of two years it would come to

$$100 (1 + .09) + .09 [100 (1 + .09)]$$
$$= 100 (1 + .09)^2 = 118.81 \qquad (5.19)$$

Knowing the initial sum and the rate of interest, one can determine the total realization at the end of the nth future year. Thus at the end of four years we have

$$100 (1 + .09)^4 = 141.15 \qquad (5.20)$$

Now turn the question around and ask: Needing to realize \$118.81 in two years at the interest rate of 9 percent, how much is needed to invest today (presently) to achieve this? The answer is

$$X (1.09) = 118.81$$

and dividing both sides by $(1 + .09)$ we have

$$V \equiv X = 118.81 / (1.09)^2 = 100 \qquad (5.21)$$

And if one stipulated a future income of \$118.81 three years into the future, its present value would be

$$V = 118.81 / (1 + .09)^3 = 91.74 \qquad (5.22)$$

Let us now get to a more appropriate example of present value. Suppose a firm is considering whether to purchase an additional unit of capital that has a projected earnings life of four years and is expected to produce a stream of net income of \$100 in each of the four years of its operation. To simplify the matter but not lose the essential message here, we assume a steady stream of earnings and we relate this investment decision to the raw purchase price (cost) of this additional capital. This decision will be made within the circumstance of an existing rate of interest, and from Table 5.4 we can calculate the worthwhileness of this investment for different interest rates—given projected earnings and cost.

Consider the existence of a 3 percent interest rate, and the calculation of the present value of each of the future years' income at that rate with the results entered in column c. We should keep in mind two points in the use of the present value formula. The first is that for a particular income stream, each part of the stream is evaluated separately; that is, as Samuelson and Nordhaus state, "in present-value calculations each dollar must stand on its own feet."[4] Secondly, the further into the future one expects the income, the

Table 5.4

Present Value

a	b	c	d	e
Year	Earnings	3%	5%	6%
1	100	97.09	95.23	94.33
2	100	94.33	90.90	89.04
3	100	91.74	86.43	83.96
4	100	88.89	82.30	79.23
Σ of present values		372.05	354.86	346.56
Cost of capital		354.86	354.86	354.86

less the worth of that income compared to current income. There is greater uncertainty attached the receipt of future income so that, in a sense, one would "pay" a smaller amount to acquire it. But we are thinking in terms of an investment of a dollar amount at a rate of interest to acquire future income; the further in time that income is to be received, the longer the time for the dollars to grow so that the less one need give today—the less its present value. This is, of course, the idea of discounting future income.

The present value (V) of the income stream at 3 percent is:

$$V = 100 / (1.03)^1 + 100 / (1.03)^2 + 100 / (1.03)^3 + 100 / (1.03)^4$$
$$= 97.09 + 94.33 + 91.74 + 88.89 = 372.05 \tag{5.23}$$

Likewise we complete columns d and e for 5 percent and 6 percent respectively.

We observe that for the 3 percent rate, the firm would be willing to pay a sum of money for the realization of future income that is greater than what it needs to pay. The sum of the present values, which is the present worth (cost) of that future income, is greater than the present cost of acquiring that income; and there is a positive inducement to undertake the investment. We would say that at 3 percent the net present value (NPV) is positive: Defining NPV as present value minus costs, giving this investment a positive net return. Alternatively, we relate the positive return to a rate of interest that lowers the implicit rental cost (price) sufficient to render this a profitable investment.

But in the context of a 6 percent rate of interest, this same capital with its projected earnings and costs would yield a negative net return and not be undertaken. We note in Table 5.4 that there is a particular rate of interest that renders NPV equal to zero; meaning, to reiterate, that the "worth" of this future income stream in terms of what the firm would be willing to spend to achieve it is, indeed, equal to what it needs to spend. This particular rate is, one might say, "internal" to the capital itself. Given the expected future income and the cost, one can always find the rate that equalizes the sum of the discounted future income to the cost. This rate is referred to as the marginal efficiency of capital rate (m); we must be aware that although both the m and rate of interest i are percentages, we must not think of them the same way—the estimate of the former does not depend on the latter. Yet the m-rate forms a guide (given the borrowing rate of interest) as to whether one would undertake an investment. Should the calculated m-rate exceed the rate of interest then the investment yields a positive NPV and would be added to the capital stock. Indeed, the higher its m, the higher the NPV and rate of return.

For a given rate of interest one can imagine a firm arranging potential investments ranked according to their m-rate (or positive NPV), and investing first in that capital good whose rate of return is highest, that is, whose m exceeds i by the most, and then bringing less worthy investments into being until one exhausts all positive incentive at the ruling rate of interest—that is, at the point where for the next unit of capital the NPV is zero, or that its calculated m-rate is equal to the rate of interest.

In Figure 5.9 we see the ranking of investment projects according to their rates of return reflective of their degree of positive net present value—given a rate of interest (i_0). But what is the rationale for the realization of lower rates of return as the firm continues to add to its capital stock? Or to put the question on a societal bases: What happens when a nation accumulates more and more capital over time, so that the production technology for the economy as a whole becomes more capital intensive or more "roundabout"?

Well, the orthodox response is that we would expect the law of diminishing returns to set in, resulting in a decline in marginal product, thereby resulting in a lower future income stream and a fall in the rate of return. As one Principles text, by Samuelson and Nordhaus, tells it:

> We would expect the law of diminishing returns to set in. As we add more fishing boats or power plants or computers, the extra product, or return on even more roundabout production begins to fall. . . . Unless offset by technological change, the diminishing returns from rapid investment will drive down the rate of return on investment.[5]

We can now set up a demand curve for capital (Figure 5.10) showing the amount of investment the firm—and, by extension, the economy as a whole—would be willing to undertake at a given rate of interest. Firms will undertake investment projects thereby increasing the capital stock as long as the rate of return from the investment exceeds the rate of interest. Of course, another way to say this is that positive inducement exists as long as NPV is

Figure 5.9

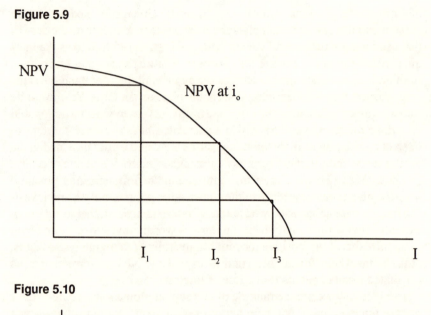

Figure 5.10

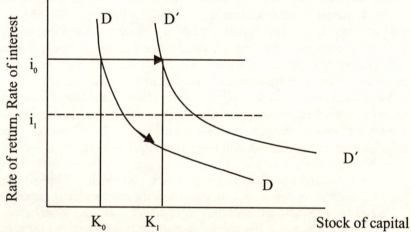

positive, reflecting the condition that the project's *m*-rate exceeds the rate of interest. However, based on the conventional wisdom, increase in the capital stock will bring with it declines in the stream of future net income, that is, the MRP, thereby reducing the rate of return and *m*-rate of the next project. Investment will then go on, up to the point where the NPV is zero or where the rate of return is equal to the rate of interest—the K_0 level. We observe how similar this description for capital is to the description of the demand for labor, where we showed that employment is increased up to the point where MRP of labor equals the wage. Here, if we wanted analogous wording, we would say that the capital stock increases to the point where the MRP of capital equals the rental price.

Looking again at Figure 5.10, we see that increasing the capital stock beyond K_0 would result in a negative rate of return from the additional investment, which essentially reflects the diminishment of the expected income stream relative to the cost of capital. Then in order to advance the stock of capital, the system would need a compensatory drop in the rate of interest, which renders the m-rate of the next investment project in excess of the interest rate, thereby turning it into a profitable undertaking. Or there would need to be some increase in the expected net income stream, which for the given rate i_0 would increase the m-rate of the additional investment, thereby giving it a positive NPV, thereby shifting the curve from D to D'. Relating our discussion to Figure 5.9, we note that a reduction in i increases the NPV for all projects, thereby shifting the curve to the right and increasing the level of planned investment.

In the usual explication of income distribution the firm is pictured as operating in competitive markets, so that it is a price-taker as well with regard to the price of inputs, and here we are talking about the price of money that it "buys" to purchase capital goods. Conventional attitude sees the role of money or the existence of cash balances in terms of serving as a transaction device or medium of exchange; it is not considered as an economic resource. That is, it is not treated as having a presence in the production function and thus performing a service in and of itself with affect on real variables such as employment and output. We will, in a later chapter, question this so-called neutral view of money, and look at the link between changes in the money supply and effects on real economic activity.

But here, in the presentation of the traditional attitude, we find the students being told the following through a text by McConnell and Brue:

> Money is not an economic resource. As coins, paper money, or checking accounts, money is not productive; it cannot produce goods and services. However, businesses "buy" the use of money because it can be used to acquire capital goods—factories, machinery, warehouses, and so on. These facilities clearly do contribute to production. Thus in hiring the use of money capital, business executives are often indirectly buying the use of real capital goods.[6]

So the demand for money, that is, loan demand, is a reflection of the demand for investment as analyzed via Figure 5.10. And in the orthodox framework the price of this money is determined through supply-and-demand mechanics.

The supply of this loanable money is presented as being composed essentially of household savings (the reader will recall that in the Principles macro discussion the calculation of a savings function is simply the reciprocal of the consumption function). The accumulation of capital is seen as being "paid for" by the society's sacrifice of current consumption; and the rate of interest is portrayed as the payment or reward for deferring consumption expenditures to make more funds available for lending. The view is that people prefer to spend their income today rather than to postpone expenditures for a later time (save today), so they must be "bribed" to delay, and the larger the bribe (the rate of interest) the greater the level of deferred consumption (savings) out of current income.

Sometimes this loanable-funds market is presented from two viewpoints. One is that of the short term, where the supply of these funds is given, and firms have pushed the demand for these funds to the point of where the PDV equals zero and the rate of return on investment is equal to the rate of interest. So the supply of funds is, so to speak, rationed out to the demanding firms, thereby exhausting the given supply. This is reflective of a market-clearing interest rate. We see this in Figure 5.11. In the absence of a change in the supply of funds, increases in the demand for investment, say, due to an increase in expected net income, will be canceled out by higher interest rates. So that at every short-run view the stock of capital is given based on past conditions. As the Principles text by Samuelson puts it: "In the short-run the economy has inherited a given stock of capital from the past, shown as the vertical SS supply of capital schedule."[7]

The other view is to look over time through the long-run lens and see that the society has been steadily increasing its capital stock being carried forward by technological change and growing markets, which pushes up the m-rate or increases the rate of return for a given interest rate (thwarting the onset of diminishing returns). Thus, over the long view, the demand for investment shifts upward, which increases the demand for loanable funds and the associated rate of interest, which shifts the supply curve of funds to the right—the supply of loanable funds increasing with capital accumulation. We see the long-run scenario in Figure 5.12.

One can perhaps conjecture that in the very long run the factors supporting higher rates of return will falter or be eclipsed as that orthodox negative element of diminishing returns makes a strong reappearance, bringing the society to a zero net accumulation status. Then one can also conceive of a long-run rate of interest that is associated with a capital stock that is no longer growing.

But let us not stray from our goal, which is the basic conventional explanation of the return to the holders of capital. We put forth this explanation culminating in the demand curve for investment in Figure 5.10. And here we

Figure 5.11

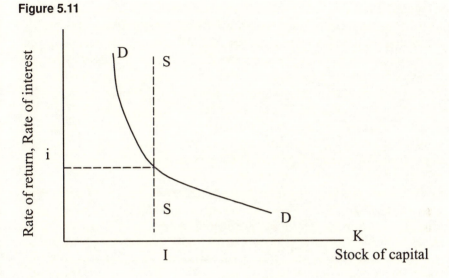

Figure 5.12

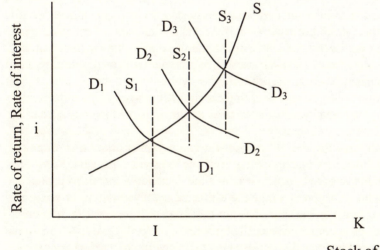

reiterate the central message: With given "costs" the rate of return (profit) is reflected in the NPV of the investment, which is the result of the expected flow of net income that is itself essentially determined by the marginal productivity of that additional unit of capital curve; in similarity to the way we treated the labor input, we see this in Figure 5.13. In accordance with the orthodox production blueprint, when we vary one input (capital) while other

Figure 5.13

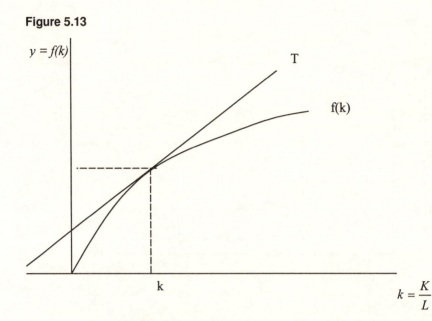

factors such as labor and technical progresses remain unchanged, we find that output per unit of labor ($y = Y/L$) reveals diminishing returns as capital per unit of labor ($k = K/L$) intensifies. And this diminishing marginal productivity reveals itself in lower rates of return and associated reduced investment demand. The rate of profit is given by the slope of the per unit of labor production function for an existing capital intensity or capital to labor ratio, and is represented by a tangent such as *RT* drawn to the function at a particular level of capital intensity.

In full knowledge of the market-determined input prices and of the prevailing technology that allows the firm to estimate the inpact on its MRP or, perhaps better stated, its net revenue flow, the firm will vary its capital and labor input to the point where the estimated revenue per unit of factor employed is equal to per unit of factor cost (recall Equation 5.7). It is on the basis of the quantity of each factor employed (reflective of its marginal product) and its price that, at a point in time, determines the compensation to each input and thereby the distribution of the nation's aggregate income.

We now have the conventional wisdom that accounts for income distribution; it does present us with a rather mechanistic (some might consider it scientific) framework that treats the "items" of labor and capital in relation to the producing entity as analogous to items of consumption in relation to the consumer. In the often used parlance, these particular producing inputs are referred to by that nondescript (melding) term "factors of production," which supposedly reflects the notion that the incomes to all factors flow from the same explanatory principle. This may lead one to conclude (as stated previously) that the relations between capitalists (the owners and suppliers of capital) and workers (the owners and suppliers of human labor power) is essentially harmonious; each makes a distinct contribution to production and receives the appropriate reward. In so far as there is an admission between them it would arise from a quarrel as to which factor should receive more of the value that is acknowledged to have been jointly created.

Yet such disputes are around us all the time; thus the antagonists do not recognize or cannot gauge the orthodox objective measure of one's contribution to production, or if they can, there is no adherence to it, having been able to relate compensation to some other base—something that we might consider hierarchical and subjective. Indeed, has it ever been otherwise? Would one really believe that the social relations between "men" in production and the distribution of the net product are guided by some objective equilibrium-maximizing rule operating through the mechanics of the markets? Or, to put it another way, that an understanding of income distribution can be resolved in terms of its being a facet of, or a special case of, the orthodox theory of price determination—that there is an analogy between product and factor markets?

Principles texts highlight this connection as they do the sameness of the description of the demand for capital as for the demand for labor, and all this to demonstrate the generality of economic reasoning. But we argue against such a uniformity on the belief that it does not lead to a clarifying principle but to a serious misunderstanding of reality. Our alternative (heterodox) understanding of income distribution has, as a central point, that there is no natural solution that implies some optimal outcome in establishing values for the distributive variable, as is implied by the marginal productivity theory of distribution. The central and realistic hypothesis is that the distributive variables of profits and wages are the outcome of a state of conflict between capital and labor, and do not, to reiterate, flow from a commonly accepted productivity principle.

Consider the wage payment to labor that we would view as a payment or a reward in exchange for work; the immediate cautionary note is that, although we use the word exchange, we should not at all think of a market context in which there is an exchange of money for things. The wage payment is not determined by outside conditions for either the purchaser of labor power or for its supplier; it is the result in almost all cases of an internal process of negotiation or bargaining (which is to say a situation of conflict) within the institutional arrangement of the workplace (i.e., the organization) itself, and the prevailing production technology (which is not to say that forces outside of the organization may not strengthen or weaken a bargaining hand). We want the reader to abandon the generality of thinking of the

Principles course where, for example, if one admits to a market for wheat with standard (orthodox) supply and demand curves and hence determines the price of wheat, then the same assumptions can be carried over to the labor commodity, with a similar construction of a labor market and an understanding of the price of labor. This is, on the basis of both the demand curve and supply curve construction, very much an escape from reality, as we will see in our presentation of the nonmarginalist (heterodox) approach to this issue.

Let us also offer some preliminary remarks about returns to this notion of capital. The student's usual understanding of this, and the way we used it in our explication earlier in this chapter, is that of durable produced goods. Capital is then defined in terms of things themselves or as produced means of production. But capital in this form comes to a production process through the use of capital in money form, which is a "property" or wealth holding. What capital is undergoes changes at different stages of an economic process. Consider a simple situation: Initially capital takes a money form as the wealth of the capitalist-owner of the firm, resulting from the net earnings of a process at a previous time. This wealth is then exchanged for means of production and labor power which are fused together in a production process to produce a new quantity of goods. If all goes according to expectations, the capitalist will realize a larger quantity of capital in money form resulting from the sale of the goods than the initial quantity of money capital that started the process. Thus:

$$\text{Money} \rightarrow \text{Commodity} \rightarrow \text{Commodities (goods)} \rightarrow \text{Money} \qquad (5.24)$$

Note that the property of the capitalist is carried through into every step of the process. Even the amount of employment is technically related to capital (as things), so that wages paid (given the wage rate) is dependent upon or can be said to come from the invested earnings of the capitalist. The notion of "capital" or of "capitalism" implies an organization of production in which there exists a specific economic relationship between the constituencies involved in production, that is, between those who own (directly or indirectly) the capital as items, and those who are employed by these owners to utilize this capital and create the net surplus or profit. It is, of course, the disposition of this surplus that is open to conflict, but whatever accrues to the owners of capital is a reflection of an entitlement to their property holdings.

There is a superficial appearance of an exchange and an emphasis of the importance of supply and demand in the Principles presentation of distribution via the circular flow mechanism. As the reader will recall, households receive income by selling their resources to firms through well-defined markets that determine their prices and household income. However, it is misleading to envision the resource seller (of money capital) as remaining apart from or outside of the producing unit that demands the resource. The act of investing money capital puts the seller into a proprietary relationship that is manifested by laying claim to a share of profits based in relation to the extent of ownership.

It bears reiterating that the term "capital" or "capitalism" reflects a production environment characterized by a class division between those that possess this proprietary stance and "own" the means of production and those that are not in this position. As we mentioned, capital in a simplistic way can be seen only in terms of things; but in a deeper sense it should be seen as things within a context of a social and economic class relationship existing in a production framework. It is only through an analysis of the relations between these social classes that we will come to a realistic understanding. It is true that capitalism is a production system, but it is also very much a social system that impacts on economic factors such as the income shares of profits and wages. Yet to understand the society in terms of class relationships is not a moral condemnation of capitalism (though orthodox neoclassical economists may like to think so); it is merely an analytical response to a specific form of commodity production that has developed historically.

We ask the reader to think of production in the early period of colonial North America, where the settlers were mainly independent artisans and farmers who owned their own capital (as tools and machines) and worked for themselves. We may refer to that early society as capitalism as the term is generally thought of: Mechanized production was used, private ownership existed, self-seeking economic activities were encouraged, and economic life was not based on personal dependence as in the feudal economic system. And yet we should not refer to it as capitalism for it was not evident of an essential and core characteristic. Capitalism, as we must come to understand the term, is a unique form of commodity production; it is only here, as Howard and King put it bluntly, that "the labor power of the producers is sold as a commodity to a capitalist who then uses it in the process of production which he controls."[8] One's concept of capitalism must have as a central reference the capitalist–worker class relationship in production.

We will elaborate on these issues by setting up a different rationale for the distribution of income, and place the entire matter within a broader context of capital accumulation and economic growth.

An Alternative Mechanism

Income to Labor

We begin by putting into doubt the very existence of the conventional notion of a labor market and consider first the demand side. The reader will recall our analysis of returns and costs of production in chapter 3, where we emphasized the existence of constant or increasing returns to scale and fixed technical coefficients, that is, fixed proportionality of inputs. It was shown that the reality of a production process is captured by the L-shaped isoquant; thus, in practically all lines of production, it is not possible to alter production levels by varying the amount of labor employed with a fixed amount of capital. And as such a substitution is generally not possible, then the whole basis of the calculation of labor's marginal revenue product as a means of determining the amount of employment that the firm would be willing to undertake at different wage rates, must be considered a pretension.

There is simply no rationale from a production view in support of the negatively sloped labor demand in Figure 5.3. Normally the curve is drawn in terms of the real wage (W/P) on the vertical, with changes in the price level being the shift variable of the curve. Now with the price level as given, we would then abandon the orthodox observation relating increasing employment to a lower real wage by labor's acceptance of a lower money wage. Again, as in our critique of the standard consumer demand theory, we have a similar conclusion in that the price of labor is not the social variable determining its "purchase"; indeed, the price effect is of a small order of magnitude.

Yet there is, ironically, a supportive line of reasoning here, even if we were to accept the standard cost structure of the firm and factor substitutability. A reduction in the overall level of money wages has the effect of reducing marginal cost, which, for given output prices, provides the incentive for firms to increase production. And as the reader will recall from the micro Principles teaching, this increase in supply causes a fall in the general price level, thereby removing much if not all of the increased demand for labor. One can see this, in terms of a left shift of the demand curve, negating the positive impact of the move on the curve. So with both money wages and prices falling, the impact on the real wage is likely to be small and so will the incentive to increase employment in response to declines in money wages. So what can conceivably occur on the firm level, where the demand for labor would vary inversely with the real wage, cannot be aggregated to the whole system with effects on income distribution and employment levels.

There is a further argument coming out of an aggregate demand framework that can be marshaled to invalidate this labor demand curve, but which is best delayed until our discussion of the systems behavior with regard to aggregate production and employment. Let us now turn to the issue of the supply curve of this presumed labor market.

Thinking back to our construction of the curve, we understood it to be based on a trade-off entered into by the individual (or in some formulations by the household) between work and leisure. That work represents a "disutility" or sacrifice of leisure for which the individual must be compensated, and that the well-being of the individual results from the attainment of some combination of hours of leisure and real income as a reflection of hours of work. And each individual (each worker) will choose to supply that number of hours of work that maximizes one's well-being. And as we recall, if the wage rate increases, the individual will be subject to a new budget constraint, which will then tell us the way one changes the choice between work and leisure. This information then translates into the individual's supply schedule for work. So as the wage rate (which is the price of leisure) increases—thereby increasing the real wage—there will be a decrease in the amount of leisure consumed, which is equivalent to increasing the amount of hours worked. Thus the individual's labor supply decision depends on the money wage and the price level, with the hours of labor supplied being an increasing function of real wages. We obtain the aggregate labor supply curve by summing the amount of hours of work supplied at each real wage overall units of labor.

Yet this direct summation to acquire the aggregate curve is valid only under the supposition that labor agents (or households) act independently of each other. But this notion of independent preferences is open to as much doubt in this context as it was in our analyses of the formation of an aggregate market demand curve. We will come back to this point.

An immediate reaction to the supply-curve construction is to question the assumption that work activity is psychologically alienating and that it is lacking in intrinsic reward. Thus the motivation to perform additional work, that is, to offer more hours of labor, is based on increased purchasing from the additional wage income. And while this may be the incentive in particular lines of work, it is simply too general a rationale and ignores other aspects of the labor supply process. An observation from Eichner here is that "it is a somewhat distorted perspective which views the individual or household as weighing the disutility from additional work against the utility obtainable from the additional income thus earned, and offering fewer hours of labor, or dropping out of the labor force entirely."[9] It is a stretching of belief for the student to relate to a circumstance that if a household suffers a decline in purchasing power due to a reduction in money wage income (say because of a mandated reduction in the wage rate or hours worked), or as a result of price increases in excess of increases in wage income, that the household responds to this reduction in its real purchasing ability in a manner that reduces it even further. Yet this is exactly what the conventional (well-behaved) supply curve dictates as it tells that as the wage rate declines there will be successive increases in the amount of leisure.

There is also the assumption that the labor unit will be employed in a work situation that allows the individual to offer a greater or lesser number of hours of work. Now while this may be the case for a household member who opts for part-time employment, say, to provide supplementary income, it is not usually the case for the primary breadwinner (or, today, we had best say breadwinners) who is offered employment for a stipulated number of hours, and thereby confronts an all or nothing choice. In the main, the reality of employment is that one does not have the kind of leisure-work (consumption) choice implied by the indifference curve in Figure 5.4. Indeed, one rarely gets to choose the amount of labor that will be supplied in the quest to maximize well-being.

Yet aside from this institutional reality, let us point to other tie-ins between work and incentives. For whatever the level of real wage, the employment of at least one member of the household is generally the only way for the household to acquire the income to meet its standard of living, that is, its needs, even if were to assume that this standard is independently arrived at and judged. Now a decline in the real wage, say via a reduced hourly money wage, will, in all likelihood, motivate the individual to work more hours, perhaps by working at a second job, in order to protect the family standard. The income effect of the lower real wage will, in reality, predominate over the price substitution effect that calls upon the individual to work less (purchase more leisure) because the price of leisure has declined. In technical language we would say that the wage elasticity of hours worked is negative.

There has been a study corroborating this income effect for male workers in the 1980s.[10] An additional piece of evidence comes from the fact that at the close of the 1990s real wages for 80 percent of the male labor force were below what they were in the recent past, and that for the majority of households it now requires more than one income earner to try to maintain the family lifestyle. The average wife is working fifteen more weeks a year then she did in the 1970s. Declining or stable real wages results in an intensifying work schedule rather than a diminution.

One must also recognize that for many there is an intrinsic reward from work itself, in that it gives a sense of worth and self-respect. Furthermore, even at a low real wage some jobs are seen as the necessary way to acquire certain skills and will not easily be abandoned for fear of then being unable to move on to higher real wage employment later on.

All in all, the reader (student) will recognize these points from his or her own experience or from observation of his or her household. Thus if we are to bring the analysis of a labor supply curve into a realistic framework, we would say that in all probability such a curve does not have the conventional upward (positive) slope, and it is not characterized by the supposed paradoxical backward-bending shape at the upper reaches of the real wage; that is, at some higher wage the worker will actually work less as a standard response, as in Figure 5.6.

We should consider a reinforcing rationale for our rejection of the supply curve. The household's standard of living, no matter for the moment how it is arrived at, will as a general observation involve the family in long-term contractual obligations reflective of past borrowing. The debt obligations must be served, so for reasons of cash flow the household will make every effort to maintain if not enhance income levels. There is no withdrawing of labor as decisions to consume and decisions to work are obviously not unrelated.

Yet the household's living standard as evidenced by its consumption pattern is not independently arrived at (recall our analysis of consumer behavior) but is formed in relation to other households with whom it perceives to have a close socioeconomic affiliation and with whom it strives not to be out of "consumption step." The household is under pressure to maintain its cash flow in order to preserve what it considers as its normal standard of living, even if were to presume little if any debt obligation. Thus, "one would expect the amount of labor to increase when a household is being subject to a drop in the real wage rate and when a drop in standards of living relative to the reference group is being perceived."[11] The essential element in determining the supply of work is acquired income needs rather than the price of work.

Figure 5.14 presents our heterodox discussion of the labor supply curve. The SL line represents the lifestyle of the individual or household, which reflects a level of financial commitments that must be met. These obligations and basic expectations concerning the continuation of the existing standard of living add up to the necessity of maintaining a certain level of real income. Then, to reiterate, when real wages fall, the breadwinners must work longer, or alternatively, additional members of the household may enter the workplace in search of part-time employment. All in all, a reduction in the real wage will induce a greater number of hours of work from h_1 to h_0, moving along the curve. When real wages rise, the labor force participation may be cut back (part-time employment may be considered unnecessary), but this response from h_0 to h_1 can be expected when the higher real wage is considered transitory. In other words, that it does not open the way to a higher lifestyle ranking.

But if the real wage increase is considered permanent, which is to say that the household believes that it can now attain a higher standard of living, then the necessary labor force participation may remain the same in relation to the higher level of real earnings, as the household shifts onto the SL' curve. Now one can conceive of a situation where a particular household has not realized a higher real wage, but where average real earnings has increased for households with whom it has always associated, that is, a reference group

Figure 5.14

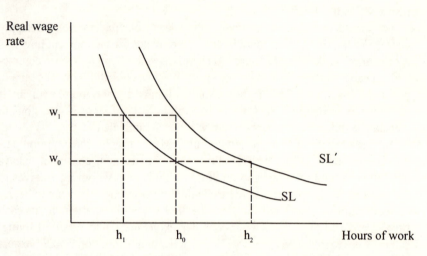

with which it is comparing itself. There would be pressure from within the household to maintain its lifestyle standing and not to fall out of step with the reference group. Again, as within our context of consumer behavior, a household's lifestyle and associated cash flow requirements are not formed in isolation. Thus we find the necessity to increase the number of hours worked from h_0 to h_2 at the real wage w_0.

As we can appreciate, the labor supply curve can take more than one shape. An increase in real earnings may reduce labor market participation or it may increase it, whereas a decline in the real wage will most certainly lead to an increase in hours worked. One can, however, rationalize an increase in participation for a given real wage. There is no uniformity to the labor supply decision that would allow one to go from an adding up of individual decision curves to an aggregate labor supply curve. Certainly we would shun the conventional positively sloped supply curve in relation to the real wage, which leaves us with Figure 5.14 at best capturing the human decision in response to changes in real earnings in the short run. And by short run we mean a time frame within which demographic factors as well as a household's ranking in the hierarchy of consumers is generally unchanging.

So we have come to the point of putting aside the orthodox (neoclassical) labor market explanation of real wages and the level of employment. We have shown that both the standard labor supply and labor demand curves are simply not constructed on a realistic institutional foundation; the whole orthodox apparatus is greatly a pretension and cannot explain the distribution of income with regard to the earnings of labor. Indeed, the labor market is not a market at all, as that term is normally understood, for as we will see, it does not possess a price-clearing (real wage rate) mechanism.

To begin with, we need to reconstruct the nature of the labor demand curve. We understand that from a firm-production viewpoint, the curve cannot relate to the marginalist's assumptions concerning the productivity of labor. It will not portray a negative relationship with regard to labor that requires a compensatory fall in the real wage to continue an increase in employment; the demand for labor curve has got to mirror a different rationale.

We recall our analysis of costs and production technology in chapter 2, where we concluded that, in the main, the modern firm (i.e., that megacorp unit) faces technical coefficients of production whereby labor cannot be substituted for capital nor capital for labor. Therefore the productivity of labor, as one will recall, cannot be a function of the amount of labor employed; it is indeed given by the technology inherent in the capital stock with which labor is employed (we do assume that the labor input possesses the requisite knowledge to work with the machinery). Let us assume an organization with a single plant representing its productive capacity, and which contains an array of machinery of a similar technology, in that as additional pieces of capital come online, they each necessitate the same increase in employment. Now it may be more realistic to assume that the megacorp's productive capacity encompasses many plants (some more recently constructed than others) where each contains a capital structure reflective of the existing technology at the time of the plant's construction. When these plants begin production, they do so with different though fixed capital-to-labor ratios. Yet even within a single plant we may, over time, find units of capital encompassing different technical coefficients (for example, different labor-to-output ratios), for where a replacement machine is brought in, it is normally not a replacement of an exact replica of itself.

But whatever the circumstance, it does not do away with the nature of the demand curve. What we need to stress at this point is that for a given level of production and thereby a degree of capacity utilization and associated employment, a lowering of the real wage rate will not improve levels of employment. The production process is such that, in general, we do not have the conventional production function that speaks of price-driven substitutability of inputs.

Improved employment levels for our megacorp will come as the result of increased demand for its product causing a greater capacity utilization, that is, utilizing a larger portion of machinery or starting up unused plants. And for the economy as a whole, higher levels of employment will come along with an increase in aggregate demand that greatly is the result of an increase in the real earnings of households. Thus in contemplating a demand curve for labor, we have what is referred to as a utilization function, relating levels of employment to the rate of capacity utilization.

Let us understand this demand relationship in somewhat more detail as viewed via its operation at the plant level. The organization will employ a level of permanent staff, or what we can consider permanent labor, with the level of this staff being related to the size of the megacorp. And we are using the term "size" as a reflection of productive capacity, whether we think in terms of a single plant or of many plants with locations in different markets. This permanent labor may consist of a legal and accounting staff, administrative and marketing personnel, and so forth. Since this labor is in place as a function of capacity, which is fixed over a period of time and over a range of production, the costs involved here are a fixed component of the organization's overall costs. Now we designate this type of employment as N_0.

In addition, there is another type of employment the level of that is connected to the degree of capacity use (not the level or size of the capacity), and for a given level of output is determined by the fixed production coefficients. We designate this "production employment" as N_v. The reader may want to review this relationship by looking at the cost analysis in chapter 2.

What is apparent is that as production increases, total employment will increase at a lesser rate, thereby resulting in an increase in average productivity, that is, the overall productivity per worker. In other words, output per unit of total employment becomes an increasing function of the rate of capacity utilization up to full-capacity operations. It is the presence of this permanent or overhead labor, combined with a constant marginal physical product of production or variable labor, that results in a percentage increase in output that exceeds that of employment, thus yielding increasing returns to labor until, one might say, all "machines" have been utilized. We see this labor productivity curve in Figure 5.15. The inner workings of this curve can be exposed by manipulating some simple relationships that the reader will find at the end of the chapter, in note 12, where we work out the labor productivity ratio.[12]

Figure 5.15 presents us with a labor demand curve anchored in the reality of the positive association between output (employment) and productivity. The mathematically astute reader, by taking the first and second derivatives of Equation 5.vii in note 12, will corroborate this association as positive and increasing at a decreasing rate as the rate of capacity utilization increases up to $U = 1$. But this is not at all related to the reasoning underlying the conventional production function that employs the largely illusionary notion of flexible production coefficients, which yields diminishing productivity due to increasing labor-to-capital ratios in response to price substitutability of inputs. And which, of course, gives us the orthodox downward-sloping labor

Figure 5.15

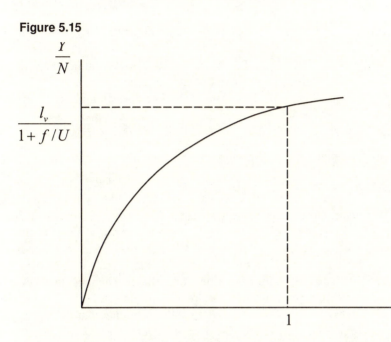

demand curve. The reader can see the look-alike curves in Figure 5.2 and Figure 5.15, but this is as far as it goes.

What happens in Figure 5.15 stems from the observation that not all of the machines, or, indeed, of entire operating plants that comprise the organization's productive capacity are of the same age or vintage, thereby embodying identical technology, giving us uniformity of the input coefficients across the whole of capacity. The reality is that the capacity is composed of machines and plants of different ages, where the older vintage capital embodies a technology that requires a greater amount of labor in association with its use, thereby resulting in a lower increase in overall productivity of labor. Thus when output increases, the capital of latest technology comes first online, carrying along a smaller production labor coefficient, and continued output increases bring older capacity online with diminishing labor productivity.

Thus we have the realism behind the slope of this labor demand curve, and we want to emphasize two points here. The change in the labor coefficient relates to the degree of utilization and associated production technology. It is not alterable for given production levels in the face of a change in relative input prices; there is, in general, no price-driven substitution of inputs in production processes. And this tells us that reduction in the money wage (or in the real wage) will not assure a zero labor surplus and thus eliminate unemployment. Indeed, it may have a nonorthodox effect by prompting a decline in the demand for labor via the wage reduction impact on effective demand and capacity utilization. But we do not want to get too far ahead of ourselves by delving into the macroeconomics of employment, as we are primarily concerned here with reasoning of income distribution. So in Figure 5.16 we bring together our nonconventional labor demand and supply curves and aggregate our thinking to envision what really constitutes the labor market.

We begin with a clearing full-employment real wage $(W/p)_F$, which is reflective of a particular demand for labor as related to the degree of capacity utilization, together with the existence of a contractual money wage and a set markup price. Now if for some reason the money wage were to fall, reducing the real wage to $(W/p)_1$, this will, as we saw in our analysis of the labor supply curve, increase the amount of labor supplied. And this higher level of available labor is in response to the reduction in real labor income. From the view of the megacorp this reduction in effective demand takes the form of reduced capacity utilization and related decline in labor demand, which only aggravates the situation. We must keep in mind that an insufficient demand for labor (i.e., a condition of excess supply) has its counterpart in an insufficient demand for goods; the level of output and employment is here constrained by demand conditions. Certainly downward flexibility of the real wage supposedly in line with market forces would reduce rather than increase employment; given the nature of price behavior in the megacorp-oligopoly world, this downward movement would take the form of a decline in money wages.

On the other hand, a real wage level of $(W/p)_2$ is associated with an excess demand for goods with its counterpart in an excess demand for labor. In line with hypothetical market forces this should lead to a higher real wage via an increase in the money wage rate. But this increases effective demand, which only worsens the labor shortage—the real wage is moving in the wrong direction.

Thus when the labor market is out of balance, the conventional assumptions concerning the movement of the real wage will only serve to further the imbalance. We conclude therefore that there is no market-clearing price (i.e., the real wage) for labor; that there are no inherent market forces working to adjust employment levels in a so-called labor market. Thus we abandon our analysis based on Figure 5.7 earlier in this chapter, which makes the money wage and level of employment, and thereby the level of wage income, an outcome of an impersonal market-clearing activity.

So what are the realities at work? We put into our psyche the reality of a workplace that is of an institutional setting both in the production of goods

Figure 5.16

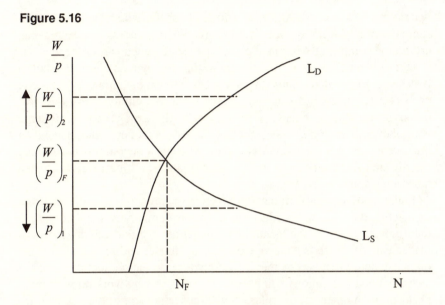

and in the supply-and-work conditions of labor, that give rise to a wage rate and rules of employment that are of a contractual arrangement as an outcome of a bargaining process. We must put aside the idea of the level of employment as an adding up of individuals selling their individual labor power in the context of an individual bargaining procedure; nor does the megacorp producing unit conceive of obtaining its labor needs in this manner.

What is purchased by the firm is a required number of labor units as determined by anticipated capacity utilization, at a predetermined wage rate, and where production takes place under stipulated workplace rules that are usually not open to interpretation or change by the individual worker. With regard to the wage rate and conditions of employment, the worker is spoken for by a union organization through an employment contract.

This organization of workers, that is, this union, is normally thought of as having as its main purpose to raise wages; while this may be so, there is a growing appreciation that it serves other beneficial purposes as well, that it is not to be seen as an organization always in a confrontational wage-negotiating posture. Much of union activity concerns itself with governance in the workplace to maintain efficiency and keep production flowing smoothly. We have in mind procedures for working out grievances that normally arise on a day-to-day basis, rules regarding particular skills for certain jobs, the monitoring of safety procedures, procedures to reduce absenteeism, and so forth. These are matters where both labor and management share the same goals, which is to maintain an ongoing employment relation that will not detract from production. And where goals are shared, the resolution of conflict is normally worked out by some agreed-upon process, for example an arbitration committee within the plant established by the parties themselves.

But supposedly the essential feature of the employment contract entails a nonshared goal that is resolved via a confrontational bargaining process; we are, of course, referring to the wage bargain. The assumption is that foremost unions aspire to raise wages and in this way to give groups of workers some control over their own incomes. So that changes in money wages depend on the outcome of this productivity bargain, which is a negotiation concerning the division of the increase in productivity and resulting profits between labor and capital.

In the modern context of mass production the reward to labor stems from its meeting the expected productivity goals or productivity standard that, in one respect, is tied to the technology inherent in the real capital, the "emplacement" of which is a management decision. But within this context the output standard may not be met if workers impede the production flow. Yet as we pointed out, unions will attempt to avoid this by working with management to hammer out the rules of governance portion of the contract. Indeed an important role of unions is to assure management of labor's adherence to the contract, because of the understanding (conveyed to the membership) that the wage level will in some degree be tied to the realization of the productivity standard.

Now this wage-level understanding is carried forward to wage increases. For example, if the plant labor–management committee calls for a change in the work rules such as reorganization of the workers at the workstations or a redefinition of skill requirements with the expectation of realizing greater productivity, this will be incorporated into the governance part of the contract. And unions will win its membership's acquiescence because of the assurance that wage increases are tied to productivity increases.

The point to be made here is that the collectivization of workers into a union organization does impart to the individual unit of labor a sense of security with regard to knowing how wages are arrived at, and what factors are essential in determining the wage increase. And, importantly, having the confidence that one's work environment and, yes, also the money wage are not going to be changed arbitrarily. The whole framework of employment impacts on productivity; so it is simply too important to be left to the capricious solution of the market and/or arbitrary managerial decision making.

Thus the stability required to maintain worker morale and a smooth production flow is, of course, not forthcoming in the orthodox context in which individual workers sell their services competitively. It is not only that the labor market in the conventional sense is institutionally unreal, but that it would yield a degree of flexibility that is unsettling to both labor and management.

In the condition of a decline in demand and labor layoffs, workers are secured in the knowledge that money wages will not fall—not only over the length of the contract but expectedly upon its renegotiation as well. In this way worker morale is maintained, and the decline in overall productivity as capacity utilization falls off is at least not made any worse by the willful disregard of established work rules. It will then pay the firm to hold the line on wages in the face of reduced demand for workers, rather than to advocate wage cuts and place in jeopardy the positive relationship that has been built up with its employees, and run the risk of employees acting to sabotage productivity standards. Again, we state the overall point that changes in employment reflect variations in aggregate demand and capacity utilization, while changes in wages will reflect the bargaining outcome concerning productivity.

It is interesting to note that a usual understanding as to how unions increase the wage rate is through showing its "monopoly face," that is, by bringing about a condition of a continued scarcity of the number of workers. And this approach is particularly identified with craft or "exclusive" unionism. This type of organization collectivizes labor along narrow lines as represented by a specific line of work or skill identification. It derives its economic strength from the fact that its membership has scarce and hard-to-replace skills. A strike action would pose a real threat to the employer because it would be extremely difficult to bring in replacement workers; yet the strike is not usually the weapon of choice for the craft union to achieve wage increases. It is the mere threat of a strike that has frequently been sufficient for the firm to cede to the union virtually complete control of the supply of the particular skilled labor.

Thus the firm would agree to employ only union workers, while the union would limit the supply of such workers through different practices. One would be to enforce long apprenticeship programs before an individual is deemed to be considered skilled and thus able to go on the job as an union member; a second practice might simply to numerically limit entry to the union and thereby entry to the work force. But whatever the practice, the basic approach is to control entry and thereby exercise greater leverage on the wage bargaining outcome.

The conventional approach to explaining the effect of this supply control is to use the standard market diagram and show a decrease in supply that, while achieving a higher wage, does so at the cost of the number of workers employed. Now if we tried this supply shift within the realism of our labor curves of Figure 5.16 we would bring about a reduction in employment as well as a lowering of the real wage, presumably through a reduction in the money wage; results that are completely counter to what is desired. But one might expect such a perverse outcome since one is employing market explanation for a situation where such a mechanism supply does not exist in the conventional sense of the term.

In the craft world what the "licensure of labor" accomplishes is a direct and powerful way to increase the wage of the particular skill, with the level of employment then being determined by the level of demand for the product employing the skill. So an increase in housing demand increases the demand for carpenters, for example, which the union responds to by providing a greater supply of carpenters as well as negotiating a higher wage to reflect the existing market conditions. Thus in terms of our heterodox labor market diagram, when the skill demand exceeds its supply, the money wage increases coupled with an increase in supply of labor and employment. We see this in Figure 5.17. The above outcome is what the union wants to achieve. So while unions are seen to be in the forefront of advocating policies to restrict the labor supply to the economy as a whole, as a means to bolster wages generally, they are also very strong advocates of the role of government to maintain and enhance effective demand.

One can say the same for industrial or "inclusive" unionism found in the mass-production world. A particular difference is that the industrial union organizes all workers of various skills and job descriptions in an industry. Indeed, it derives its strength from this inclusion; for it then has the power to deprive the firm of its entire production labor force. Also the labor contract in the mass-production workplace will include much detail concerning work rules and procedures that, along with the technology inherent in the plant, impact on productivity, as we mentioned previously.[13] In the craft workplace productivity essentially depends on the level of skill exercised on the job; hence wage contracts are very skill-specific where differences are related to levels of training and experience over which the union has some control.

An additional point regarding these union organizations is that the industrial union required the assistance of the political process to succeed (the passage of the Wagner Act in 1935). The union's weakness was that it could not demonstrate its monopoly face through licensure restrictions since the job performance of most of its organized workers (at least in earlier years) required little skill. Hence the union's bargaining power and its contract enforcement capability was weakened, since the firm could always call upon replacement workers.

As Williamson stated, "Accordingly, incumbent workers in those industries were unable, without political assistance, to reach and enforce supra-

Figure 5.17

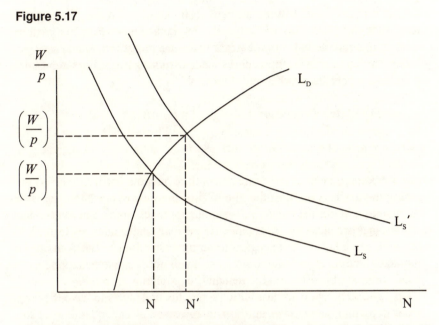

competitive wage bargains because potential entrants for their jobs would undo them."[14] "Inclusion" needs the underpinning of law to exercise power, while "exclusion" derives its power from the control of a relatively small number of workers with generally nonreplaceable skills.

As we bring this discussion to a close, we are left with the realization that, as a general view, there is no market explanation for the wage level overall, or, indeed, for a specific kind of employment. The conventional attitude was that the theory of the determination of wages is but a special case of the general theory of value—wages simply being another price. But it is untenable to make this transition, even if one were secure in the belief that output prices are determined in free markets via the conventional or well-behaved supply and demand structure. The human characteristic of the labor market makes the analogy not at all viable; as we know from the earlier analysis of pricing and consumer behavior, the marginalist underpinning of the market construction to explain prices is a misunderstanding of the behavior of the economy both from the firm and the consumer standpoint, much less having it extended to the pricing of labor. And it is interesting to observe that even when discussing the impact of imperfect competition on wages, implying those union models of raising wages, there remains a dependency on the usual demand and supply curves. But we now understand that such curves cannot, by their very design, be employed to express the behavior of the commodity in question.

So if it is not the conventional market model that explains the price of labor, then we must conclude that the explanation reflects the various institutional-contractual arrangements that, one might say, bind labor according to particular work procedures while assigning reward based on rules agreed to by both the worker and the firm.

Income to Capital (Property)

A Critique of the Orthodox Approach

It would perhaps be helpful for the reader to review our earlier analysis concerning the determination of the rate of profit—in particular the discussion surrounding Figures 5.12 and 5.13—for our approach to this issue will reject the marginal productivity explanation. If the marginalist analysis proved, in the main, to be hollow with regard to an understanding of the demand for labor and the formation of the wage rate, it will not prove to be any better in an explanation of profits and the demand for capital.

Let us continue with some additional recollection, so as to have the basis of our departure, as we take up the nonconventional understanding of this profit distribution of the product. When we presented the orthodox modeling of income distribution, we came to understand that at the core is the idea that the pricing of capital and labor is but a particular case of value theory in general, and that input factor prices are determined by their relative scarcities, with this determination being made through a market as a reflection of supply-and-demand conditions. All factor incomes are seen to be the result of an exchange process and to flow from the same explanatory principle. It is then but a short step to consider as essentially harmonious the relationship between the capitalists, that is, those who own property (capital) or the means of production and receive profits, and workers who receive wages. All this is underpinned by the benign capital–labor relation that each makes a distinct marginal contribution to production and receives the appropriate reward. To put this another way: The orthodox approach conceives of the relation between labor (workers) and capital (owners of the "machinery" of production) as one of a "social relation of exchange" or, we can say, a quantitative exchange of market-determined equivalents—a given amount of labor supplied for a specified wage, or a given amount of capital supplied in relation to a profit share. There is no sense of conflict over the distributive shares in this vision, as it is all technically and objectively determined via these "free" market exchanges. And as we showed earlier, this approach comes wrapped in terms of an aggregate production function that, specifically with regard to the reward to capital, shows the rate of profit being a function of the marginal product of capital. It is reflective of variations in the degree of capital intensity, that is, the capital-to-labor ratio. Well, we have extricated an explanation of the wage rate from this framework. Let us see how we would deal with the rate of profit.

If we would think of profits, for the moment, in physical terms, then it emerges from a production process as the surplus product in excess of what the process uses as input in the production of its own output. The surplus resulting from a previous time period of production will, at the outset of the current period, "purchase" labor and raw materials (which is the output of other firms) to begin the process anew. The use of this previously generated surplus or profit is then the expenditure or the act of investment by this capitalist-manager of accumulated goods that the individual or firm has legal title to as a result of a property relation. If there is an exchange going on here, it is that the capitalist is exchanging the surplus from oneself as an owner to oneself as a producer with the intention of realizing an equal or greater surplus. We do want to emphasize that the ratio of the realized surplus to investment is determined by the technology inherent in the production process; it is not subject to an inexorable law of return.

Let us overview our image at this point: We eschew the notion that the reward to factors of production is the result of an exchange process that is guided by marginalist considerations. Indeed, as we previously mentioned, we would do away with that anonymous term "factors of production"—which implies some objective equality of treatment in assessing the rewards to labor and capital—and replace it with the particularity of "worker" and "capitalist," thereby implying that the payment to each flows, fundamentally, from their particular role in production. The capitalist's relation to production rests upon the ownership of the means of production, that is, on the legal entitlement to the physical structures that make production possible and generate income. This capitalist-agent receives income (i.e., profits) as a right in conjunction with ownership of this income-producing property. The whole of this profit, which arises from within the production process, is appropriated by the capitalist; it is not a matter that the amount taken is somehow justified by the productivity of what has been previously committed. Certainly labor (clearly in the guise of an organization of workers) may very well challenge capital's claim to the total of this surplus; the strength of this challenge will be reflected in the share of profits that labor is able to extract in the form of a higher wage. Now we would like to see the impact of change in the distribution between profits and wages on the relative prices of commodities, and as well to relate this division to subsequent production levels. In this latter connection we will unhinge an understanding of the rate of profit from its microeconomic setting where, to say again, the rate of profit depends on the scarcity of capital relative to labor, and place it within a macroeconomic theory of income distribution.

Yet before setting up this different framework, we need to look at "technical arguments" that caused the very foundation of the orthodox understanding to be put aside, thereby lending strong credence to the heterodox (non-micro) explanation of the relative prices of capital and labor.

The reality of a general presence of fixed technical coefficients makes untenable the approach that systems of production can be ordered according to different degrees of mechanization, that is, different capital-to-labor ratios. One cannot model the real world of production by placing an aggregate notion of capital (in conjunction with labor) into an aggregative production function, and then consider the marginal product of this capital in response to changes in its quantity per capital as determining the rate of profit. Yet even if we were to assume technical substitution of production coefficients, we would still face an impasse as to how to get hold of an aggregate measure labeled "capital." In what unit is capital to be measured so that we can assess different quantities of it in relation to a level of labor input?

This question did not come up with regard to the labor input. We can, without feeling too uncomfortable, assume similar type workers and measure aggregate quantities of it in terms of man-hour units or efficiency units and then (as convention tells us) assess the marginal product of a change in such a quantity to arrive at the demand curve for labor and the wage rate. Thus the quantity of labor within the aggregate production function stands apart from its wage rate price; then one can, at least conceptually, reckon the result of a change in this labor input quantity as a determining feature of its price. The question now is, can the capital input be treated the same way? Can we find a unit in which capital may be measured as a number that is likewise independent of its rate of profit "price"? But why are we asking this question; what is unique about capital?

Let us go back for a moment to labor: If we have two people, we can express their relation to production (i.e., to represent them in terms of activity) in terms of cumulative man-hours of labor; if we double the number of people, we can express this totality as a doubling of man-hours worked. But say that we have two machines, what term would we use to express their presence in production? Well, to say that a process has an "investment" of or "contains" within it two machines does not convey any activity; it is the same as saying that a production process contains two people. Indeed, machines, being inanimate objects, cannot be expressed in terms of a unit of activity, since they have no life apart from the man-hours of labor applied to them.

But what can be done is to express the presence of these in the alike "unit" (i.e., number) of their value; we can then think of the production process as containing, or having invested in it, a monetary value that becomes productive when related to labor hours of work. Then one, supposedly, should be able to measure the production results of changing this value relative to a given level of man-hours of labor to a means of arriving at the rate of profit. In taking this tack, we seemed to have answered our question; we have found a unit in which machines can be measured in relation to production, and it is a number that, at first glance, stands apart from the rate of profit reward earned by the capital itself. We can then insert capital into a production function, along with labor, also measured in suitable units, to explain the level of aggregate output. And to reiterate the essential point of conventional factor pricing, we would take the marginal product of the change in this value capital to determine the profit reward accruing to the owner of this capital as it is manifested on the surface by the change in aggregate output with respect to "machine capital."

Yet in a simpler way of considering the matter, imagine going into a plant and observing an array of machines of different types, and being asked to represent this heterogeneity of machines as a single unit representing the quantity of capital embodied in this plant. Certainly the response would not be that this plant contains a number of machines of, say, A, B, and C types, which, in terms of labor, would be like saying that this plant contains a particular number of human beings each of a different weight, telling us nothing about an input to a production process. In what unit will these diverse pieces of equipment be measured so as to come up with a "quantity" of capital that is put into a production arrangement in conjunction with a quantity of hours worked? Well, as we indicated, the measure would need to be a value of capital. Without belaboring this point any further, there is no way to measure a quantity of capital except by calculating these quantities in value terms.

But the solution to the problem (as to how to locate a quantity of capital such that it can be assigned to an aggregate production function) immediately creates another and more serious problem. Capital as a unit of equipment with a particular output capability is obviously not a natural unit similar to a unit of labor or that of an acre of land with a given fertility; it is a produced means of production, created within a production process out of labor and other produced means, which are themselves produced with labor and capital and so forth.

A given quantity of capital is calculated in value terms, telling us that this value is equal to the price times the quantity, as would be the value of the stock of capital that served as input to produce this capital, and so forth. Now at whatever point one enters this "production chain," the price of the capital output would be determined by the wages of labor plus the earning of a rate of profit on the investment of the means of production, whose price itself contains a rate of profit. Thus the price depends on the distribution of income given the mechanics of production. We see that it is not possible to conceive of a quantity of capital, the value of which is independent of the rates of profit and wages. But unless this can be done, valuation placed on the capital stock does not stand apart from the distribution of income, which the quantity of capital (in value terms) after being incorporated into an aggregate production function is supposed to explain. As I stated in another work, "How then can we talk in terms of the slope of the production function, now for a given value of capital per capital, determining the rate of profit, when the value is itself not determinable in the absence of knowing what the rate of profit is; there is nothing in and of itself that we can take the marginal product of."[15] The conventional (micro-based) approach leads us into a state of circular reasoning in that we have to know the rate of profit in order to determine what the rate of profit is. To reiterate: The value of a stock of capital depends on prices, and prices will depend on the distribution of income, that is, on the relation between the wage rate and the rate of profit. Let us see an example of this.

Suppose we have the production of two commodities produced in separate A and B sectors; to begin with, we assume that profits as a designated payment to a particular class of individuals does not exist, so that all the net output—which is the value of output minus the value of inputs used up in production—accrues to labor, that is, equals wages. Such a system might be as shown in Table 5.5. Now we emerge from this "rude" state to one in which a class of capitalists come onto the scene who own the means of production used in these processes, and will thereby share in the net output. Say they do so to the receipt of 25 percent on the value of their invested capital, and that this rate of profit is allowed for by a reduction in wages (i.e., the wage rate) of 50 percent. The value of the output in each sector must now consist of the value of the input (which is the same as originally as we assume no change in production technology), the wage bill, plus profits at the 25 percent rate. This situation emerges as shown in Table 5.6. Prices have changed from the original condition to reflect the new state; we see that the combined value of the same "quantity" of commodities has increased from 2,000 to 2,050 and, importantly, that the relative prices of the two outputs have changed. And this change in relative prices, which results from a change in the distribution of income (the wage rate fell by one-half), occurs simply because the proportions in which labor and capital inputs are combined are different in the two sectors. It can easily be shown that if the input proportions were the same, relative prices would not change from their original position. Students are normally instructed that changes in relative prices are essentially the result of consumers exercising their power via changes in

Table 5.5

	Value of used-up inputs	Wages	Price
A sector	800	200	1,000
B sector	600	400	1,000

Table 5.6

	Value of used-up inputs	Wages	Profits	Price
A sector	800	100	200	1,100
B sector	600	200	150	950

demand; however, our analysis of pricing led us to see that shifts in demand are not primary in determining relative prices. And now we can appreciate that price changes as reflected in markup behavior are not only related to concerns regarding capacity needs, but may also reflect distributional changes that speak of the conflict outcome between labor and capital.

Furthermore, we have assumed in our example that a reduction in the wage of one-half will result in a rate of profit of 25 percent; but we can in fact work up a relationship that shows how far the rate of profit will in fact rise for a particular wage reduction, given the production technique inherent in the reality of interrelated productive processes. One can start from a situation where the wage is equal to one, that is, when the whole of the net product goes to wages, and then see what happens to the rate of profit and prices as the wage is reduced. It would take us too far off the road to become involved with the extraction of such an equation, but its message about distributional changes and relative prices, as it bears on the choice of technique that would be undertaken in production, has given rise to a more general criticism of the conventional marginal productivity approach to factor pricing. This criticism, in its generality, is more powerful than that arising from the difficulty of placing an aggregate quantity of capital into a production function. Eichmen says, "For it denies the very logical foundation of a demand curve based on marginal productivity (not only for capital, but for all factor services), and thus it vitiates the explanation of the distribution of income based, as the orthodox explanation is, on the determination of prices for factor services, through the market, as a reflection of supply and demand conditions."[16] The reader is reminded of the conventional view whereby one reads the rate of profit as the slope of the aggregate per capita production function; that is, as being determined by the marginal product of capital at a point on the function. The design of the conventional function showed production processes (i.e., different "quantities" of capital-to-labor ratios) changing continuously with the rate of profit; the implication is that a change in the rate of profit is associated with a change in the technique of production, and only one technique (and not the same one) is in use at each possible level of the rate of profit. This produces our smooth aggregate production curve, negatively associating techniques of production with higher capital-to-labor ratios and the rate of profit. It is this entire construction that has, to say the least, been called into question, but let us be more emphatic (to reflect the fundamental theoretical change here) and say that what we termed this "powerful critique" has caused the orthodox (neoclassical) design to be put aside as a representation of a realistic and coherent explanation of income distribution. It will serve us well to briefly consider this critique before embarking on an alternative road.

The thrust of this critique is seen in a situation that is referred to as one of capital-reswitching (or double switching). This is a circumstance in which we find the possibility that a particular technique of production is cost minimizing or the most profitable of all possible techniques at two separated values of the rate of profit, even though other production processes were most profitable at rates of profit in between; then it will be switched back to the original technique (the original capital-to-labor ratio). But let us read Pasinetti's description of such a possibility:

> . . . In other words, if at a rate of profit r_1, method a is the most profitable technical method of production, and if at a higher rate of profit r_2 ($r_2 > r_1$), technical method b (for producing the same commodity) becomes the most profitable one; method a may again become the most profitable technical method at an even higher rate of profit r_3 ($r_3 > r_2 > r_1$).[17]

What this possibility does, to say again, is to demonstrate that it is not possible as a general rule of technique choice, to "order" technical methods of production in such a way that their choice is a monotonic (i.e., related to in a uniform way) function of the rate of profit as the latter is varied from zero to some maximum. And, of course, this dismantles the framework of the conventional aggregate production that was constructed as the assumed "truths" of the association between lower rates of profit and higher capital-to-output ratios, leading to the understanding that the distribution of income is explainable by knowing the supply of input factors of production and their marginal productivities.

We consider an example of this reswitching phenomenon that involves the use of "circulating" capital.[18] By this we mean a type of capital that in time goes through (circulates) different processes to be utilized with differ-ent amounts of labor in each process. And as it completes one process, it changes its form from what it was originally so as to become the capital of the next process, and so forth until the capital is no longer recognized as such, as it has changed into a final good.

Say we produce a unit of champagne with a process (α) requiring 7 units of labor to make one unit of brandy in one period; then this one unit ferments by itself to become one unit of champagne in one more period. What is the cost of producing the unit of champagne as the final product at the end of the second period? Well, as we now know, it would be equal to the value of the "invested" capital (the brandy), which itself was produced under a particular distribution of income. So its price would have to be reckoned at (or be reflective of) an existing rate of profit plus the earning of a rate of profit on the input of that capital in the second period. Then at an extreme of the rate of profit being 100 percent and assuming a labor unit cost of $1, we have the cost of a unit of cham-pagne as:

$$L_\alpha w (1 + r) + r [L_\alpha w (1 + r)] \qquad\qquad (5.25)$$

Where:

L_α = labor input with α technique
w = wage rate
r = rate of profit

So:

$$7 (1 + 1.00) + 1.00 [7 (1 + 1.00)] = 28$$

In this α technique, brandy does not require champagne as an input for its own production either directly or indirectly.

Now presume an alternative process (β), requiring the input of 2 units of labor in one period to produce 1 unit of grape juice, which in one additional period ripens by itself into 1 unit of wine, and in the third period 6 units of labor are employed to produce 1 unit of champagne from this 1 unit of wine. We have two techniques for producing the same commodity—all cham-pagne is interchangeable. What is the cost of a unit of our final product em-ploying method β, assuming the same distribution of $w = 1$, $r = 100$ percent? This cost will consist of the initial "investment" of the two units of labor plus the earning of the rate of profit on this investment; secondly, the investment of the value of the grape juice plus the rate of profit on this, and carried into the third period, the cost of the wine plus the additional 6 units of labor, all yielding a rate of profit of 100 percent. Thus:

$$(1 + 1.00) [8 + 6] = 28 \tag{5.26}$$

which is reflective of the final period of production that required an input of $8 of wine plus $6 of labor. Both techniques yield the same price (cost) per unit of final product, given our particular distributional relationship. To see this another way: We can say that for the particular wage bill in either process, both processes are equally profitable in that each yields the same rate of profit. Thus for the β process the value of the net product, which we consider now as the price minus the value of the labor input, is $28 - 12 = 16$, which is equal to 100 percent of the value of the capital input itself (reckoned, of course, at the prevailing rate of profit).

We consider the point where $r = 100$ percent and $w = 1$ as a switchpoint; for at a distribution other than at the "point," the system would choose one of the two processes that is less costly, which is to say, will yield—for the given wage rate—the higher rate of profit. We can see what choices are being made in Figure 5.18 where the prices of the unit of champagne derived with each technique are related as a ratio. At an extreme of $r = 0$, only labor and wage costs matters, and as α requires 7 units of labor over all production periods compared to β's 8 units, technique α wins out as being less costly with the price ratio being 1.1. As we can see, the ratio will exceed one as the rate of profit becomes positive (though diminishingly so) up to the switchpoint rate of profit of 0.5; thus over this range of the rate of profit it is process α that is adapted as it is least costly, thereby yielding the greatest level of profits for the given wage rate. For rates of profit in excess of 50 percent the switch is to the β process as it gives the lower cost of production; indeed, β dominates for rates of profit up to 100 percent as $p_\beta/p_\alpha < 1$. For example, at $r = 0.6$ we find $p_\beta = 17.7$, $p_\alpha = 17.9$. But for still higher rates of profit in excess of 100 percent, it is technique α that is switched back to, as β shows up to be the more costly method of production. So, overall, for low rates of profit up to 50 percent it is technique α that predominates, and for a rate of profit in excess of 50 percent it is technique β that is switched to, and for still higher rates of profit in excess of 100 percent it is technique α that is switched back to.

Our rather simple circulating capital example reveals that there is, indeed, no monotonic relationship between lower rates of profit (reading Figure 5.18 in reverse) and associated production processes that are more mechanized and involve a greater quantity of capital per unit of labor, or have become in some sense more roundabout. The reader may recognize the term round-

Figure 5.18

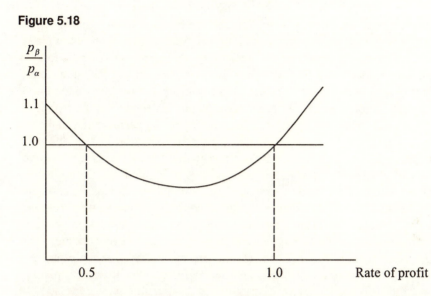

about from the Principles text, which relates it to the extensive use of tools of production at all stages leading up to the final good production, thereby involving overall a longer span of production stages compared to a less roundabout more direct production process. What we have shown is that the production process that is least costly and used at high rates of profit, only to come back to be used again at low rates, is the less roundabout, shorter time span process. And this result is certainly at odds with the orthodox message inherent in the aggregate production function alleging that as the rate of profit falls, the technology in use is always the more roundabout, reflecting higher levels of capital intensity.

We want to mention some points at this juncture, and to repeat some thoughts. One can also demonstrate this reswitching of techniques with the use of a durable (fixed) capital goods model,[19] so that this critique of the orthodox (neoclassical) explanation of the prices of factor services is of a general nature. Secondly, this "technical" attack, if you will, on the apparatus of an aggregate production function as an explanatory vehicle of income shares, could be considered as being beside the point; that is, beside the realistic observation that in the main, production processes are carried on with fixed technical coefficients. Yet the willingness to accept an alternative approach requires more than the recognition of an existing misfit between what the theory purports to explain and "what is going on out there," since those who defend traditional theory can always come up with singularly "special" cases where it can be sustained.

What is required is a thrust on the basic design and message of the established model that purports to explain income distribution in terms of supply and demand, thus rendering it a particular facet of price theory generally. What we have shown is that this approach is defective. Consider the following observation made by Kurz and Salvatori: "The demonstration that a fall in the wage rate (i.e., a rise in the rate of profit) may lead to the adoption of the less 'labor intensive,' that is, more 'capital intensive' of the two techniques, destroyed, in the minds of the critics of traditional neoclassical theory, the whole basis for the neoclassical view of substitution in production."[20] Contrary, then, to what an aggregate production function tells us, the direction of change in input proportions cannot be related unambiguously to changes in relative factor prices. And although the production function and its distributive message cannot be sustained, it still is in practice. Kurz and Salvatori say, "The disquieting fact remains that in economics propositions that have been proved wrong are still used by many of its practitioners."[21] A glance at economic texts in the area of income distribution, unfortunately, sustains the above quote. Well, we now begin down an alternative path toward a different theory of distribution to, hopefully, lessen the state of miseducation.

The Rate of Profit: A Heterodox Approach

The overall framework is that income accrues to economic classes of people as a consequence of their particular role in a production process, and as the result of the conflict between them over the division of the net product (there is no uniform explanatory principle for an understanding of distributive shares). We have alluded to such an economic society previously in this chapter during our heterodox discussions of the wage rate; now we want to explore this framework in a more formal manner to derive an explanation for the rate of profit.

We begin by drawing the relationship between economic class activity and income distribution within a macroeconomic context and, under some simplifying assumptions, clearly revealing the essential linkages. We consider the gross domestic product (GDP) of a closed private-sector economy (thus excluding any foreign trade or government expenditures and taxation influences on earnings). The value of the product then consists of consumption and gross investment expenditures, where the latter is equal to the purchases of fixed capital (machinery, buildings, and so forth) and any change in inventories, and the former consists of the value of consumption expenditures by the economic classes of people in our two-class society. Thus the national income is divided between our two classifications as income to workers consisting of wages and salaries, and income to capitalists, that is,

Table 5.7

Income	Expenditures
Income of capitalists (profits) + Income of workers (wages & salaries)	Gross investment + Capitalists' consumption + Workers' consumption
= National income	= Domestic product

those who possess legal entitlement to the means of production. But it may be best to think of the latter in a broader sense as income to property, encompassing interest and rent as well as profits (though we will put all of this into profits).

As the reader is well aware from the Principles description of the GDP, there are two ways of looking at aggregate output. One is to see the GDP as the sum of expenditures in purchasing the output, and the other is in terms of income derived from the creation of the output. This gives the following balance sheet of our simple economy, shown in Table 5.7, in which we distinguish between capitalists' and workers' consumption spending on the expenditure side.

An inherent simplifying assumption, which may stand out by simply looking at our balance sheet, is that workers' income is taken to be equal to workers' consumption expenditures; that is, workers are assumed to do no saving, or as it is usually put, workers spend what they earn; of course, the workers' propensity to save is not zero, and we will at a later point consider the impact of this piece of reality. But for now, in keeping with our assumption about workers' savings, it then follows that profits are equal to gross investment plus capitalists' consumption expenditures. And since the capitalists' income is what we can call profits, then it follows that capitalists earn what they spend. Thus:

$$P = C_c + I \tag{5.27}$$
P = Gross profits
C_c = Capitalists' consumption
I = Gross investment

Yet this relationship calls up a question about the causality involved here. As Kalecki puts it, "Does it mean that profits in a given period determine capitalists' consumption and investment, or the reverse of this?"[22] The answer depends on which of these items in this profit equation is directly subject to the decisions of capitalists. Certainly the capitalist (really the megacorp) can decide to engage in an increased level of investment spending, but one cannot decide to earn greater profits for a given level of expenditure. The level of profits depends on the technical intersector relationships and accompanying set of relative prices, which, as we have seen, assumes a given distributional relationship. But assuming no changes in these elements, then a greater level of capitalists' expenditures will result in a greater level of gross profits. We keep in mind that these profits are reflective of the organization's pricing (markup) policy in relation to its cost structure, with its net profits being mirrored in the negotiated outcome regarding the distributive shares.

Thus it is the capitalists' consumption and investment decisions that determine profits and not vice versa. For if it were otherwise and capitalists were always to spend what they earn, profits would then be the same from period to period. But clearly the level of profits is not stationery. Although profits in the proceeding period are an important determinant of the expenditure decision, capitalists (organizations) in general do not decide to invest in a given period precisely what they have earned in the period before. One reason may be that previous investment decisions may turn out not to have been warranted by realized demand conditions resulting in an unexpected accumulation of inventories. This may prompt a level of expenditures below that of earned profits (which failed to meet expectations), which will further reduce the volume of profits in the subsequent period. The point here, as Kalecki notes, is that "the real gross profits in a given short period are determined by decisions of capitalists with respect to their consumption and investment shaped in the past subject to correction for unexpected changes in the volume of stocks."[23]

The attempt to come up with an investment function that captures the complex set of factors, in addition to accrued profits, that affect the investment decision has been characterized as reminiscent of the search for a will-o'-the wisp. One approach in the light of this has simply been to consider investment as independently given, being driven by the investment zeal or the animal spirits of entrepreneurs, where realized profits and the availability of finance are no small considerations. But for us, at this point, we will make use of the relationship that the volume of capitalists' expenditures governs the volume of profits, which, itself, is an influence on future spending. And we should be thinking here of essentially capitalists' investment expenditures that result in a positive net investment or a level of capital accumulation.

What emerges from our simple classification of Table 5.7 is that capitalists as an economic class have the power to increase their own incomes. They can increase the share of the national income that comes out in the form of profits simply by increasing the investment outlay which, based on the multiplier, creates a higher level of income. In other words, their actions will not only raise the level of aggregate output but also increase their share of this output as well as to provide an enlarged level of employment and total wages. Yet interestingly, considering the causality of the profits in Equation 5.27, as Kregal says, even if capitalists "consume their profits in high living rather than investing, they do not suffer a reduction in their profit income."[24] The income of capitalists (again as an economic class, not, of course, in terms of an individual) is maintained independently of how it is spent.

We want to relate our simple distributive shares discussion to the division of the national output between consumption (wage) goods and capitalists' goods. This will expose an essential underpinning for that equilibrium GDP outcome that is encountered in the Principles course analysis of the Keynesian aggregate expenditure model. We take a different tack by desegregating the economy into a three-category exposure, with each of the three types of goods being produced in identifiably different sectors of the economy; we want to look at the relationship between the flows of goods and of incomes between these sectors.

We have a sector I producing capital or investment goods, a sector II producing consumption (luxury) goods purchased by that class of people whose income consists of profits, and a sector III producing consumption goods for workers purchased with their wage income. The income to sector III is equal to the sales value of the purchases by the workers in all three sectors. We can then picture the level of profits in III as being equal to the value of its output minus its wage bill, which is itself equal to the purchases of its own work force. Then the amount of its profits must be equal to the value of its sales to the workers in sectors I and II, that is, equal to the wages paid in I and II.

The profits in II are equal to the value of sales, which is determined by the proportion of profits earned in sectors I and III that capitalists spend on consumption goods minus its wage bill. This difference represents any and all additional capitalist consumption good produced for its own use, but we have to see this as being equal to its profits, of which a portion will be used for investment purposes, that is, purchases from I, and a portion to be used to satisfy producer's demand for consumption goods. To complete our three-sector description, the profits in I will be equal to its sales to firms in II and III—again equal to some proportion of total profits earned in these sectors—which must cover the labor costs of production; thus all additional investment goods produced for the sector's own use represent the excess of sales over costs, with this profit difference purchasing both capitalist consumption goods and investment goods.

Now what are some aggregate observations that we can draw here? First of all that the profits of the three sectors combined must be equal to the combined value of the output in sectors I and II, while the real value of the combined wages for all sectors must be equal to the amount of workers' consumption goods produced in sector III. And this is because of the aggregate demand flow where only the totality of profits is available to purchase the output of sectors I and II, and only the wages earned in all sectors are available to purchase the output of sector III. Secondly, aggregate profits over the whole system will be equal to the sum of profits in sectors I and II plus the corresponding wages paid that determines the profits in sector III. Thus aggregate profits will be equal to the combined value of capitalists' spending, which mirrors the value of production in sectors I and II and, with given production processes, the corresponding levels of employment and total wages. Again, the combined decision regarding capitalists' consumption and investment spending determines aggregate profits. And thirdly, let us bind the sectors in terms of employment. Assuming that the distribution of income between wages and profits is given for all sectors, then production and employment levels in I and II will determine the level of employment in sector III. For a given level of the GDP, the level of employment in sector III will be such that the profits in real terms (that is, the surplus production in a physical sense as being the output level over what is sold to the workers in this sector) will be equal to the wages (in real terms) of the workers in I and II, reflecting production and expenditure in these sectors. Thus the activity of this economic class of individuals referred to as capitalists or entrepreneurs determines aggregate employment as well as profits.

It appears that an understanding of the introductory Keynesian aggregate model of income and employment (normally related in two-sector terms) requires the simultaneous tracking of two necessarily related phenomena: one is the distribution of the national product between the sector outputs, and the other is the supportive distribution of the national income between wage and profit shares. Over the three-sector model the flows are:

$$GDP = Kc + WOc + I \qquad (5.28)$$
$$Y = W + P \qquad (5.29)$$
$$WO_c = W \qquad (5.30)$$
$$K_c + I = P \qquad (5.31)$$
$$\text{Then } P - K_c + S = I \qquad (5.32)$$

Where:

WO_c = Wage goods consumed by workers
K_c = "Luxury" goods consumed by capitalists

In the two-sector model we neglect luxury consumption goods production (such expenditure would in any event be of negligible impact as compared to expenditure for investment goods) and presume that all capitalists' income is saved and equal to investment expenditure. In this simpler model it is invest-ment spending that simultaneously determines the aggregate volume of profits and savings. Thus:

$$GDP = WO_c + I \tag{5.33}$$
$$Y = W + P \tag{5.34}$$
$$WO_c = W \tag{5.35}$$
$$P = S = I \tag{5.36}$$

Thus an equilibrium level of GDP (via what Principle texts describe as the expenditure–output approach), which is better referred to as a stationary state of economic activity, coexists with a particular profit share stemming from a previous period's level of investment expenditures (we overview the economy in terms of two sectors). We now bring in our understanding of pricing and recall that in the main, firms bring these profits about by their ability to determine the margin of prices relative to average prime costs. The profit result of this markup pricing policy will, in the stationary state con-text, trigger an equivalent level of investment spending that determines the distribution of income between profits and wages and thereby the same divi-sion of the output between wage goods and investment goods. Yet there must also exist a level of the real wage that results from the aggregate determina-tion of prices by organizations (capitalists) in relation to the overall conflict outcome determining the money wage. In the equilibrium state this level of the real wage gives rise to a level of aggregate demand by workers in both sectors equivalent to the output of the workers' consumption goods sector. We must see that in the stationary condition the economic outcomes in terms of aggregate employment (determined as we know by the activity of capital-ists' expenditures), that of the capital stock, that of the profit share in na-tional income, and that of the level of the national product itself are all constant over time, which reflects the constancy of the flow level between the distribution of income and the distribution of output.

Now our approach is to link distributional factors such as the markup price policy and degree of monopoly on the capitalists' (i.e., firms) side in a theory of profits, and the institutional conflict arrangements on the workers' side in a theory of wages, to production and employment. This means that we are adding an essential element of understanding (a different Principle if you will) to the usual exposition of the basic Keynesian aggregate demand model. What are the usual linkages in the introductory Keynesian model?

Well, we have a level of investment expenditures (assumed to be exogoneously determined) without a related theory of profits, and a consumption function that makes consumption expenditures by all the constituents of the economy related to the level of national income, and thereby masks the particular nature of one's economic role and type of income received. The aggregate expenditure so structured then determines production and employment, which then leads to the question of what happens to prices given the determined level of demand. Yet as we can recall from our analysis of pricing, prices are generally not determined via a market apparatus by demand shifts.

However, our current analysis takes a different approach by putting first a realistic micro foundation for the macro result. This approach, in effect, realizes that firms (i.e., capitalists) not only have the ability to determine the aggregate level of investment expenditure, but they also have the power to set the markup price at which they will sell their output that, when combined with the level of aggregate demand, determines the quality sold. And this, given the negotiated money wage, determines profits and the real wage. And it is the level of profits that is an essential ingredient in the making of investment plans. One must begin, then, with a realistic micro analysis to adequately understand the equilibrium state of the Keynesian macro expenditure and employment model. The sequence of analysis should not start with the effect of investment expenditures and demand on prices and then go to income distribution, but should begin with the influence of prices and profits on investment decisions and then go to the subsequent distributional shares and aggregate demand and employment.

Having placed "distributional factors" into front focus, let us now work up an expression for the profit share. Starting with the presence of a luxury consumption goods sector, we determine the capitalists' consumption relationship as:[25]

$$K_c\,(t) = bP\,(t - \lambda) \qquad\qquad (5.37)$$

where in Kalecki's words, the λ "indicates the delay of the reaction of capitalists' consumption to the change in their current income"[26]—their profit income. We have simply a lagged consumption function where the marginal propensity (b) is positive, and we would consider it to be appreciably less than one. This latter point is in keeping with the pivotal role played by this class of "persons" to impact the economy via their expenditure on investment goods. The reader finds quotation marks around the word persons because it is all too easy to really consider the term persons as individual beings. While this can certainly be the case, it is, however, a more realistic image to consider capitalists as enterprises, so that we can speak of Equation (5.37) as the firm's use of that portion of profits for purposes other than to finance the expansion of (or to keep intact) the state of productive capacity.

Be that as it may, we now substitute this consumption expression into the capitalists' spending equation (5.37) to obtain

$$P_t = I_t + bP_{t-\lambda} \tag{5.38}$$

Profits at time t are determined by current investment expenditures and profits at an earlier time $t - \lambda$ (we can consider $\lambda = 1$). And by the same reasoning profits at $t - 1$ are determined by investment in $t - 1$ plus profits at yet an earlier time $t - 2\lambda$ as

$$P_{t-1} = I_{t-1} + b\,(P_{t-2\lambda}) \tag{5.39}$$

and so on. Profits at time t are then linearly related to investment expenditures stretching back in time $(t, t - \lambda, t - 2\lambda)$. It can be shown that the further back in time one goes the less influence does that expenditure have on the determination of current profits. As Kalecki puts it: "Profits will thus be a function both of current investment and of investment in the near past; or, roughly speaking, profits follow investment with a time lag."[27] So

$$P_t = f\,(I_{t-i}) \tag{5.40}$$

where i is the approximate time lag involved (say one period). Now substitute Equation 5.40 for the value of P_t in Equation 5.38, so that

$$f\,(I_{t-i}) = I_t + bf\,(I_{t-i-\lambda}) + A \tag{5.41}$$

In our stationary state equilibrium condition the level of profits that implies that the level of investment expenditure is maintained from period to period, thus:

$$I_t = I_{t-i} = I_{t-i-\lambda}$$
$$I_t = I_{t-1} = I_{t-2} \tag{5.42}$$

Then Equation 5.41 would read

$$f\,(I_t) = I_t + bf\,(I_t) \tag{5.43}$$
or
$$f\,(I_t)\,[1 - b] = I_t \tag{5.44}$$
and

$$f(I_t) = [1 / (1 - b)] \cdot (I_t) \tag{5.45}$$

and then from equation (5.40) for a level of stable investment expenditures, we read the determination of profits as

$$P_t = [1 / (1 - b)] \cdot (I_{t-i}) \tag{5.46}$$

What 5.46 does is to reduce the number of determinants of profit to the one element of lagged investment, for it "contains" the other element of capitalists' consumption that depends on past profits that are themselves determined by lagged investment.

Interestingly enough, Equation 5.46 can be read to determine to what extent the current profit level is attributable to the manner of capitalists' expenditure. If we take $b = 0$ so that capitalists invest all, then lagged investment determines profits, which equates with current savings, which equals current investment, which determines profit and equivalent savings some periods into the future, and so forth. The sequence is such that savings (via current investment) determine future profits; savings and profits are equal and codetermined as a function of past investment. And we think here of a stationary state where, as we mentioned before, investment and thus savings and also profits are constant through time.

But capitalists will most likely decide to engage in expenditures in a given period that exceed earnings of the proceeding period; we can express this circumstance by assuming now that $b > 0$ and thereby adding a luxury goods flow. Profits are

$$P_t = I_{t-i} + b (I_{t-i}) \tag{5.47}$$

which may result in a stationary circumstance at a higher level. And this brings up an interesting situation that, in all reality, further reinforces a sequence that is opposite conventional assumptions. Say we are in a stationary condition and there is a sudden increase in investment spending that leads to higher savings and profits, which will also increase by the same amount. But the luxury consumption flow (if it did not exist before) will come online only after a time lag, and thereby continue to add to expenditures and profits after the initial rise in investment and savings comes to a halt. So the peak in profits comes after the peak in savings. The point we want to make here is that it is not savings that limits or determines investment and profits as conventional thinking tells; it is rather the reverse. And we can make this point quite evident by thinking in terms of the capitalist as our "organizational firm." The markup pricing policy will determine how much net cash inflow (business savings) will be generated relative to sales. But what will actually be realized once the margin is set depends on the actual strength of sales, that is, on the level of aggregate demand that is reflective of the level of investment and consumption spending. Thus savings are seen to be determined essentially by capitalist activity; to say again, it is profits and hence savings that are then determined by investment.

We will, in a subsequent chapter, look somewhat deeper at this causality, certainly with regard to the basis for savings. But the reader at this point can discern that the Principles' discussion of an equilibrium level of income lacks an essential understanding; it is not the aggregate level of income to which one should relate a savings function to determine the level of savings that is in support of investment that, itself, is normally presented as exogoneously given. Or, if it is put into some functional relation, one does not see profits in the equation. Of course, what is needed (and we might consider this principle as a modification of the Principles of Economics approach) is a calculation of savings in relation to the relative shares in output.

But here, at the close of this chapter on distribution, let us construct the equation revealing the profit share. Realizing that we are considering distributive shares, we understand that the wage and salary bill (W) will change in relation to the change in national income via the impact of the change in aggregate demand on employment levels. Thus for a given level of the national product of the private sector (we maintain the assumption of a negligible government sector) we have:

$$W = \alpha(Y) \tag{5.48}$$
with α positive and < 1

And the wage and profit shares are:

$$\alpha = W / Y, 1 - \alpha = P / Y \tag{5.49}$$

with the difference between Y and W being profits P, we can then state:

$$Y_t - P_t = W_t = \alpha(Y_t) \tag{5.50}$$

$$\text{So } Y_t (1 - \alpha) = P_t \tag{5.51}$$

$$Y_t = P_t / (1 - \alpha) \tag{5.52}$$

And from (5.46):

$$P_t = I_t / (1 - b) \tag{5.53}$$

Combining (5.53) and (5.52) has us solve for the level of the national output as

$$Y_t = [I_t / (1 - b)] / (1 - \alpha) \tag{5.54}$$

$$Y_t = I_t / (1 - b)(1 - \alpha) \tag{5.55}$$

Now some minor manipulation allows us to determine the profit share. We know that b is the capitalists' propensity to consume out of profits, so $(1 - b)$ would be the capitalists' propensity to save, which we write as (s_K). And from (5.49) we recognize the second term in the denominator of (5.55) as the profit share in output. All this comes together as:

$$Y_t = I_t / [s_K \cdot (P_t / Y_t)] \tag{5.56}$$

$$\text{Or } Y_t \cdot P_t / Y_t = I_t / s_K \tag{5.57}$$

$$\text{And } P_t / Y_t = (1 / s_K) \cdot (I_t / Y_t) \tag{5.58}$$

Assuming the extreme case of what is known as "classical thriftiness" (to highlight the essential role of that capitalist class), we have the propensity to save out of profits being unity; thus, to reiterate, a volume of profits creates an equal volume of savings. With $s_K = 1$ equation (5.58) reduces to:

$$P_t / Y_t = I_t / Y_t \tag{5.59}$$

Profits as a share of output mirrors the level of capitalists' expenditures (here totally composed of investment) as a share of output. And the level of profits automatically creates the savings to maintain the necessary subsequent level of investment expenditures. However, to maintain this stationary condition of income and employment implies the presence of a real wage that maintains the requisite level of aggregate demand. And this means the ability of capitalists (in reality the megacorp organizations) to hold to profit margins (the existence of a price markup) that continue to provide the necessary savings to accommodate the value of the investment-to-output ratio at the given level of employment.

We now appreciate that an understanding of profits and of the profit share must be derived from a macroeconomic context that emphasizes the interdepence between a level of aggregate demand and the distribution of income between profits and wages, which is reflective of the activity of economic classifications of "people." And this activity reveals itself in the form of realistic micro foundations, whether it be in the mechanics of arriving at the money wage or that of the ability of producers to control the price margins over costs and their simultaneous control of investment. What must be recognized is that there are no inexorable laws of production that determine the distribution of income; that distribution is to be explained through an understanding of the economic institutional arrangements of society. We contrast this view with the conventional formula for the profit share, which reads

$$P / Y = [(\Delta Y / \Delta K) \cdot K] / Y \tag{5.60}$$

with the "mechanistic" explanation stemming from that marginal productivity law governing output and factor utilization.

Furthermore, the introductory economic course exposes the student to distribution within a micro setting under the label of the pricing of resource markets, as if this follows naturally the analysis of pricing of commodity markets. Of course, the usual explanation of what goes on in both settings is greatly an exercise in miseducation. But what makes matters worse is the compartmentalizing of thinking; when students are subsequently brought to an aggregate market discussion, the proceedings are normally divorced from any distributional micro understanding.

In our alternative endeavor we not only propose a contrary to traditional explanation of the distributive shares, but show that such an explanation is indispensable for an understanding of macro outcomes. In the next chapter we deepen our understanding of this framework.

Notes

1. Paul Samuelson and William Nordhaus, *Economics*, 14th ed. (New York: McGraw Hill, 1992), p. 20.

2. C.E. Ferguson, *Microeconomic Theory* (Homewood, IL: Richard Irwin, 1969), p. 116.

3. Alfred Eichner, *A Guide to Post-Keynesian Economics* (White Plains, NY: M.E. Sharpe, 1979), p. 103.

4. Samuelson and Nordhaus, *Economics*, p. 212.

5. Ibid., p. 274.

6. Campbell McConnell and Stanley Brue, *Economics*, 13th ed. (New York: McGraw Hill, 1998), p. 607.

7. Samuelson and Norhaus, *Economics*, p. 274.

8. M.C. Howard and J.E. King, *The Political Economy of Marx* (London: Longman, 1985), p. 46.

9. Eichner, *A Guide to Post-Keynesian Economics*, p. 111.

10. See the analysis in Marc Lavoie, *Foundations of Post-Keynesian Economics* (Aldershot, UK: Edward Elgar, 1992), p.220.

11. Ibid., p. 223.

12. We have the level of employment as

$$N = N_o + N_v \tag{5.i}$$

and the given technology yields

$$N_v = \frac{Y}{l_v}, = N_o = \frac{Y}{l_o} \tag{5.ii}$$

where l_v and l_o are the required input coefficients per unit of output for each type of employment. The ratio of actual output (Y) to full-capacity output (Y^*) is

$$U = \frac{Y}{Y^*} = \text{degree of capacity utilization} \qquad (5.\text{iii})$$

The actual level of output is given by

$$\begin{aligned} Y &= [N - N_o]\, l_v \\ &= N_v l_v \end{aligned} \qquad (5.\text{iv})$$

Thus the overall production per worker is

$$\frac{Y}{N} = \frac{Y}{N_v + N_o} = \frac{N_v l_v}{N_v + N_o} \qquad (5.\text{v})$$

and from 5.ii and 5.iii we can state

$$Y^* = \frac{Y}{U}, \text{ so } N_o = \frac{Y}{U l_o} \qquad (5.\text{vi})$$

Then

$$\frac{Y}{N} = \frac{N_v l_v}{N_v + \frac{Y}{U l_o}} = \frac{N_v l_v}{N_v + \frac{N_v l_v}{U l_o}} \qquad (5.\text{vii})$$

Now dividing 5.vii by l_v and with some manipulation we arrive at

$$\frac{Y}{N} = \frac{l_v}{1 + \frac{l_v}{l_o}} \qquad (5.\text{viii})$$

The greater the rate of capacity utilization (U) the larger the decisive term on the right side of 5.viii and the larger the productivity per worker.

We can come to this conclusion somewhat more directly by dividing 5.v by. So:

$$\frac{Y}{N} = \frac{l_v}{1 + \frac{N_o}{N_v}} \qquad (5.\text{ix})$$

For a given rate of capacity utilization the level of productive employment will be some proportion of what it would be at full-capacity operations, that is, when $U = 1$. Then:

$$N_v = U(N_v^*) \qquad (5.\text{x})$$

So we write 5.ix as

$$\frac{Y}{N} = \frac{l_v}{1 + \dfrac{N_o}{UN_v*}}$$ (5.xi)

Yet N_o stands as a fixed ratio to at $U = 1$ operations, and will fall to this fixed position as utilization rates increase. We left this fixed rates be given by (f) as

$$N_o = f(N_v*)$$ (5.xii)

Then we can restate 5.xi as:

$$\frac{Y}{N} = \frac{l_v}{\dfrac{1 + f(N_v*)}{UN_v*}} = \frac{l_v}{1 + \dfrac{f}{U}}$$ (5.xiii)

Again, the greater U the greater the overall productivity up to $U = 1$. It is the last term on the right side of 5.xiii that labels the vertical axes in Figure 5.15.

13. An example of how work procedures can alter productivity was seen at the Maytag appliance corporation. Originally a complement of four workers at four workstations had each assembled an entire refrigerator door. This meant that there had to be a full set of parts at each station. But a change in procedure now has the same four workers produce ninety more doors per hour, which was roughly a 15 percent productivity increase.

What happened was that the four workers now positioned themselves around a lazy-Susan contraption, with the plastic door mold circulating by each worker. As it does, each worker adds one metal part, so that about every thirty-seven seconds a finished door comes off the revolving table. At each station there is only the part that is needed rather than keeping a full set of parts at every station.

The result is that labor costs per unit of production are reduced, thus enabling the firm to squeeze out more revenue per hour of pay. This type of procedural change, as well as the speed of the assembly line, was worked out by a productivity committee of which we spoke. These kinds of adjustments translate into increased profits and rising wages and, importantly, overall stable prices, as has generally been the case in the growth experience of the 1990s.

14. Oliver E. Williamson, *The Economic Institutions of Capitalism* (New York: Free Press, 1985), p. 254.

15. Stanley Bober, *Recent Developments in Non-Neoclassical Economics* (Brookfield, VT, and Aldershot, UK: Ashgate, 1997), p. 63

16. Eichner, *A Guide to Post-Keynesian Economics*, p. 51.

17. Luigi L. Pasinetti, "Changes in the Rate of Profit and Switches of Techniques," *Quarterly Journal of Economics* LXXX (November 1966).

18. Based on the model by Paul A. Samuelson, "A Summing Up," in *Quarterly Journal of Economics* LXXX (November 1966).

19. See the analysis in Pasinetti, "Changes in the Rate of Profit." Also the discussion in Stanley Bober, *Modern Macroeconomics* (London: Croom Helm, 1988).

20. Heinz D. Kurz and Neri Salvatori, *Understanding Classical Economics* (London: Routledge, 1998), p. 245.

21. Ibid., p. 254.

22. M. Kalecki, *Theory of Economic Dynamics* (New York: Rinehart, 1954), p. 45.

23. Ibid., p. 46.

24. J.A. Kregal, "Income Distribution," in *A Guide to Post-Keyesian Econonics*, ed. Eichner, p. 53.

25. There is normally a constant term in this consumption function that is taken to be subject to long-term changes, though constant in the short term. We omit this term for presentation simplicity; and as we are discussing matters within a stationary state, this omission is of no consequence.

26. Kalecki, *Theory of Economic Dynamics*, p. 53.

27. Ibid., p. 54.

6
Distribution—Extending the Analysis

Before going forward, let us revisit Equation 5.58 to be certain of an important point. To say that capitalists' savings propensity (s_K) is equal to unity is to tell us that capitalists are consuming all of their profit income in the form of investment expenditures, which translates to Equation 5.46 in the previous chapter as $b = 0$. And this is normally what is envisioned by the phrase "capitalists get what they spend," saying to us that profit will be equal to the value of the investment goods purchased by them. For profit levels to be stationary in time, capitalists would need to invest in every period an amount equal to what they had in the preceding period. But capitalists can decide to spend all profit income on noninvestment goods (luxury wage goods), or spend a profit in some proportion between wage goods and investment goods; in this latter circumstance profit earning would exceed investment expenditures in the same proportion as the profits are used to purchase luxury consumption goods. As far as profit income is concerned, it is maintained independently of how it is spent.

With this reinforcement, let us look again at Equation 5.46. Should $b = 0.5$, then the decision has been to spend half of the preceding period's earnings on investment projects and half on luxury living; thus one-half of current profits is attributable to consumption expenditures, with terms in the parentheses of Equation 5.46 being reduced by one-half below its value in the event $b = 0$, and the investment term would best be replaced with a consumption goods expression. Of course, via Equation 5.58 with $s_K = 0.5$, the I_K/Y_t is reduced by one-half. The reader should see Equation 5.46 or 5.53 as lookalike expressions to the multiplier equation in the macro Principles course; it is just that, for the term $(1 - b)$ does not here signify a "leakage" but an alternative profit generating expenditure.

Again, let us restate Equation 5.58 of the proceeding chapter—here as Equation 6.1.

$$\frac{P_t}{Y} = 1/s_K(\frac{I_t}{Y})$$

(6.1)

Should $s_K = 0.5$, then realized profits as a proportion of income is twice that of investment expenditures, with the difference resulting from a consumption out of profit flow. In that case, and with a careful interpretation, Equation 6.1 can be considered as a profit multiplier expression. To reiterate: Capitalists are spending an amount equal to earnings of the last period, and resultant earnings therefrom are independent as to the type of expenditures. Another way to make our point is to say that the share of profits (and thus the share of wages) in income is determined once the capitalist's propensity to consume and the ratio of investment to output are known. We see that backing away from the strong (extreme) assumption that all profits are saved (thereby allowing for a capitalist's consumption flow) causes no problems for an understanding of the profit share.

However, the implication of dropping the extreme assumption concerning "workers" for an analysis of the profit share is not that straightforward. And, we recall, the strong assumption regarding this class of people is that expenditure is equal to their income (i.e., that as an economic class they are presumed not to accumulate "property" through current savings, nor are they presumed to draw on any past accumulation to supplement their expenditure). How would the presence of workers' savings affect our understanding of the determination of the profit share? Initially we want to look at the matter in terms of savings propensities out of different classification of income, keeping with the notion that the different types of income accrue solely to different economic classes of people.

With income divided into the classifications of wage income (W) and profit income (P) we have aggregate savings (S) as

$$S = s_W(W) + s_P(P)$$

(6.2)

where s_W and s_P are the savings propensities out of wage and profit incomes respectively, with the assumption that $1 > s_P > s_W$. This enables us to "calculate" the ratio of savings to income and expose its relation to the distribution of the level of income rather than to the aggregate income level itself, which, as the reader will recall, is the approach taken in the Principles course construction of the Keynesian aggregate expenditure model. With $Y - P = W$, then from Equation 6.2 we see

$$S = s_W(Y - P) + s_P(P)$$

(6.3)

$$= (s_P - s_W)P + s_W(Y)$$

(6.4)

and dividing by income (Y) gives

$$\frac{S}{Y} = (s_P - s_W)\frac{P}{Y} + s_W \tag{6.5}$$

On this analysis the savings ratio is determined once the share of profits, and the savings propensities of the different economic classes, are known. This may be made even clearer by restating Equation 6.3 to read

$$\frac{S}{Y} = s_P(\frac{P}{Y}) + s_W(1 - \frac{P}{Y}) \tag{6.6}$$

Relating the equation for aggregate savings to the Keynesian equilibrium condition for a given level of capitalists' investment expenditure, we have

$$I = (s_P - s_W)P + s_W(Y) = S \tag{6.7}$$

which, upon dividing by Y, yields

$$\frac{P}{Y} = \frac{1}{s_P - s_W}(\frac{I}{Y}) + \frac{s_W}{s_P - s_W} \tag{6.8}$$

Equation 6.8 can be made less cumbersome by stating it as

$$\frac{P}{Y} = \frac{\frac{I}{Y} - s_W}{s_P - s_W} \tag{6.9}$$

What these equations are telling us is that allowing for the reality of savings out of the wage classification of income (i.e., the general case) does not change our previous observation that for the Keynesian equilibrium condition of $I = S$ to be satisfied through time (the stationary condition) and hence maintain an existing employment level, there needs to extend a particular distribution of income between profit and wages, such as to yield the requisite level of savings in "support" of the investment expenditures that maintains the level of aggregate output. Thus our previous structuring of this Keynesian condition can be considered as special or limiting cases that we restate for a quick comparison with $s_W = 0$, $s_K < 1$; Equation 6.8 reduces to our case of

$$s_K(\frac{P}{Y}) = \frac{S}{Y} = \frac{I}{Y}$$

or

$$\frac{P}{Y} = \frac{1}{s_K}(\frac{I}{Y}) \tag{6.10}$$

and where $s_W = 0$, $s_K = 1$ we simply have

$$\frac{P}{Y} = \frac{I}{Y} \tag{6.11}$$

While the general case does not change the essential distributive underpinning of the equilibrium condition, it does present a different alignment in comparison to a state where $s_W = 0$.

The presence of savings out of wage income means a lower share of wage goods in aggregate output; workers are reducing their expenditures on wage goods relative to capitalists' expenditures. This reduces capacity utilization in the wage goods sector that results in reduced profit levels at the existing mark-up price and may over time bring about a reduction in the administered price itself. But however the mechanics, the result of $s_W > 0$ is to reduce profit margins in the wage good sector, which then reduce its ability to purchase investment goods, thereby reducing demand and profit margins in the capital goods sector. A look at Equation 6.9 reveals that savings out of wages reduces the profit ratio below the ratio of investment expenditures to output and thereby the volume of capitalists' savings (keeping $s_P = 1$); in essence it would seem that capitalists are getting less than what they spend, which may very well motivate a reduction in their own spending. We might conclude that the reality of $s_W > 0$ breaks down the Keynesian equilibrium state, sending the economy into a condition of underemployment as a reflection of insufficient aggregate demand. In other words, savings out of wages could misalign the distribution of income in terms of too great a reduction in the profit share to maintain the condition of $I = S$.

But this negative impact need not happen providing that s_W does not exceed an upper bound, and that the real wage rate (i.e., the profit margin as determined by the level of prices with respect to money wages) is flexible with respect to changes in demand. The lower expenditure on wage goods relative to investment goods should lead to a fall in the relative price of wage goods, thereby increasing the purchasing power of workers and yielding them a higher real wage and simultaneously a fall in profit margins. Thus the presence of $s_W > 0$ is, over time, counterbalanced by a higher real wage such as to negate any demand insufficiency. The system can maintain a full-employment level of output in the presence of the complication (of positive savings out of wage income) by adjusting the distributive shares via real wage (profit margin) flexibility. Thus in a comparative look at two full-employment stationary states (one when there is positive savings out of wage income and the other when such savings are zero), it is the difference in income distribution that maintains the requisite level of aggregate demand, and releases the required level of savings to be absorbed by the investment-to-output ratio that maintains the equilibrium condition. And, to reiterate, we would see a higher wage share in output in the state where $s_W > 0$.

Yet a cautionary word is in order. The presence of savings out of wages is not inimical to the employment equilibrium condition, providing that such savings are small in relation to savings as a percentage of profit. As we can see directly from Equation 6.9, a worker's savings ratio in excess of the ratio of investment expenditures to output evidences an economy with a zero or negative share of profit, which eliminates an economic class that is defined by the nature of its profit income. Yet in a practical sense a condition of

$$S_W > \frac{I}{Y} \tag{6.12}$$

would send the economy into a state of chronic underemployment, and indeed overwhelm any real wage adjustment. Conceptually the society could over time devolve into a one-class (workers' state?) economy. We will not pursue this interesting hypothetical scenario, though the reader may see this as an additional justification to exercise those fiscal and monetary policies to stave off the condition of insufficient demand and underemployment. Yet to call upon to such policies is to acknowledge a misalignment of the distribution shares.

We can also characterize our stationary condition as one with an unchanging rate of profit in relation to the existence of a particular investment-to-capital ratio; in this condition the level of the capital stock (as well, the size of the labor force) is unchanging with gross investment equal to replacement expenditures. With the rate of profit (r) as

$$r = \frac{P}{Y} \cdot \frac{Y}{K} \tag{6.13}$$

then by multiplying this with Equation 6.8 we have

$$r \equiv \frac{P}{K} = \frac{1}{s_P - s_W}(\frac{I}{K}) - \frac{s_W}{s_P - s_W}(\frac{Y}{K}) \tag{6.14}$$

giving us the rate of profit corresponding to the stationary equilibrium $I = S$ condition. Again, our special cases emerge (similar to Equations 6.10 and 6.11) on the basis of $s_W = 0$, $s_P = 1$. Thus

$$r = \frac{1}{s_P}(\frac{I}{K}) \tag{6.15}$$

and

$$r = \frac{I}{K} \tag{6.16}$$

There is an additional complication as a result of acknowledging workers' savings that we need to consider if we are to gain a full understanding of its effect. Historically, in the development of the analysis, capitalists are placed in an advantageous position in that they do possess savings (in line with their essential task to accumulate capital); thus their purchasing power is large relative to their actual expenditures. While it is true that they earn what they spend, it is also the situation that capitalists, as a class of people, are in a position to spend in excess of what they earn. The level of profits may then be considered as one of several variables inducing a level of capitalists' expenditures—essentially investment expenditures. The connection between expenditures and income is far less rigid than what was supposed for workers, by which one really means a class of people that do not receive income from property.

For the latter it was considered that their reserve of purchasing power (i.e., savings) was small or nonexistent; the connection between expenditure and income was treated as being quite rigid. And we can understand this approach, since it was thought that the only expenditure by workers was for wage goods. Thus an act of not spending all of one's income was seen as an investment act of hoarding, since these monies would not be purchasing anything and would only serve to reduce one's standard of living. Indeed, the function of this class of persons is to spend all on the purchase of wage goods in order to maintain and reproduce themselves, that is, to provide the system with its labor force. Thus workers are considered to spend more if they earn more, and are forced to spend less when they earn less; in any particular period their purchasing power was considered no greater than their expenditures.

But as we have been talking about, there is savings out of nonproperty (wage) income, and this is not an irrational act of hoarding; furthermore, in our stationary condition this volume of savings, when added to that of capitalists, maintains the Keynesian equilibrium condition and the requisite investment-to-output ratio. Yet the fact that workers' savings end up in the hands of capitalists (firms) to be used mainly for purposes of investment expenditures, is obviously not the result of a gift transfer, nor are these savings forced and then confiscated by the state as the transfer agent. So the question is, what are workers purchasing with their savings? What is it that is motivating workers to accumulate property in the form of money capital? The answer, obviously, is that they are purchasing a portion of the profits earned by the capitalists' investment expenditures; and as a class of people, workers will receive profit in proportion to the savings contributed. We can put our point here, as I noted in a recent book, as follows: "If workers as a class of people are not to follow the attribute normally assigned to them, namely, to spend all they receive, then they must be seen as being rewarded for the transfer of their savings to capitalists by receiving a part of capitalists' income, i.e., profits."[1] The trouble with our previous discussion admitting to $s_W > 0$, is that we simultaneously held to equating the difference between classifications of income with the difference between economic classifications of people. But the approach that workers do not receive nonwage income implies that their savings are somehow given away freely, or that such savings are taken from them (by the state?), and as they are thus "robbed" of ownership, there is nothing to reward. Of course, this is an unreality; for as Pasinetti says, in any type of society, "when any individual saves a part of his income, he must also be allowed to own it, otherwise he would not save at all."[2]

The reader can imagine a transfer of savings by workers to a capitalist—better yet to think of a transfer to a firm—which serves as a part of the firm's total investment expenditure. Workers, in a sense, will then claim ownership of that portion of the capital purchased by their transferred savings, and receive that portion of the total profit income attributable to or created by their share of the capital. Pasinetti goes on to say, "This means that the stock of capital which exists in the system is owned by those people (capitalists or workers) who in the past made the corresponding savings. And since ownership of capital entitles the owner to a rate of interest, if workers have saved—and thus own a part of the stocks of capital (directly or through loans to capitalists)—then they will also receive a share of the total profit."[3]

There are then two concepts in an analysis of income distribution: that of the distribution of income as between the wage and profit classifications of income, and an analysis of income between the worker and capitalist classification of people. These two concepts (as between categories of income and categories of people) coincide, as we have seen, in the particular case in which there are no savings out of wages. But in the reality of such positive savings, we will need to reformulate the analysis to account for the distribution of categories of income as between economic classes of people, and see what effect this has on the determination of the profit share and the rate of profit.

We maintain the basic divisions:

$$S = S_W + S_P \qquad (6.17)$$

$$Y = W + P \qquad (6.18)$$

However:

$$P = P_{W0} + P_K \tag{6.19}$$

Letting W_0 stand for workers, as we are using W to represent wage. The K symbol does double duty here: As a subscript it relates to capitalists (as people or firms), and as a capital letter as part of a ratio it stands for capital (as instruments of production).

Aggregate savings must now read

$$S = s_{W0}(W + P_{W0}) + s_K(P_K) \tag{6.20}$$

By substituting the division of profit into the income statement 6.18, we find aggregate wages as

$$W = Y - P_{W0} - P_K \tag{6.21}$$

which upon substituting into Equation 6.20 gives an expression for savings as

$$S = S_{W0}(Y) + (s_K - s_{W0})P_K \tag{6.22}$$

The $I = S$ equilibrium condition as a proportion of income emerges as

$$\frac{I}{Y} = s_{W0} + \frac{(s_K - s_{W0})P_K}{Y} \tag{6.23}$$

And following the same procedure that led to the profit share and rate of profit outcome of Equations 6.8 and 6.14, we now find

$$\frac{P_K}{Y} = \frac{1}{s_K - s_{W0}}\left(\frac{I}{Y}\right) - \frac{s_{W0}}{s_K - s_{W0}} \tag{6.24}$$

$$r_K = \frac{P_K}{k} = \frac{1}{s_K - s_{W0}}\left(\frac{I}{K}\right) - \frac{s_{W0}}{s_K - s_{W0}}\left(\frac{Y}{K}\right) \tag{6.25}$$

Note the degree of similarity: the right-hand sides of 6.24 and 6.25 are the same as 6.8 and 6.14, though here they yield different (and limited) results. This reinforces the observation that the way in which we previously arrived at the profit share (and also the rate of profit) was mistaken, since it was based on an erroneous consideration of workers' savings. With what we now see as the correct understanding of such savings, the analysis results only in a partial ratio (Equation 6.24), and thereby gives the distribution of income between classifications of people and not between classifications of income. Having determined the ratio of capitalists' profit to income, one can then ascertain the share of workers' income (consisting of wages and profits).

To arrive at an expression for the aggregate profit ratio we would need to add workers' profits as a share of income to both sides of Equation 6.24. Thus:

$$\frac{P}{Y} \equiv \frac{P_K}{Y} + \frac{P_{W0}}{Y} = \frac{1}{S_K - S_{W0}}(\frac{I}{Y}) - \frac{S_{W0}}{S_K - S_{W0}} + \frac{P_{W0}}{Y} \tag{6.26}$$

And we would also want to obtain an expression for the overall rate of profit in the economy, that is, a ratio of total profits to total capital. This requires that we add the rate of profit (interest) earned by workers on their investments to of capitalists; as we similarly adjust Equation 6.25:

$$r \equiv \frac{P_K}{K} + \frac{P_{W0}}{K} = \frac{1}{S_K - S_{W0}}(\frac{I}{K}) - \frac{S_{W0}}{S_K - S_{W0}}(\frac{Y}{K}) + \frac{P_{W0}}{K} \tag{6.27}$$

Both Equation 6.26 and 6.27 go through a degree of algebraic manipulation to arrive at the final expressions for the determination of the aggregate distribution of income and rate of profit. The reader will find this worked out in an endnote.[4] Here we set down two equations resulting from these manipulations that open the way for some very important conclusions.

Regarding the aggregate rate of profit, Equation 6.27 works through to:

$$\frac{P}{K} \cdot \frac{S_K}{I}[I - S_{W0}(Y)] = \frac{1}{K}[I - S_{W0}(Y)] \tag{6.28}$$

With the very realistic assumption that workers' savings out of their income does not constitute the whole of savings (i.e., investment) in the economy, that is, $I - S_{W0}(Y) \neq 0$, and by dividing 6.28 through by $I - S_{W0}(Y)$, we arrive at

$$\frac{P}{K} \cdot [S_K \cdot \frac{1}{I}] = \frac{1}{K}$$

and

$$\tag{6.29}$$

$$\frac{P}{K} = \frac{1}{S_K}(\frac{I}{K})$$

And with regard to the aggregate profit ratio, Equation 6.27 works through to

$$\frac{P}{Y} = \frac{1}{s_K - s_{wo}}\left(\frac{I}{Y}\right) - \frac{s_{wo}}{s_K - s_{wo}} + \frac{P}{K}\left[\frac{s_K s_{wo}}{s_K - s_{wo}}\left(\frac{K}{I}\right) - \frac{s_{wo}}{s_K - s_{wo}}\left(\frac{K}{Y}\right)\right] \tag{6.30}$$

This foreboding-looking equation (6.30) will, with some work, reduce itself to

$$\frac{P}{Y} = \frac{1}{s_K}\left(\frac{I}{Y}\right) \tag{6.31}$$

The reader immediately recognizes that Equations 6.29 and 6.31 were encountered earlier numbered 6.10 and 6.15, where they were considered "special" cases due to the particular assumption of $s_w = 0$. Now they reappear as a result of taking into account the presence of workers' savings and their receipt of a share of existing profit. The results are general in that they are no longer dependent upon making any particular assumption regarding the propensities to save of workers; these outcomes, when constructed out of the reality of positive workers' savings, are certainly more satisfying.

But it is the message that is most striking. As we are now aware, the maintenance of the stationary condition with its Keynesian savings–investment equality requires the underpinning of an appropriate distribution of income and associated real wage rate, so as to generate the required investment expenditures and thereby the level of income that, so to speak, feeds back to maintain the equality of aggregate demand and aggregate supply of commodities.

In the formation of these "internal balances" the activity of workers, in terms of their savings propensity, plays an irrelevant role. We draw our attention again to the result, that while $s_W > 0$, this term does not appear in the outcomes of Equations 6.29 and 6.31. Certainly workers' savings will influence the disposition of the level of profit between themselves and capitalists, but workers do not at all influence the level of profit. In other words, the fact of positive savings out of wages will impact the distribution of income as between classes of people, but does not impact the distribution as between the classifications of income. It is, of course, the latter distribution that is strategic, since it is the level of profits that is the essential agent that generates the required level of investment expenditures and an associated level of savings. Here it would be helpful to reiterate a point (which drew our thinking away from the standard approach): It is not savings that determines investment, but rather the reverse, that investment determines savings via its impact on profits.

The startling result that workers' propensity to save does not play a role in determining total profit (it is, as well, irrelevant with regard to the overall rate of profit) that is the determining factor in maintaining the equilibrium condition, and, as we shall see in the next chapter, it is as well the essential propellant of economic growth, would compel us to take a close look at the logic behind the results of Equations 6.29 and 6.31. The fact of maintaining an equilibrium level of output in the presence of positive workers' savings, and its reflection in the equality of the Keynesian $I = S$ association means, as we mentioned earlier, that such savings do not behave as a depressing factor to aggregate demand and profits. Workers' savings must then be acting to complement that of capitalists in the maintenance of the equilibrium level of investment expenditures.

Suppose we start with the fictional scenario in which workers transfer their savings as a gift to capitalists. They would receive no part of existing profits generated by the capitalists' investment of their total savings. Capitalist activity determines total profits; and as they own all the capital (i.e., savings), they receive all the profit. This fictional case is as if we had only one class of savers, that is, $s_W = 0$.

But, as we pointed out, in the reality of matters, workers will receive a share of existing profits (as a reward for the investment of their savings via loans to capitalists); the amount of profits received will be in proportion to the amount of savings they provide (in proposition to the ownership of capital). Thus, for our two categories of people, we have

$$\frac{P_K}{S_K} = \frac{P_{W0}}{S_{W0}} \qquad (6.32)$$

So that for each category, profits are proportional to savings. Pasinetti stresses that this relationship "does not depend on any behavioral assumption whatsoever; it simply and logically follows from the institutional principle that profits are distributed in proportion to ownership of capital."[5] From 6.32 we can write:

$$\frac{P_{W0}}{s_{W0}(W + P_{W0})} = \frac{P_K}{s_K(P_K)} \qquad (6.33)$$

If we take that the workers' propensity to consume is the same whether out of wage income or profit income, then the makeup of their income will have no effect on their total savings (or for that matter on their total consumption). And, as well, the savings behavior of workers will have no effect on the aggregate level of savings in the economy.

When workers save out of profits, they do so at a lesser rate than capitalists would have saved out of these profits had they not distributed them to workers. But to this lower savings ratio in relation to profit income, one must add the same savings ratio in relation to wage income; this will result in a total level of workers' savings that by itself would be the same as the savings on the part of capitalists out of those workers' profits (at the higher rate) had the capitalists retained them. Thus the sharing of profits with workers will not alter the aggregate level of savings. Another way to see this, is that the higher level of workers' consumption out of profit income as compared to that of capitalists (had capitalists maintained these profits), is offset by their savings out of wage income. All we are saying is

$$s_{w_0}(W + P_{w_0}) = s_K(P_{w_0})$$

$$\text{or}$$

$$s_{w_0}(W) = s_K(P_{w_0}) - s_{w_0}(P_{w_0})$$

(6.34)

And expression 6.34 reflects the necessary balance in the division of the output between consumption goods and investment goods, as this division relates to the division of income between profits and wages. This reinforces our understanding of the strategic role played by that capitalist economic class; they have the investment decision power, and through it, they determine the investment-to-output ratio and the overall level of profit. But in doing so, they determine the level of profits accruing to workers, given their savings propensity. According to Pasinetti, "Whatever the workers may do, they can only share in an amount of total profits which for them is predetermined; they have no power to influence it at all."[6] And it is aggregate profits that form the basic font for savings and play an essential role in the investment decision.

As we bring this chapter on distribution to a close, it may be useful to remind ourselves that these discussions of pricing and distribution enable us to achieve an understanding of the supportive economic balances for that very aggregative Keynesian equilibrium condition. That is, it allows us to peer below the surface data, and realize that such macro elements as investment, savings, consumption, and the categories of income, if we are to properly deal with them, are the result of subaggregative behavior of groupings of economic classifications of people. We may well think of the capitalist in terms of the large organizational enterprise with its executive group making the key decisions regarding pricing and investment expenditures. Though with smaller start-up companies, or even large firms that are family-owned, the term capitalist may still be envisioned in terms of an individual. But no matter, we are considering a grouping of economic entities in the society whose income is derived from profits, as differentiated from a group of people whom we referred to as workers. Yet this workers term is a general designation by which we refer to those individuals whose income from work is in the form of wages. But not all income from work takes this form; for example, there is obviously such income in terms of professional earnings and salaries of executive and professional employees. However, no harm is done to our analysis; we simply lump all of these nonprofit earnings into the wage category.

The essential thought is that it is the activity of that profit-earning group that generates the investment and the subsequent "productive distribution" of income, that is, the division between profits and wages. We would reiterate that the activity that generates the profits will also create the equilibrium level of savings.

We now have a sense of the economic balances—for example, the ratio of investment-to-income, that of savings-to-income, and that of profits-to-wages (relationships that are hidden from view when observing the most aggregative data)—that need to be struck in the maintenance level of economic activity. And in the context of the stationary state this level—whether we consider it in terms of employment, production, or its representation as given by the stock of capital equipment available to society—continues to exist through time. But in reality what may be a desirable economic state at a certain point will not be so through time. Certainly in a society of change when the population and capital stock are increasing, and where technological advances are occurring, we need to reformulate the Keynesian stationary state into a framework that reveals the economic circumstances enabling the society to maintain the full-employment of a growing resource base through time.

Notes

1. Stanley Bober, *Recent Developments in Non-Neoclassical Economics* (Brookfield, VT, and Aldershot, UK: Ashgate, 1997), p. 305.
2. Luigi L. Pasinetti, "Rate of Profit and Income Distribution in Relation to the Rate of Economic Growth," *Review of Economic Studies* 29 (1962): 270.
3. Ibid.
4. We see some of the steps toward obtaining the aggregate role of profit. The proportion of the total capital stock "owned" by workers ($\frac{K_{w0}}{K}$) is

$$\frac{K_{w0}}{K} = s_{w0}[\frac{Y}{I} - \frac{1}{S_k - S_{w0}} - \frac{S_{w0}}{S_k - S_{w0}}(\frac{Y}{I})] \tag{6.i}$$

which can be simplified to

$$\frac{K_{w0}}{K} = \frac{S_k S_{w0}}{S_k - S_{w0}}(\frac{Y}{I}) - \frac{S_k}{S_k - S_{w0}} \tag{6.ii}$$

Now we add the workers' rate of return, which is $\frac{K_{w0}}{K}$, to that of capitalists:

$$r \equiv \frac{1}{S_K - S_{W0}}\left(\frac{I}{K}\right) - \frac{S_{W0}}{S_K - S_{W0}}\left(\frac{Y}{K}\right) + r\left[\frac{S_K S_{W0}}{S_K - S_{W0}}\left(\frac{Y}{I}\right) - \frac{S_K}{S_K - S_{W0}}\right] \qquad (6.\text{iii})$$

which becomes

$$r \equiv \frac{P}{K} \cdot \frac{S_K}{I}(I - S_{W0}(Y)) = \frac{1}{K}(I - S_{W0}) \qquad (6.\text{iv})$$

Postulating that workers' savings out of their income, now consisting of wages and profits, do not constitute the whole of savings invested (that is, $I - sw_o(Y) \neq 0$, then by dividing 6.iv by $I - sw_o(Y)$ we obtain the equations in 6.29.

5. Pasinetti, "Rate of Profit," p. 273.
6. Ibid., p. 274.

7

Growth Economics and Distribution

Introduction

What do we mean by that often spoken, popular term economic growth? As a working definition, we could say that the subject of growth deals with how a society achieves increasing levels of real aggregate output over long periods of time. It is an understanding of how an economic system translates the expansion of its potential real GDP into actual increases in real output. The reader will recall the use of the production-possibilities curve as a way to demonstrate the need to make economic choices—the "what is to be produced" question—where the position of the curve at a point in time reflects a given level of production capability. Soon after, the discussion involves an awareness that at a later time period the curve will have shifted outwardly, so that any choice point on the outer curve reveals greater output levels than any point on the inner curve. And this is because over time the society will find an increase in its ability to produce due to a greater level of economic resources coupled with ongoing technological progress.

Implicit in all this is that as the possibilities curve moves outwardly, telling us of the increasing potentiality of production, the actual choice point will always be found on the outmost curve. Also, that the long-run view of economic performance is one of growth, and we mean a circumstance where the ongoing evolution of the society's capability of production is mirrored in its actual secular growth rate of output.

We would, perhaps, all agree with Samuelson and Nordhaus's assessment that "economic growth is the simple most important factor in the economic success of nations in the long-run."[1] The subject of economic growth is of primary importance for some obvious reasons. It is clear that if the population is growing, real income must also grow. A lack of growth in real output will simply translate into a reduction in living standards, which itself may negatively affect population growth. At the very least, then, if the society is to maintain a given living standard, income must grow in proportion to population. But success means more than this; it means that over time the society realizes a rising standard of living for an increasing population, and clearly this requires the growth in real income to exceed that of population—there has to be an increasing real GDP per capita. Furthermore, from the point of view of employment, real income must grow. The increasing labor force stemming from the growth in population requires income to rise fast enough to absorb the addition to the labor supply into production. Otherwise, one can imagine a society that is evidencing an insufficient rate of growth, and thereby developing an increasing core of unemployed labor that, sooner or later, may have political repercussions.

This is a good point at which to briefly remind ourselves how, in the previous chapter, the framework for the analysis was the stationary state. That is, we developed the conditions to maintain the level of employment (let us say full employment) and income through time. The level of the capital stock was unchanged, that is, there was no positive net investment; and income was maintained at a level sufficient to maintain full-capacity operations of the existing capital stock, which, of course, translates to the given employment level.

But here, in the framework of growth, all of the economic elements are expanding. The labor force is expanding; and given a relationship between the size of the capital stock and employment levels (we will want to look at the effects of technological change on this), then capital must be accumulating to maintain full employment, and the level of real income needs to be increasing proportionately to avoid idle capacity that will lead to a downward spiral in employment and income. Those balances (the ratio between economic elements) that in the previous chapter structured the stationary state will again be instrumental in maintaining economic growth. But all of the economic quantities along a given growth path grow in time and at the same proportional rate of growth, so that all of the ratios among them remain constant. Here, as the reader recalls, we are talking about the savings-to-income, profits-to-wages, investment-to-income, and the rate of profit as some of the ratios that need to be kept in proper balance if the society is to realize sustained growth at a consistent proportional rate.

But does an advanced industrial society realize economic change in such a fashion? It will behoove us to take a look at the experience of the United States over the span of the twentieth century and to consider whether an analysis framed on a steady growth-rate approach is a helpful and reasonably realistic model for us to understand the underlying issues.

When our view sweeps over Figures 7.1a and 7.1b (portraying annual and quarterly movements) we cannot help but be impressed with the image of the sustained increase in aggregate output over the long period of time—output having increased by a factor of twenty-five since about 1900. Yet this upward movement, when viewed through the up-close shorter time lens, say that of annual changes, is not continuous at all. What is actually experienced are the consistent wavelike patterns in economic activity referred to as business cycles. These are recurrent fluctuations that evidence the characteristic of much variability in the duration of the entire cycle—say as measured peak to peak—as well as the duration of either the expansion or contraction phase of the cycle. In general, to use a more technical description, we can say that cyclical fluctuations are nonperiodic in nature. Also, this variability is characteristic of the degree of amplitude or the severity of change in economic activity when taken over the cycle as a whole, or over a particular phase; usually one is concerned with the amplitude of the contraction of the cycle for obvious economic and political reasons.

Look at the cyclical experience over the century, which we divide into the time period from 1900 to 1945 and from 1945 to the present, in order to allow a bit more insight into Figure 7.1a. Fluctuations were more characteristics of the first part of the century in terms of frequency, duration, and severity of change. Between 1900 and 1945 the economy went through eleven cycles with an average duration of forty-eight months, as measured from trough to trough. But perhaps more telling is an average duration of economic downturns of eighteen months, with this number being severely influenced by the Great Depression of forty-three months from 1929 to 1933, resulting in the largest cyclical contraction of the century. What is striking though is that one does not see extended peacetime periods of economic growth; the two major periods of expansion occurred during the war years of 1914–1918 and 1938–1945, though there was an expansionary period of fifty months from 1933 to 1937.

The cyclical experience in the postwar period has been different. Compared to the eleven expansions and eleven contractions in the prewar period back to 1902, the postwar expansion has been one of nine recessions and ten expansions; more important is the fact of the change in the average length of expansions and contractions, which has led to a large increase in the amount of time that the society spends in periods of economic growth relative to the time it spends in economic declines. Since the end of World War II, expansions have lasted more than five times as long as contractions. During this period the average duration of expansion and recessions was fifty-nine months and ten months respectively. Looking at the data somewhat differently, we find that expansions on average lasted 4.5 years while prewar expansions lasted less than 2.25 years on average. Again, the more telling point is that the average length of recessions has been halved in the post–World War II

Figure 7.1a

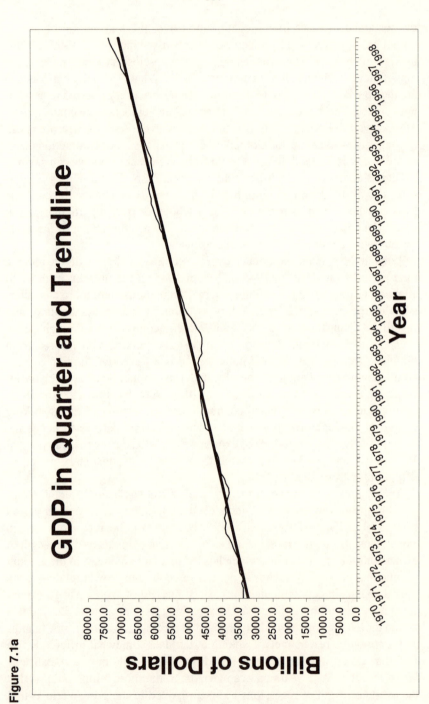

GDP in Quarter and Trendline

Billions of Dollars

Year

Figure 7.1b

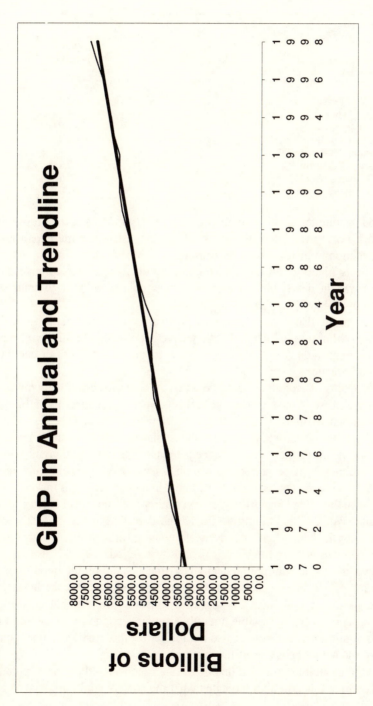

GDP in Annual and Trendline

Table 7.1

Time period	Depth (%) GNP constant dollar
July '53–May '54	−3.3
August '57–April '58	−3.2
April '60–February '61	−1.2
December '69–November '70	−1.1
November '73–March '75	−5.7
January '80–July '80	−2.6
July '81–November '82	−3.3
September '90–March '91	−1.6

period, lasting ten months compared with twenty months in the prewar era.[2] At this writing we are in the midst of the longest peacetime expansion in U.S. economic history; with its beginning in March 1991 the expansion is now in its ninety-ninth month. To date, the only expansion to have lasted longer was the nearly nine-year expansion associated with the Vietnam War, which in all likelihood will be surpassed.

We should also note a feature of postwar contractions aside from their brevity of duration, which is that they have been relatively mild with regard to their amplitude. Table 7.1 gives us a measure of the depth of decline of eight contractions since 1950.

The reality of economic existence is that the society is continually traversing through a phase of the business cycle; this is what we see in terms of the short-run experience. But one does want to overview the movement of the economy over long periods of time to arrive at the persistent underlying movement; that is, to see the net result of the cyclical experience over time. To this end, one can apply techniques of varying sophistication to arrive at the trend or secular movement. This movement turns out to be linear in nature, telling us that economic activity in the United States has grown at a fairly constant rate over long periods of time. We see this "trend-line fit" as the dark line in Figure 7.1; what is comforting is that, overall, the cyclical variations around this line tend to be subdued—this is clearly evident in the postwar period.

So while the economy in its actual existence is not on the trend line, it is shown not to deviate much from it. Then our frame of reference for the analysis of economic growth, which is that of a constant, proportional growth-rate experience, is very acceptable not only as an understanding of the trend line as a statistical creation, but is also not too far off the mark as an understanding of the actual behavior of the system.

In the usual interpretation this trend line is considered as one of potential GDP, where this potential indicates what the society could produce as a result of consistently fully utilizing its growing resource base. Thus the shorter-term (one to four years) cyclical variation can be reckoned as interruptions (as a result of some economic misalignment) of the underlying growth pattern. In this chapter we come to understand the conditions (and thereby realize the difficulties) for maintaining the economy in a state of growth, which may yield some insight about the causation of the cyclical fluctuation. These conditions yield a theoretical construct to help us interpret the trend movement of the economy, which, over the postwar period, is not that far removed from the actual course of events.

Some Growth Economics

Let us begin at a time where the economy is in a full-employment condition (around the cyclical peak), as mirrored by that Keynesian $I = S$ equilibrium condition. From this point forward our concern is to maintain this full-employment system, given that the growth rate of the labor supply is a demographic-sociological fact. This assumption of exogeniety, as it is commonly referred to, simply implies that the growth rate of the labor force is uninfluenced by the behavior of other components of the economy; for example, the rate of growth of the capital stock or that of technological change—in a later analysis we will have reason to question and alter this assumption. Of course, a level of employment spills out in the form of a level of production, as production requires the inputs of the capital and labor within a production process. Now with the labor supply growth rate assumed as given, the structure of full employment through time requires the society to grow its stock of plant and equipment in line with the realized growth in its labor supply so that the growth in production goes on without the appearance of a labor surplus and growing unemployment or that of a labor shortage. The strategic element is that of the rate of capital accumulation; by which, as we recognize, we mean the rate of growth of capitalists' (in the broader term, business) investment expenditures.

We do not know, as yet, the conditions that give rise to this rate of capital accumulation; but assuming that such is the situation, then it is considered that the economy is in a steady-state, or, as it is at times referred to, a balanced-growth existence. And to be sure of our terminology, we mean a model of the economy in which all of the variables are growing at same constant rate, so that although there is an absolute expansion, every element remains in the same proportion to each other. We do keep in mind that the idea of steady-balanced growth is a way to analyze some of the issues associated with a growing economy; it is not a name for an observed reality, but it is certainly a fair approximation.

The growth path is developed within the context of a production arrangement; we are after all viewing the change in output over time. We utilize an aggregate production function of the fixed coefficient type, which was analyzed in chapter 2. Repeating the basic design, we mean that the amounts of capital (K) and labor (L) required to produce any given flow of output are given. This leads to the form of the production function as

$$Y = \min\left[\frac{K}{v}, \frac{L}{b}\right] \tag{7.1}$$

We are adopting for the aggregate economy the isoquant image for the single producing unit that was the focus of discussion in chapter 2. And as we are thinking in macro terms, it does bear reiterating the point that this type of production mechanics allows either capital or labor to remain "unemployed." Given a certain rate of capital accumulation, only one flow of output can be produced (in conjunction with the technically required labor input) however much more labor is available.

Yet the increase in aggregate output over time does not stem solely from increases in the quantities of capital and labor employed; it is very much related to the presence of technological progress that, as an ongoing phenomenon, affects the performance of the economy via a rate of increase in the productivity of labor. It is not only a matter of an increase in the number of employed "hands"; but it is the rate of increase in the effectiveness of those hands that is central in understanding the growth path. However, this increase in the effectiveness or productivity of labor results mainly from an increase in the stock of knowledge (which is what we mean by technological progress) that is continuously infused into the production processes of the economy via the expansion of the capital stock and the related increase in the level of employment.

In the usual approach, at least initially, growth analysis is carried on within a highly aggregative basis. One speaks of the growth of the capital stock, thinking in terms of, let us say, a uniformity of machines or that of the productivity of labor, as if this effect is absorbed by all of the employed labor at any point. We will, in our initial look at the mechanics of growth, take the same tack. But it is important to understand what is assumed here in focusing on the basic elements. It is that technical progress is "disembodied"; in that, as new equipment is added to the capital stock, the improvements in technology that accompany it can, so to speak, be passed back to be absorbed by all of the existing capital. And this means that the increased labor productivity on the newly installed equipment will result in an advance of labor productivity overall. The growth of the economy is thus not limited by the actual growth of the labor force. But we are going to step away from the presence of technological progress—merely as a first look—and consider the characterization of the growth path as it relates to the growth rate of the actual quantities of inputs.

We begin by asking the following: At what rate must the economy grow if it is to create a level of aggregate demand such as to absorb (i.e., to keep fully utilized) the increase in production capacity resulting from positive net investment (i.e., from a rate of capital accumulation)? Given the nature of the production function, we understand that an increase in the capital stock will, in its full operation, result in a particular increase in the level of employment, so that the extent of this latter increase will indeed depend on the degree of utilization of the economy's added capacity.

Thus the question we have posed draws our attention to the dual effect of investment expenditures. It does determine the actual level of income via the Keynesian multiplier process, but it simultaneously increases the maximum potential income level that the economy must generate. The idea is to understand the conditions under which the actual level of income (via an adequate level of demand) will be equal to that necessary to absorb the increased capital stocks resulting from net investment.

Thinking back to the Principles of Economics presentation of the employment and aggregate expenditures analysis, we recall that employment is treated as a function of income (demand); full-employment income level is maintained if the system (indeed, business expenditures) is "persuaded" to invest sufficiently—equal to planned savings—thereby maintaining the necessary level of aggregate demand.

As an example, let us say that the full-employment income level is $200 billion, with an aggregate saving relationship of $s = 0.25$. Should planned investment expenditures be $50 billion, the economy then reflects the Keynesian condition and maintains the existing level of output and aggregate demand. The reader is now aware that behind these total numbers exists a "correct" distribution of income, in particular, the ratio of profits-to-income that greatly determines the overall savings propensity and gives rise to the requisite investment spending. But the point to be made is that this level of expenditures that seemingly maintains an adequate level of demand will show up as representing a state of insufficient demand. The level of spending that maintains a demand sufficient to fully employ the existing capacity will, in and of itself, cause that capacity to enlarge. We are talking about net investment expenditures, which is an act of capital accumulation with its attendant increased output capacity. Certainly the continued existence of the $200 billion income level will represent a state of insufficient demand relative to the system's production capability, leading to subsequent Keynesian unemployment results. We should not consider employment as a function of national income, but assume instead that employment is a function of the ratio of national income to productive capacity. The problem with the Principles analysis of the Keynesian system is that it does not take into account the essential and elementary fact, to reiterate, that investment both generates income and increases productive capacity. This means that the economy must always be realizing an increasing level of investment spending so as to generate a high enough increase in national income to avoid the emergence of excess capacity. A level of spending equal to realized savings that results from a previous level of investment expenditures will not do. Recalling our analysis concerning capitalists' behavior, we are saying that they will need to invest (and consume) in a given period in excess of what they earned in the preceding one.

Before setting out numbers to illustrate the growth path, we want to consider the relationship between the rate of capital accumulation and the rate of increase in the total economy's productive capacity. We begin with investment proceeding as $I_t = s(Y_t) = S_t$ (starting from the short-term Keynesian equilibrium) and let the notation σ be the ratio of the potential increase in national output to this increase in the capital stocks, that is, net investment. Sigma is a productivity ratio; that is

$$\sigma = \frac{\delta Y}{\delta K} = \frac{\delta Y}{I} \tag{7.2}$$

It represents the potential increase in production made possible by a dollar's worth of investment or increase in the capital stock in conjunction with other available resources, mainly labor. Domar refers to sigma as representing the "potential social average investment productivity,"[3] which he states as

$$\sigma \equiv \frac{\frac{\delta P}{\delta t}}{I} \tag{7.3}$$

But we must be cautious as to what this σ entails. The point is that this is an estimation of an aggregate effect; it indicates the increment in capacity of the whole economy per dollar of investment, and not only of the newly created capital taken by itself. Furthermore, the σ term in Equation 7.2 is not to be read as that lookalike marginal productivity of capital of orthodox analysis; we are not holding other inputs constant here. The calculation of σ allows for whatever increase in other inputs is necessary (given the prevailing technology) to accompany the increase in capital that results in a potential increase in national product. Underlying this productivity ratio is the assumption of our fixed input coefficients production function with constant capital-to-labor and capital-to-output ratios.

The most direct way to proceed is to assume that the increase in the production capability of the economy in total is a reflection of the increased production inherent in the addition to the capital stock. It follows that

$$\frac{\Delta P}{\Delta t} = \sigma_I \tag{7.4}$$

which is the growth of potential output in the system. And this carries some interesting implications. First of all, it assumes that the growth of associated inputs, particularly that of labor, is of the correct magnitude so that labor need not be drawn off from existing (older) plants, thereby reducing productive capacity. But in saying this, we are really assuming that older facilities are not going to find their outputs reduced because they have high-cost production relative to the newer facilities that reflect the additions to the capital stock and contain the latest technology. The notion of older capital not becoming technologically obsolete means that technological progress is absorbed by all older working capital; it is, to reiterate, disembodied. Thus our understanding of depreciation would need to be defined in terms of the cost of replacing a physically worn-out asset (one incapable of absorbing technological improvements) rather than that of economic replacement. Of course, the reader may question (and correctly so) this overall view that as investment proceeds and new projects with a productive capacity are built, then nowhere in the economy is production capacity reduced; that is, no older plants are either junked or, more realistically, taken out of production. We consider the issue of technological change, and this possibility, in some detail in the following chapter.

But we keep in mind that our search is for the conditions making for a full-employment growth path; this will revolve around the existence of an appropriate rate of growth in national income (or aggregate spending) to ensure that the additional productive capacity originating in a level of investment does not turn out to be one of excess capacity. Full employment will be maintained in the face of a growing labor force because of a particular rate of growth in national income, which results in an increase in demand and actual capacity utilization, equal to the growth of society's productive capacity. And the growth of the full-capacity income (demand) will absorb into employment the increase in the labor force based on our fixed input production technology. We reiterate that this assumes no reduction in productive capacity (and associated release of labor) somewhere in the economy as result of an increased level of investment and emplacement of newly created capital.

There are really two growth rates of real output that we need to recognize: One ensures the continuous utilization of a growing capital stock at full capacity; the second is a rate of growth that is necessary to ensure the full employment of a growing labor supply. These two growth rates need not necessarily be equal; full-capacity growth may be insufficient to absorb into production the annual increments in the labor supply and/or the labor rendered unemployed due to technological progress. There may be a downside to such progress, an analysis of which would have us question the notion of a general embodiment of technological change. Yet the approach taken at this point to set out the growth path is that of the two growth rates, the former as a prerequisite to, and identical with, the latter. That the society will not be suffering a secular growth in unemployed labor despite the full utilization of capital.

Before moving on, let us restate this supply side of our story. From (7.2) we can write

$$\sigma_I = \sigma\left[s(Y)\right] = \Delta Y \tag{7.5}$$

the term $\sigma\left[s(Y)\right]$ indicating the total increase in productive capacity from the sum of net investment undertaken in time (t) equal to $s(Y_t)$. Then full-capacity income growth requires that

$$\Delta Y_t \equiv Y_{t+1} - Y_t = \sigma\left[s(Y_t)\right] \tag{7.6}$$

national income in year $(t + 1)$ should exceed that of year t by the amount of added capacity resulting from the investment in year t. And the burden of increasing the level of income (aggregate demand) rests with the "behavior of capitalists" in terms of an increasing level of investment expenditures, which as we understand is itself tied to the distribution of income. This brings us to the expression for the demand side of the growth relationship.

The reader is undoubtedly familiar with the simple Keynesian multiplier expression that tells of the amount by which a change in investment expenditures (normally presented as an out-of-the-blue autonomous change) is multiplied or magnified to determine the change in equilibrium of real output and expenditure. Thus from the view of a change in aggregate demand we write

$$\Delta Y = \frac{1}{s}(\Delta I) \tag{7.7}$$

The change in investment expenditures does double duty: It increases the overall productive capacity of the economy, while it also increases the level of aggregate demand. Thus the existence of full-capacity utilization requires that demand grow at a rate equal to the system's increased productive capability, which, of course, implies that the economy must evidence a particular rate of growth of investment expenditures—as the propelling force—to bring about this equality. Thus with the use of Equations 7.4 and 7.7 we have

$$\frac{1}{s}(\Delta I) = \sigma \, I \tag{7.8}$$

which, by sample manipulation, as a result of multiplying both sides by s and dividing by I yields

$$\frac{\Delta I}{I} = s\sigma \tag{7.9}$$

Given the economywide productivity ratio (σ) and the propensity to save (s), investment and income must grow at the annual percentage rate of σs in order to assure the full utilization of the addition to the economy's productive capacity. What will be happening is that the actual increase in aggregate demand will be equal to the increase in the system's productive capability, thereby avoiding the presence of excess capacity that would depress future investment and employment.

Thus full-capacity growth rate will vary directly with the quantity of investment s, and with the productivity enhancement character of the investment (σ). The greater the value of sigma the greater must be the rate of income growth to absorb the higher capacity created in association with a given investment expenditure. But this productivity of investment is very much the result of new knowledge and the speed at which this knowledge translates into new production technologies. Yet the pace of innovation is itself interwoven with the rate of capital accumulation; it is reasonable to suppose that a society where capitalists are eager and quick to abandon tried production methods, and to adopt new techniques, is necessarily one where the rate of capital accumulation is large and (as we now understand) vice versa. Though let us consider these as separate influences on the requisite rate of investment growth.

We have the essential observation by Domar: "If sufficient investment is not forthcoming today, unemployment will be here today. But if enough is invested today, still more will be needed tomorrow."[4] It is Equation 7.9 that tells us the required "still more" rate of increase; the reader understands that in this movement both investment and income are both growing at a constant proportional rate.

Table 7.2

Output Growth

Year	Capital stock	Potential output (Y)	Actual output (Y)	Consumption	Investment
			Panel A		
1	400	100	100	88	12
2	412	103	103	90.64	12.36
3	424.36	106.9	106.09	93.36	12.73
4	437.09				
			Panel B		
1	400	100	100	88	12
2	412	103	100	88	12
3	424	106	100	88	12
4	436				
			Panel C		
1	400	100	100	88	12
2	412	103	102.3	90.02	12.28
3	424.28	105.45	104.69	92.12	12.57
4	436.85				

Let us consider an arithmetic example to demonstrate the economic affect of the required, and of a less-than-required, rate of investment growth. Table 7.2 is constructed on the basis of an aggregate savings ratio .12 and a productivity ratio (σ) of .25 telling us that an expenditure of one dollar of net investment creates .25 of additional productive capacity.

We begin with panel A in year 1 where the system is in short-term Keynesian ($S = I$) equilibrium, with full utilization of the given (400) capital stock. The appropriate level investment (12) that maintains the full-employment condition in year 1 will enlarge the capital stock and the productive capacity (potential output) from 100 to $\sigma I = 103$ in year 2. In order for this potential to be realized as actual output in year 2—so as not to become excess capacity—investment expenditures in year 2 will have to grow by an amount equal to σ_s so as to bring about a growth in aggregate output and demand that fully absorbs the increased capacity stemming from the previous period's investment spending. With Equations 7.8 and 7.9 we have

$$\frac{1}{12}(\Delta I)=0.25(12)$$

$$\Delta I=0.36$$

$$so: \frac{0.36}{12}=0.12(0.25)=0.0. \tag{7.10}$$

Investment expenditures will need to increase by 0.36, which is at a growth rate of 3 percent, in order (via the multiplier mechanism) to propel an increase in aggregate demand in year 2 that fully absorbs the higher capacity of the economy. The potential output of 103 will become actual output as a result of a higher level of income and demand (consisting of $I = 12.36$, $C = 90.64$) stemming from the appropriate rate of investment growth. So at the end of year 2 the economy is again in short-term equilibrium, but the investment act in getting to this point has itself caused a still higher level of capital stock and productive capacity in year 3, necessitating that expenditures increase by an additional 3 percent to 12.73, which, by maintaining the necessary increase in expenditures in year 3, will again result in capital and capacity growth in year 4, and so forth. An economic system that is maintaining full employment of its growing labor force in association with the full utilization of its capital stock, requires that the level of investment expenditure itself be growing. To put this another way: The capital stock must be growing through time in order to maintain the full-capacity use of higher stock of capital at a point in time. Ironically, the stock of capital must always be increasing to avoid the problem of having accumulated too much capital.

Revealing what is behind this arithmetic narrative, we want to recall our discussion of the distribution shares in chapter 5. We arrived at the profit share via equation (5.58), which we restate here

$$\frac{P_t}{Y_t} = \frac{1}{s_K} \cdot \frac{I_t}{Y_t} \tag{7.11}$$

Now assuming the extreme case of $s_K = 1$ in order, as we pointed out, to highlight the capital accumulation role of the capitalist class, then a volume of profits creates an equal volume of savings, which reduces matters to (repeating Equation 5.59)

$$\frac{P_t}{Y_t} = \frac{I_t}{Y_t} \tag{7.12}$$

Profits as share of output reflects the level of capitalists' investment expenditures; and while the level of profits creates the savings to support a subsequent level of investment, that subsequent level must exceed the previously realized level of profits (savings). Businessmen must always want to invest an amount in excess of previous earnings, which itself will lead to higher levels of demand and earnings. It is this which distinguishes our growth framework from the stationary state analysis.

However, should businessmen elect to undertake investment spending equal to previously earned profits (savings)—in essence maintaining the Keynesian stationary equilibrium—they will quickly find that they have spent too little. We see this very clearly in panel B of Table 7.2, where we find a growing disparity between the level of demand and productive capability of the economy. While a level of expenditures may be appropriate at a point in time to restore at full employment and increase capacity usage, that same level of spending cannot be appropriate over time as it builds in the very basis for its excessiveness. And as such, subsequent spending and demand will fall below the previous insufficient levels, further darkening the economic picture. It would appear that unless investment and output are continually increasing, they will decrease; the system cannot, for any length of time, be expected to maintain a zero growth rate in investment expenditures.

In panel C we see that it is not only a matter of a growth of expenditures, but of growth at the proper rate. We note that a too slow growth rate (one of 0.024) simply results in a slower increasing disparity between the growth in aggregate demand and productive capacity.

Our overall concern is with the capacity growth effect of investment, and with determining that rate of capital accumulation (and thereby the rate of income growth) that prevents this effect from inhibiting the steady expansion of the economy. In a technical sense we know what this rate of increase must be, yet we do not see how it would be motivated. In other words, there is no investment-demand expression that tells us about the actual behavior of investment. What is it that might be said to induce capitalists to increase their expenditures by that required percentage in each time period? Which, if they do so, will make certain that all additions to the capital stock, in the aggregate, will be absorbed into production. At the risk of being repetitive, we remind the reader to recall the Principles of Economics analysis of the Keynesian aggregate demand model where the level of income is a function of investment $[Y = f(I)]$, and the required rising income and demand is a function of a rising rate investment operating through the multiplier process. To restate:

$$\Delta Y = \frac{1}{s}(\Delta I) \tag{7.13}$$

But this increase in investment is itself not unrelated to the realized change in the level of economic activity; it is essentially a reflection of an induced behavior. If we are to take that Keynesian point-in-time equilibrium $(S = I)$ condition into a growth framework, then this equality must be maintained in the face of a growing capital stock; which means that the level of aggregate demand must grow at some necessary rate. Now it is one thing to stipulate in a sort of technical way what this rate must be, but one does obtain a richer understanding of equilibrium growth by having explicit behavioral assumptions that would, under the right conditions, result in equality between all increments of planned savings and investment, thereby maintaining the required rate of income growth.

This equality of the changes in investment and that of savings as the system proceeds along the growth path does leap out at us from what we know to this point, even though we have not explicitly considered those ex ante or expectational (planned) behavioral equations concerning investment or savings. We can see this straightaway. Equation 7.9 can be rewritten as[5]

$$\Delta I = s\sigma_I \tag{7.14}$$

And we know from 7.7 and 7.8 that the capacity absorption increase in income must be

$$\Delta Y = \sigma_I \tag{7.15}$$

Then for the increase in the capital stock not to turn out to be excess capacity we have

$$\Delta I = s\sigma_I = \Delta Y = \sigma_I$$
$$= s(\Delta Y) = \Delta S \tag{7.16}$$

Yet we want to see this in a "behavioral" way, which brings us to Roy Harrod's famous growth model or to "Mr. Harrod's Dynamics"; this model, together with Domar's independently produced similar analysis, takes its place at the start of modern growth theory.[6]

We need to be clear about Harrod's assumptions. First, that the level of savings during any period of time t is taken to be a simple proportional function of national income received during that period. This is in keeping with the usual highly aggregative macroeconomic view; we set down this very familiar expression so as to have the tools of the analysis in front of us. Thus:

$$S_t = s(Y_t)$$
$$0 < s < 1 \tag{7.17}$$

a constant average, and hence marginal propensity to save. Here the reader should feel somewhat uneasy, recalling our analysis of income distribution in chapter 6, which had us consider Equation 6.17 as too broad a statement, needing to be replaced with the understanding that income (Y) is equal to the two broad income classifications of wages (W) and profits (P) with their constant average (and marginal) propensities to consume. We restate Equations 6.2 and 6.5:

$$S = s_W(W) + s_P(P) \tag{7.18}$$

Leading to:

$$s = \frac{S}{Y} = (s_P - s_W)\frac{P}{Y} + s_W \tag{7.19}$$

Now if we take the special case (as we referred it) where $s_W = 0$, we have the level of savings as a proportion of income equal to:

$$\frac{S}{Y} = s_K(\frac{P}{Y}) \tag{7.20}$$

And in the more special case of $s_K = 1$, we find

$$s = \frac{S}{Y} = \frac{P}{Y} \tag{7.21}$$

Reminding ourselves about the realities of income distribution and savings will help us to read the Harrod analysis with more understanding. His assumption concerning savings in expression 7.17 refers not to intended or planned savings but to actual savings; since actual savings may differ from intended savings (in Harrodian terms), the income of the period turns out to be greater or lesser than expected. But we underpin this by saying that what is essentially determining the level of savings is the level of realized profits, which may certainly turn out to be other than expected. While we look at the model within Harrod's own framework, we do want to keep alongside our distribution analysis.

Second, there is the assumption about the labor force that it will be growing at a constant proportional rate. And this rate is to be taken as "exogenous" in that it is uninfluenced by the behavior of the other variables of the economy. In Harrod's discussion there is a growth rate that speaks directly to the maintenance of full employment.

Third, there is the presence of technological progress that is assumed, as well, to grow at an exogenous rate and is considered to be purely "labor-augmenting." It is not only a matter of an increase in the numbers of the labor force in the production of output, but it is also a matter of an increase in the efficiency of the increasing number of hands; this combination gives us what is known as the growth rate of the effective labor force. In the following chapter we consider the entire matter of technical progress and the nature of its embodiment.

Fourth, we come to the assumption regarding the production function and interpretation given to the capital-to-output ratio. In consideration of the retrospective literature, it is fair to say that Harrod did mean to deliver his message within the framework of our previously discussed fixed input coefficient production function; and that the fixity of the capital-to-output ratio is to be reckoned as a consequence of the technology reflective of the productive processes of the economy. It is then not a matter that capital and labor are technically substitutable (that the orthodox production function with its diminishing returns configuration holds true) but that in practice they are "fixed" due to the inflexibility of factor prices, in particular the rate of interest. And even if input prices were flexible, price-driven factor substitutability would be of little consequence, due to the assumption that the investment demand schedule is highly inelastic with respect to changes in the rate of interest. All in all, Harrod believed that it would be fruitful to base the model on the premise of a constant capital-to-output ratio, with this constancy being dependent on technology. One would like to think that Harrod, even that many years back, recognized the overall inapplicability of the orthodox production function. With this in mind, there are then two views of this ratio in the model; one is simply a relationship showing the ratio of the stock of capital to the flow output; or more meaningfully, the ratio of the actual addition to the stocks divided by the actual addition in output. We write this as

$$K = v(Y) \tag{7.22}$$

With the assumption

$$\frac{K}{Y} = \frac{\Delta K}{\Delta Y} \tag{7.23}$$

Another conception, and one that is at the heart of the growth movement, places this technical relationship into a "behavioral" setting. It is placed there by asking the following: What level of investment expenditures would businesses (in the aggregate) be motivated to undertake given the realized increase in the level of income and demand? What determines planned or ex ante investment? Harrod's assertion is that the desire to undertake investment depends on how quickly income is rising; that planned investment in time period (t) is equal to some constant proportion (v_r) of the amount by which income in period (t) exceeds that of the previous period $(t-1)$. Thus:

$$I_t = v_r(Y_t - Y_{t-1}) \tag{7.24}$$

which is a variation of what is known as the acceleration principle, where (v_r) is the acceleration coefficient.

We want to be clear about this acceleration idea by again stressing the distinction between the stock of capital and the "flow" of investment or the additions to that stock. For a given level of output, a particular stock of capital (in association with a level of employment) is required and is in place to produce it. But if production is going to increase, additions to the stock will be desired (indeed, will be required given the input coefficients); so while the level of the stock of capital relates to the level of production, the additions to the stock relate to the rate at which output is growing. The faster the realized rate of growth in production (income) the more entrepreneurs will want to invest.

With these explicit assumptions in tow, we derive the growth movement of the economy. First of all, a question needs to be asked of the acceleration principle: Why would the system plan a level of investment expenditures the impact of which, in terms of added productive capacity and income, will be realized in the future, on the basis of the currently experienced change in production? And the logical response is that firms are expecting that the realized growth will be carried forward to the next time period. Harrod's planned (behavioral) investment notion explicitly introduces the expectations factor as an important underpinning of the growth path. The reader should see that $(Y_t - Y_{(t-1)})$ of the acceleration equation is really an expected change in income and demand. Investment decisions taken now relate to events in the future; these decisions must then be based on expected future events (sales and/or profits). As we will see, the secret to the growth trajectory is to bring into being a growth rate of output whose realization assures fulfillment of these expectations at each point in time. Or, to put it another way, that in the aggregate, the level of investment expenditures that were undertaken is a level that firms would have wanted to undertake given the realized growth in income.

But first we step back to look at what has come to be known as Harrod's fundamental growth equation from the viewpoint of a truism, that is, that of an ex post or realized condition. From our accelerator equation we know that a realized increase in output prompts a particular level of investment spending that, in light of the elementary macro-equilibrium condition, will be equal to current savings $s(Y_t)$. Thus:

$$v(Y_t - Y_{t-1}) = s(Y_t) \tag{7.25}$$

with the actual or realized rate of income G written as

$$\frac{Y_t - Y_{t-1}}{Y_t} = G \tag{7.26}$$

and dividing both sides of 7.25 by vY_t yields

$$\frac{s}{v} = \frac{Y_t - Y_{t-1}}{Y_t} \equiv G \tag{7.27}$$

We have in 7.27, Harrod's equation, an identity expression; should $s = 0.10$ and $v = 3$, the growth rate is 3 percent. One notices that the percentage change expression is not the mathematical version; it results from the unlagged savings assumption. Should we presume a lagged savings function as $S_t = s(Y_{t-1})$, the constant proportional rate expression would be defined as

$$G = \frac{Y_t - Y_{t-1}}{Y_{t-1}} \tag{7.28}$$

It makes little difference for our understanding of the workings of the growth path whether the savings function is lagged or not, but for an arithmetic representation, which we get to at a later point, we would clearly need to assume the lagged version.

We must be careful in interpreting expression 7.27, for while it is the basic growth equation, it is not the expression of it that reveals the propelling force behind the realized growth rate. What we have in 7.27 is the change in the level of output in time t as a result of an expenditure action taken in a previous period. Thus the actual result in t is merely a manifestation of the technical relationship associating the incremental change in the capital stock to that of income. It is simply a reflection of that Keynesian $I = S$ condition. Thus:

$$v = \frac{I}{\Delta Y}$$

$$\frac{\Delta Y}{Y}(v) = s$$

$$\frac{\Delta Y}{Y}\left(\frac{I}{\Delta Y}\right) = s \tag{7.29}$$

and $\quad I = s(Y) = S$

But this is obviously not what Harrod wanted to convey. To give insight as to the underlying support to the growth path and to impart, one might say, "theoretical content" to the fundamental equation, we need to return to our previous discussion of the acceleration equation and rephrase v in terms of v_r. Recall that the v_r expression for the investment coefficient places such expenditures into a behavioral setting. The investment equation became a statement expressing entrepreneurs' requirements or desire for additions to the capital stock given the actual growth in income and output. And the point we made was that this level of desired investment (i.e., this investment ex ante) depends on how the realized growth rate plays upon expectations concerning economic growth in the subsequent time period.

Let us assume that the realized growth in output in t was equal to expectations formed in $t - 1$. In this circumstance the right investment decisions were made in $t - 1$ in the sense that the right amount of additional capital was put in place to produce the incremental output. Such a realized or actual rate of growth is considered a warranted growth rate (G_W) in that the investment decisions previously entered into are, indeed, warranted by the currently realized increase in income and demand. Or to put the matter another way: If output grows at the G_W rate, then the actual increase in the capital stock will equal the increase that businesses require in order to realize the full utilization of capacity, that is, if they are to be satisfied that the level of the stock of capital is appropriate for the production of the current level of output. It is clear that if output grows at the warranted rate, then the actual capital stock will conform to the desired capital stock and thus assure the fulfillment of expectations.

Now at this point, that is, facing the next time period $t + 1$, Harrod argues that if growth expectations in t were correct based on realized growth in $t - 1$, then expectations about events in $t + 1$ will similarly be based upon realized growth in time t. In a simple way, expectations are formed on the basis of past experience; if that past experience was one of a warranted rate of advance, then according to Harrod, it will "leave entrepreneurs in a state of mind in which they are prepared to carry on a similar advance."[7] Since previous investment was validated by the realized growth in income and demand, producers will anticipate a similar advance in the following period and will execute an investment decision that will, indeed, perpetuate the existing growth rate. Of course, this "execution" occurs through the particular value taken on by our investment coefficient (v_r), which, in a technical manner reveals the necessary increase to the capital stock to provide an increase in capacity equal to the projected increase in output and demand. Thus if the economy is experiencing a warranted rate of growth, expectations are being fulfilled in every time period as a reflection of the behaviorally induced investment being equal to realized savings.

To say again: Given the values for s and v_r, all savings will be invested (absorbed) if the actual growth rate of output (G) equals the warranted rate (G_W), and this absorption will cause capacity growth to equal that of output, thereby leaving the capital-to-output ratio unchanged. Thus:

$$\Delta K = I = v_r(\Delta Y) = s(Y)$$

$$\frac{\Delta Y}{Y} = \frac{s}{v_r} = G = G_W \tag{7.30}$$

The induced investment that producers undertake must be the amount that the investment coefficient (the v as a technical relationship) indicates is needed to provide the added capacity to increase income by the expected change.

By this time the reader may have become quite suspect of the society's ability to realize a constant proportional growth rate and, if it should experience this steady-state condition, whether it is maintainable for any length of time. This distrust is not a far-off notion, as we keep in mind that the realized growth rate (G) is the result of investment and output decisions flowing from a vast number of firms; and they are not, in any lockstep fashion, all going to be satisfied with their estimate of demand and hence with their past investment decisions (all will not be experiencing $G = G_W$). Induced investment by some firms may be greater or lesser than that called for by the investment coefficient due to previous misjudgments regarding forecasts of demand and capital needs.

We need to keep before us two main features of this warranted concept. First, it is a growth rate that, on balance, leaves all producers satisfied with their production and investment decisions. Some may be disappointed, finding production in excess of estimated demand, while others will see sales expectations resulting in a deficient level of inventories and capital stock. Hamberg says, "But—and this is the critical point—the disappointments and resulting reactions on the part of some firms will, in the aggregate, just be cancelled by the shortages and subsequent reactions of other firms."[8]

While this "on balance" understanding is a necessary (realistic) condition for the steady-state (G_W) experience, it is insufficient. In addition, there is that behavioral assumption that when all firms, in the aggregate, are satisfied with the actual rate of growth (i.e., their expectations have been met), they will be induced to make new investment decisions to cause the same rate of growth to be continued in the following period. An actual growth rate that is a warranted rate is one that is constant.

We will want to highlight the potential difficulties to maintaining steady growth and consider how the economy might respond to an interruption of the steady growth condition. That is, what might we expect to happen if for some reason income and demand does not grow fast enough? If the system is then thrown off the growth path, will it stabilize itself at a lower level of growth, or will the behavior of firms be such as to plunge the economy into a downward spiral of growth levels to a point of absolute declines in output and employment. The reader can certainly appreciate the need to be aware of a slackening of the pace of economic activity and, in terms of policy, to try and forestall a possible unhinging of the economy.

Before considering these matters, it will behoove us to set out an arithmetic example of steady growth so as to perhaps make clearer what is involved, and to have some numbers to illustrate what may happen if the system goes awry. We express the rate of change from period to period as a ratio; thus the rate between Y_t and Y_{t-1} is stated as $\frac{Y_t}{Y_{t-1}}$, and a comparison can be made between this rate and that of the previous period in the form:

$$\frac{Y_t}{Y_{t-1}} = \frac{Y_{t-1}}{Y_{t-2}} + f(U_{t-1}) \tag{7.31}$$

where $U_t - 1$ is the state of production relative to demand in period $t - 1$. Should the system be realizing an unintended or unexpected reduction in inventories reflecting the condition that it had not invested and produced at a sufficient pace in $t - 1$, it will plan to increase the growth in investment expenditures and hence cause a realized growth in t to be proportionately greater than that in $t - 1$. The expected rate of increase in output is more than proportionate to the increase in the immediate past period; it is equal to that realized income plus what we might call a "correction factor." Then:

$$U_{t-1} = Y_{t-1} - D_{t-1}$$

and

$$f(U_{t-1}) > 0 \text{ as } U_{t-1} < 0 \tag{7.32}$$

and in this circumstance planned investment in time t would exceed actual savings. And this results from the circumstance that in $t - 1$ actual investment is less than planned investment by the degree of unexpected inventory disinvestment, telling us that expected demand is less than actual demand.

When we put this together more obviously by identifying the demand (D) components in the previous period, and keeping matters simple, we have

$$C_{t-1} = b(Y_{t-1})$$
$$I_{t-1} = v_r(Y_{t-1} - Y_{t-2}) \tag{7.33}$$

since the v_r term is the ratio of realized or actual demand relative to production, we can substitute this ratio directly into Equation 7.31 and write:

$$\frac{Y_t}{Y_{t-1}} = \frac{Y_{t-1}}{Y_{t-2}} \cdot \frac{D_{t-1}}{Y_{t-1}}$$

so: $\dfrac{Y_t}{Y_{t-1}} = \dfrac{Y_{t-1}}{Y_{t-2}} \cdot \dfrac{bY_{t-1} + v_r(Y_{t-1} - Y_{t-2})}{Y_{t-1}}$

$$(7.34)$$

and $\dfrac{Y_t}{Y_{t-1}} = b + v_r\left(\dfrac{Y_{t-1}}{Y_{t-2}}\right) - v_r$

And what we are asking of the last equation in 7.34 is a straightforward question: Given the expenditure coefficients b and v_r, what rate of increase in income and demand would need to have occurred in Y_{t-1} so as to fulfill expectations? That is, that the increase in investment and output was justified (warranted) by the realized growth in demand, thereby engendering a rate of increase in expected output in Y_t equal to the actual rate of growth in Y_{t-1}. And it is the expenditure behavior, in the aggregate, mirroring these expectations, that results in an actual growth rate equal to that of the immediate past period.

A past growth ratio of 1.075, that is, $\frac{Y_{t-1}}{Y_{t-2}} = 1.075$, reflective of expenditure coefficients $b = 0.85$, $v_r = 2.15$, will result in a constant proportional growth path as

$$\frac{Y_t}{Y_{t-1}} = 3(1.075) - 2.15 = 1.075 \qquad (7.35)$$

At the risk of belaboring the point, the .075 rate is a steady-state condition in that it evidences the correct working out of past expectations at every point, thereby motivating an expenditure response that sustains the growth experience. To say that a past level of expenditures is always appropriate in terms of the realized growth in demand can simply be put as

$$b(Y_t) + v_r(Y_t - Y_{t-1}) = Y_t$$

$$Y_t(b - 1 + v_r) = v_r(Y_t - 1)$$

and $\qquad (7.36)$

$$\frac{Y_t}{Y_{t-1}} = \frac{v_r}{b - 1 + v_r} = 1.075$$

The reader certainly recognizes this Keynesian equilibrium condition, now carried forward through time whereby the levels of output and demand are increasing absolutely at a constant rate of change.

However, even if the system were able to achieve and maintain this desirable state, it does not in and of itself imply that the actual experience is that of maximum growth rate. By this we mean a pace of increase in output and demand resulting from (or permitted by) the full utilization of a growing resource base coupled with the growth of technological progress. It is one thing to have demand grow at a rate that absorbs into production the increase in productive capacity (our terminology being the G_W or σ_s ratio); it is not necessarily the same to have real income grow at a rate that would ensure the full employment of a growing labor force where "productivity per pair of hands" is in all likelihood itself increasing. The working out of past expectations will bring into being an increase in expenditures that in net terms will increase productive capacity; now given the "fixity" of the production coefficient, it would be most desirable that the proper utilization of the growing capital stock necessitate an increase in employment equal to the rate of increase in the labor force. And that the rate increase in demand always be sufficient to absorb the increase in production from a consistently fully employed labor force. We have a way of describing a maximal growth rate whereby the actual growth of the economy is prescribed by the growth of the labor force. Harrod considers this maximum as a "natural" or (ceiling) growth rate, labeling it as G_n. Again at the risk of repetitiveness, it is the maximum rate of growth that the economy can achieve given the full employment of the labor force. Thus one view of this maximal steady-state condition is

$$G = Gw = \frac{s}{vr} = \frac{\dot{L}}{L} = n = Gn \tag{7.37}$$

where n is the rate of increase on the labor force L.

We say "one view" because clearly Equation 7.37 is a restricted notion of "maximum" as it emphasizes the accumulation of inputs (the labor force) neglecting a central element in the growth process, that of technological change. As we stated previously, it is not only a matter of an increase in the number of hands absorbed into the production process, but of an increase in their productivity; and it is this combination that gives the growth of what we considered as the effective labor force. The most obvious way to handle this is to suppose that this labor-augmenting progress is growing at some exogenously determined rate (λ); thus the natural or maximum growth rate would now read:

$$G = G_W = \frac{s}{v_r} = n + \lambda = G_n \qquad (7.38)$$

It is the maximum growth rate that the economy can achieve, given the growth of the labor supply and productivity. Again, we make the point that the full employment of an effective labor force growth rate stands in contrast to the warranted or equilibrium growth rate, which is a full-capacity growth rate only.

While there is no doubt about the importance of this technology input, a question can be asked of the way in which it is normally handled—certainly within our effective labor force notion. The higher level of output per pair of hands does not fall only on the new entrants to the labor force working with the additions to the capital stock which may contain some innovation, but falls over the entire labor force. Reinforcing an earlier point, this is an example of what we mean by disembodied technical progress. Yet to be more precise, we can relate disembodiment in terms of the time a particular input becomes part of the productive process. An innovation is disembodied if it increases the productivity of the productive inputs independently of the date on which the particular unit of the input is brought into use. If an invention increases the efficiency of the productive system by improving the quality of all capital goods, whether they are installed before of after the invention, or of all labor, whether they enter the work force before or after the invention, we have disembodiment. If the invention increases productivity only through the inputs that are brought into use after the date of the innovation, then the change is "embodied," residing only in those units of the capital stock that contain the most recent technology.

If we hold to disembodiment, then we can speak in terms of an overall effective labor force, or of an aggregate capital stock of some sameness of efficiency. Every technological change can be absorbed by all of the working capital. While this might be easier to handle analytically, it is realizing this at the expense of some reality. We certainly do not believe that any part of the capital stock becomes technologically obsolete, nor that the increase in productivity falls uniformly across all employed hands. There is then, in reality, no uniform effective labor force, nor should we conceptualize the capital stock as alike capital, thereby not having to distinguish between different facilities embodying different technologies.

What the disembodied vision asks us to accept is not only that it is like manna from heaven in that it somehow appears and spreads itself over the entire growing population of inputs, but that its appearance does not even require that the inputs be growing—there is no connection here. That is, even if capital and labor were constant, output would drift up at a constant proportional rate to this unaccounted for presence. But these are matters for later discussion (in the following chapter); here we continue with the usual—disembodied—nature of the warranted growth path and bring up some matters that may present roadblocks to steady growth.

The most obvious is perhaps that of expectation. We reiterate the basic assumption: If the economy on balance is satisfied with a realized income growth, that is, past investment and production decisions are warranted by the current experience, new expenditure decisions will be induced such that the same rate of growth will be continued in the next period. But why restrict entrepreneurial behavior to such a "limited exuberance"? Certainly if businessmen are jubilant over how well the economy is performing, and profits have met expectations, it would seem to be an equally valid assumption to expect a rate of growth in year $t + 1$, such that $G_{t+1} > G_t$ even though $G_t = G_W$. An interesting question is what would happen if the economy were to depart the steady-growth path due to excessive optimism? Will the system in $t + 1$ simply adjust so that $G_{t+1} = G_W$, or will the society witness a different kind of experience?

On the basis of this exuberance, the pace of increase in investment and production in $t + 1$ will cause a rate of income growth that exceeds the higher optimistic expectations. As there does exist a rate of increase in production (given the coefficients of demand) that would be warranted by the subsequent rate of growth in income, it stands to reason that a rate in excess of this would not be. Paradoxically, this higher pace of investment expenditures will, on balance, leave producers in a situation of not having invested enough. It is true that there will be dissatisfaction with past decisions, but for the satisfactory experience of the economy having outperformed expectation. And this may be expected to produce an even greater rate of expected income growth with an even greater growing condition of underproduction.

We illustrate this expectations-driven upward departure from steady growth using our warranted growth example. Suppose the system realizes a growth rate of 8 percent between Y_t and Y_{t-1}, exceeding the warranted growth rate yearly ratio of 1.075. What might we expect the growth ratio to be between Y_{t+1} and Y_t? Thus $Y_t = 108$, $Y_{t-1} = 100$, and using the format of the last equation of 7.34, we have:

$$\frac{Y_{t+1}}{Y_t} = 3\left(\frac{108}{100}\right) - 2.15 = 1.09$$

(7.39)

and $Y_{t+1} = 108\,(1.09) = 117.72$

Carrying this one further step we see:

$$\frac{Y_{t+2}}{Y_{t+1}} = 3(\frac{117.72}{108}) - 2.15 = 1.12 \tag{7.40}$$

and so forth—though within limits.

In this cumulative upward departure it will behoove us to see the paradoxical economic situation. If production is increased too rapidly, the system will find that it has produced too little. "While an increase in output which is more rapid than warranted will increase the quantity to be sold, it will increase demand even more and so the result will be underproduction."[9] The adding of further "optimistic fuel" to previous optimism results in a self-sustaining upward growth departure.

Of course everything we have been saying about expectations can work in reverse, as the coefficient of expectations takes on a negative value. Here we have a paradoxical situation; where the economy does not increase production rapidly enough, it will have produced too much, setting up a condition of a self-sustaining downward growth departure from the warranted path.

Over the years the literature has spawned much debate concerning this seemingly unstable characteristic of a sustainable growth path. It is the basic view of the Harrod–Domar growth dynamics that not only will a departure of the actual growth rate from the warranted rate not correct itself, but will produce even larger departures. Yet this need not necessarily be the case. But from the point of view of the expectations element, we would be comfortable in saying that once the economy goes off the rails, it may very well be quite difficult to get it back again—we would need to break the "expectations of divergence."

We also alert ourselves to the distribution of income element that is the essential support of the steady growth path. As we made mention, this element is normal, hidden under the macroaggregates of the growth analysis; yet the correct alignment of profits and wages as proportions of the growing level of output assures the proper growth of aggregate demand and, most important, that of investment expenditures. And it is instrumental in providing the requisite level of savings. It must be remembered that what governs the future justification of current expenditures is the future growth of income. But this future growth is the very result of current expenditures based on expectations concerning the growth in income and profits. Anything that may threaten to reduce profits could trigger pessimism regarding the growth of future earnings, and hence reduce the growth of actual investment expenditures, which would be enough to derail the growing economy.

It may be all too easy, certainly, in a period of ongoing full-employment prosperity (assume $G = G_W = G_n$) for labor to press for a larger proportion of the total product, perhaps citing the huge and growing level of profits. Yet this may be quite shortsighted, as it could lead to a reduction in the growth of income with negative employment effects. As the economy is steadily progressing, both wages and profits are growing but must remain in correct alignment to each other as proportions of the growing economy.

The idea one hears much about concerning a move toward a more equitable distribution of income may be fraught with misunderstanding. Of course, there is no economic obstacle to this, as we have put aside the orthodox justification of income inequality in terms of productivity differences. But the danger is treating changes in income distribution (or that of income equality) independently of other factors. At the aggregate level we know that any desired growth rate requires a particular utilization of the resources of the system for investment. At the same time, income must be distributed between wages and profits, such that total income less expenditure on consumption goods (i.e., profits) must equal the value of aggregate investment expenditures that propels the system. There is then a particular distribution of income between profits and wages that supports the desired growth rate.

As we said, this link is not very obvious, and the society should be quite wary at attempts to bring about a more equitable distribution of income (on the surface a laudable goal) that could very easily upset the growth experience.

Should the economy continue its present sustained upswing to July 2000, it will have expanded for 112 months making it the longest expansion in U.S. history. As such, this "smooth" advance mimics quite will our steady-state economy. The annual growth rate between 1990 and 1998 has been around 2.5 percent, with the unemployment rate being driven down to a thirty-year low of about 4.2 percent of the labor force. We would also add that investment expenditures as a percentage of GDP averaged 17 percent over the years 1990 to 1997. But there is a disquieting note to this good experience of the 1990s. In terms of GDP growth by decades, we find the 1990s experience about equal to that of 1980s, but below that of the 1970s, where the growth rate was 2.8 percent, and certainly well below the 4.1 percent rate of the 1960s. So that over a period of forty years the growth rate has been slipping; it has been thought that this is greatly due to the very weak increase in productivity gain, that is, the increase in output per worker. This productivity slowdown can be seen by the fact that the gain in output per worker increased at a rate of 1.1 percent compared to increases of 1.2 percent in the 1980s, 2.2 percent in the 1970s, and 3.4 percent in the 1960s. There is uncertainty as to why this is happening and how to reverse this growth slowdown. While steady growth in and of itself is desirable, it is the pace that may give concern; it may very well be that the productivity issue is the key, which means essentially the presence of technological change and how it becomes infused into the production process. There is a question as to why the technological advances in our so-called time of the "information revolution" do not show up in our average annual productivity-gain numbers.[10]

In this chapter we delved into the fundamental models of steady growth, and thereby the reader should have an understanding of those economic balances maintained beneath the surface that sustain the macrogrowth numbers. But we need to go further and look in some detail at that important technological change element in the growth experience. How do we represent its presence in a production process, and how much has it been thought to contribute to growth? Is there a relationship between the rate of capital accumulation and the pace of improvements in technology that is thought to feed back to the growth process itself? In the following chapter we turn to these issues.

Notes

1. Paul Samuelson and William Nordhaus, *Economics*, 14th ed. (New York: McGraw Hill, 1992), p. 546.
2. The prewar term goes back to the beginning of the business cycle chronology, encompassing the period from 1854 to 1939.
3. Evsey D. Domar, *Essays in the Theory of Economic Growth* (New York: Oxford University Press, 1957), p. 74.
4. Ibid., p. 101.
5. Since we are talking in terms of a movement through time, it would have been more accurate to replace our delta term with

$$\frac{dI}{dt} \text{ and } \frac{dY}{dt}$$

showing the rate of change per unit of time. But for simplicity we use ΔI and ΔY.
6. Harrod's writings are many, but essentially: R.F. Harrod, *Towards a Dynamic Economics* (London: Macmillan, 1948). Also, "Themes in Dynamic Theory" *Economic Journal* (September 1963). And there is Domar cited in note 3, especially essays 3 and 4. Elucidating commentary on these models can be found in Daniel Hamberg, *Economic Growth and Instability* (New York: W.W. Norton, 1956). Also William J. Baumol, *Economic Dynamics* (New York: Macmillan, 1951). More recently, Stanley Bober, *Recent Developments in Non-Neoclassical Economics* (Brookfield, VT, and Aldershot, UK: Ashgate, 1997).
7. Harrod, *Towards a Dynamic Economics*. In talking about past experience, we are saying that the rate of increase in output anticipated to occur in t is proportional to

the rate of increase realized in the immediate past period $t - 1$. Writing these rates of change as a ratio we have

$$\frac{Y_t^a}{Y_{t-1}} = m\left(\frac{Y_{t-1}}{Y_{t-2}}\right)^2$$

where

a = anticipated.

In the model $m = 1$ so that:

$$Y_t^a(Y_t - 2) = (Y_t - 1)$$

$$Y_t^a = \frac{(Y_t - 1)^2}{Y_t - 2}$$

which is a fancy way of saying that one expects the most recent rate of growth to continue in the next period.

8. Hamberg, *Economic Growth and Instability*, p. 105.

9. Baumol, *Economic Dynamics*, p. 46.

10. When these words were written we did not see appreciable productivity gains. But recently, productivity increases have been showing up strongly, with non-farm business productivity increasing by 5 percent in the last quarter of 1999.

8

The Issue of Technological Change

The Accounting Matter

We begin by observing the conventional accounting for the technological change element. From our analysis of growth models we know that the pace of advance of the economy is propelled by the rate of capital accumulation, that is, net business investment expenditures, the rate of growth of the labor force, and that of technical progress. However, these elements are understood not to partake equally in the growth rate of real GDP; they are weighted by their particular contribution. But how are these weights determined?

A way to go about this is to have the weight of labor, say, determined by the proportion of national income going to wages. Yet we have to be rather careful here. It is all too easy to assume (as orthodoxy would have us do) that the wage rate reflects the marginal productivity of labor, with the wage bill being determined in a labor market setting. But as we have argued (in our distribution chapter), that is, to say the least, an unsound vision. We have shown that overall there is no labor market in the conventional sense, and that the wage outcome is mainly the result of a conflict situation. So we have to say that the proportion of income going to labor reflects the bargaining outcome, whereby labor was able to extract a wage rate that it believed reflected its contribution to production. But this is not at all that of a marginal productivity determination or explanation.

So let us have that the growth rate of the labor force is weighted by three-quarters and that of capital by one-quarter, roughly in line with the proportion of national income going to wages and profits. This gives the equation of growth accounting as

$$G = 3/4\, G_L + 1/4\, G_K + \text{TC}$$

$$\text{TC} = \text{Technological Change} \tag{8.1}$$

And on a per capita basis we have

$$G_y = 1/4\,(G_k) + \text{TC}$$

$$y = \frac{Y}{L}, k = \frac{K}{L} \tag{8.2}$$

What Equation 8.2 tells us is that should (TC) = 0, then the growth in output per capita would be one-quarter less than the growth in capital per capita (referred to as capital deepening); this, as conventional analysis would explain it, is a reflection of diminishing returns to capital. The analysis asks us to accept the orthodox output per capita production function of Figure 5.13 of our chapter on distribution.

Now accepting this framework, the contribution of technical progress comes up as a residual after the other input components have been calculated. One can then distinguish, supposedly, between how much of the growth in output per capita is attributable to an increase in capital deepening, and how much is due to advances in technology. Let us follow through with an arithmetic example. In the period between 1900 and 1991, the capital stock grew by 2.5 percent per year while the labor force grew by 1.3 percent per year, with the growth in output being 3.1 percent. On a per capita basis and assuming capital's contribution to growth is equal to 0.25, we derive the following growth equation.

$$G_y = 1/4\,(G_k) + \text{TC} \tag{8.3}$$

$$1.8 = 1/4\,(1/2) + \text{TC}$$

$$1.8 = 0.3 + \text{TC}$$

$$\text{TC} = 1.5$$

Samuelson and Nordhaus say, "Thus of the 1.8 percent per-year increase in output per worker, about 0.3 percentage point is due to capital deepening while an astounding 1.5% per year stems from T.C."[1]

While we certainly would acknowledge the essential contribution of technology to economic growth, we would reject the way in which it is conventionally accounted for by our arithmetic example. It cannot, except by a very limited understanding of the term technical change, be reckoned as a "leftover" or residual; it does not stand apart from the nature and growth of the

Figure 8.1

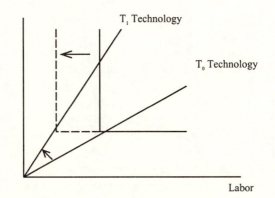

capital input itself. Of course, our critique stems from previous discussions where we urged the abandonment of the traditional output per capita production function. In the modern economy we do not encounter production processes that speak of diminishing returns to capital; we do not have price-driven factor substitutability in the conventional sense of moving along a production function. The notion of the deepening of capital carries a message of ongoing change in the technique of production that, in the reality of fixed input coefficients, reduces the labor input required per unit of capital as capital is being accumulated. For if this were not the case, then the historically observed trend of the growth in capital outpacing that of the labor force would lead to capital redundancy (which may occur for effective demand reasons and not normally due to a labor shortage). The problem more likely to be encountered by society is technologically driven redundancy in the labor force.

What happens is the amalgam of capital accumulation and latest technology, which reduces the fixed labor coefficient as it increases labor productivity. In Figure 8.1 we see this labor-augmenting technical progress via our fixed factor proportions function where we have an increase in the capital-to-labor ratio.

Figure 8.1 speaks in terms of the same capital coefficient operating with a reduced labor input. Thus even if we imagined no capital accumulation so that investment expenditure equals replacement, it is realistic to assume that the replacement machine is, in most instances, not an exact replacement of the machine being replaced, but contains an up-to-date, different technology.

What are we to make of that 1.5 percent TC (in and of itself) contribution to the growth in labor productivity? We would say that it is an artificially correct result being based on production assumptions that, as we have argued, are very much at odds with real world production processes. The orthodox production function with its smooth factor substitutability and diminishing returns characteristic should finally be put aside. The idea of being able to gauge the effect on the growth of output per unit of labor as one increases the capital-to-labor ratio, all other elements not changing, is an arbitrary (and artificial) way to adjust numbers. To repeat, production processes simply do not sustain this vision. And the notion of assigning capital's contribution of one-quarter on the basis of capital and/or labor being paid their marginal product is, in general, a widely used pretension. So while it is very encouraging to see growth in the capital stock per worker and a long-term increase in output per worker, there is no way to separate in reality the impact of technological change from the growth of the capital stock itself. Technical progress does not come from nowhere to be added on to the data as a residual; it is not possible to segregate variations in output per unit of labor due to technical change from those due to change in the growth of capital per head. Capital formation must be seen as the vehicle for bringing the latest technology to the production process. At the risk of overstating our point, the reader is asked to think again of the orthodox production function evidencing (supposedly) diminishing returns to output per capita in response to change in the capital-to-labor ratio; now it must take a strong suspension of disbelief to believe that it is the same type of capital containing the existing technology that is being accumulated per head along the function. And when technology does change, it appears from the outside to imbue the existing input ratio with a greater output. In other words, the economy is portrayed as having been shifted from one production function to another.

Perhaps one should simply accept a finding such as an increase in output per unit of labor without attempting to splice it, which may, not withstanding all good intentions, do harm to a realistic interpretation. Yet there have been several attempts to isolate the technical change and knowledge factor contributions to economic growth.

An often-referred-to study is the one by E.F. Denison where he analyzed the sources of growth over the 1948 to 1989 period, when the U.S. economy had grown at average rate of 3.3 percent per year. What showed up was that the growth of inputs as such, that is, that of labor and capital, accounted for 1.9 percent of the total growth rate; while the growth of output less the growth of the weighted sum of the inputs, which accounts for the growth in the productivity of labor amounted to 1.4 percent per year. This was a residual factor attributable to elements such as education, innovation, and so forth. Overall, this particular study concluded that capital growth accounts for 37 percent of output growth, while technological change and education make up 42 percent of total growth and more than half the growth in output per worker.[2]

Tracing growth over the years 1929 to 1982, Denison found that 28 percent of the increase in real national income was accounted for by technological advance, while only 19 percent was attributable to the growth in the quantity of capital. The whole vision of this separation, to say in other words what we have been stressing, is that a worker will, subject to diminishing returns, be more productive when equipped with more capital, and there is a residual factor that will make more productive a given combination of machinery and worker. But this flies in the face of real-world production processes. What happens is that as capital formation takes place, the new capital requires a lower labor coefficient due to the technical change built in to the new equipment. Of course, this increases labor productivity, and it is not accountable by something "leftover." But perhaps we are being a bit too stringent here.

If one includes in technological change matters such as education and training and improved resource allocation, then these can improve labor productivity for a given worker-to-machine ratio. But these are of minor consideration compared to the improvements in output due to some inherent change in the operations of the capital good itself. Productive innovations are in the main embodied in new equipment, which is tied up with the rate of capital growth.

The Usual Representation of Change

Let us now look at the traditional representation of the residual nature of technical change or, to use the more common term, technical change as "neutral." The idea is that technical advance will allow more of a commodity to be produced for a given input ratio of capital to labor, or that a smaller level of inputs within the existing ratio can produce the same level of output. As we said, this neutral advance shifts the aggregate production function upward with the new function being superior to the old. Making use of our orthodox production function in terms of output per worker, we see this in Figure 8.2. Without going over what is by now familiar ground, we have argued that the functions in Figure 8.2 are not representative of the reality of production processes in the economy—they cannot form the core of our understanding. However, we can portray this notion of neutrality with the use of our fixed coefficient production function, which reflects the stylized fact of production in the real economy—consider Figure 8.3. As we mentioned, neutrality would allow one to reduce the quantity of capital and labor within existing proportions and maintain the same level of output.

The problem then is not with the representation, but, as we have been saying, with the notion of neutrality itself. Shifts in the production function reflecting neutrality leave the marginal rate of substitution between inputs

Figure 8.2

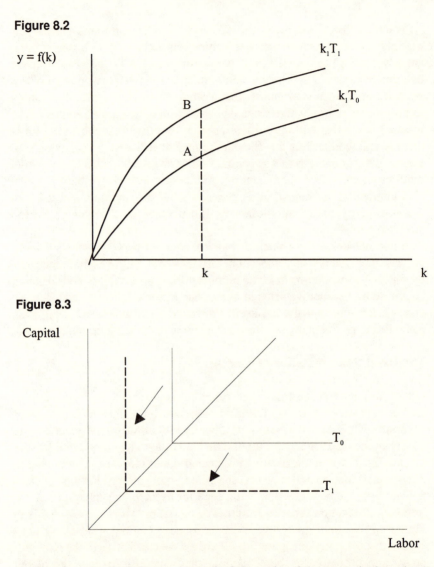

Figure 8.3

unchanging, that is, it leaves untouched the ratio of the "marginal product" of capital to that of labor. Thus the aggregate production function may be written as

$$Y = f[A(t)K, B(t)L] \qquad (8.4)$$

Output is not a function of the quantities of capital and labor or of the capital-to-labor ratio (k), but it is a function of "effective" capital to "effective" labor in response to technical change. Capital and labor are multiplied by factors A and B over time t, so that it is as if they both increased in quantity thereby enabling greater production levels. Of course, there is no increase in quantity, but capital and labor have augmented their production capability by equal quantities represented by $A(t)$ and $B(t)$. This representation of technical progress is said to be Hicks-neutral, which, to repeat, is saying to us that at a constant value of the capital-to-labor ratio, the impact of technical change is to leave unchanged the marginal product of capital to that of labor. This perhaps gives another view of that arithmetic residual technical change number.

Another characteristic of this type of technical change is that since it carries the associated assumption (at least in its orthodox representation) that factors of production are paid their marginal products, and as there is no change in the ratio of marginal products, then a neutral change is one that does not change relative income shares. Of course, a particular relationship between wages and profits must be maintained as an essential underpinning for the steady growth condition, so as to provide the required savings; but this income distribution is institutionally hammered-out, if you will. It is not a technical result of reading input income off the slope of a production function reflecting, as we said, that inputs are paid their marginal product.

One further point reflecting this neutral change that we can read from Figure 8.2 is that it is the entire curve that is shifting up, implying that all productive processes are affected by the technical change. That is, while the change is occurring within a circumstance of a particular capital intensity in use, it is absorbed by all other processes. And it is this aggregateness or disembodiment that certainly heightens one's doubt about this neutral manner of handling technical change. Normally one reads a point on the function in Figure 8.2 as saying that all processes are reflective of the same capital intensity, so that a technical change is incorporated with the same impact throughout the entire economy. But this interpretation does not move us further along with regard to a realistic framework for the assessment of this technological change element.

All in all, we need another way to get hold of the impact of technical progress. And we do have an alternative approach in terms of the notion of an "effective labor force" that we encountered in the Harrod growth model analysis. To recall: It is not merely a matter of the growth of the labor force, as such, as a central element in the process of economic growth, but it is very much a matter of expressing or measuring the labor supply in efficiency units, which is in terms of the growth in productivity of a unit of that labor supply. And what we can refer to as this labor-augmenting progress is presumed to be going on at an exogeneously determined rate λ. Writing this out in a production function, we have

$$Y = f[K, B(t)L] \qquad (8.5)$$

Where B is the labor-enhancing factor growing at the rate λ per unit of time t. Again, to point up the obvious, while population growth causes there to be two units of labor where there was one previously, this labor-augmenting progress causes one man to be able to do twice what he could have done previously. Together they give us what Harrod referred to as that natural rate of growth (Equation 7.38 in chapter 7), the G_n.

What is attractive about this approach is that the effect of technological progress is not neutral in the sense of uniformly impacting all inputs, but is reckoned to spill out in the form of enhanced labor productivity only. Yet this increase in output per unit of worker is the result of new technology embodied in the added machinery employing additional units of labor. We do not mean here a sense of an increase in productivity that results from more "learning by doing" on existing or even on additional machinery, which has the implication that the additions to the capital are of the same "type" as the existing capital.

The overall reality of a technologically different capital as capital is being accumulated carries a negative as well as a positive impact. The addition to the capital stock reduces the labor input that it requires for its operation while, of course, simultaneously increasing the output per worker. But this is not how the Harrod technical progress is usually put forth, as we can see directly from Figure 8.4, which is a repeat of Figure 5.13 from our chapter 5, with associated orthodox characteristics. So we have a production function (f) in the absence of technological progress, with the presumed declining productivity increases as capital per capita increases; and the marginal product of capital being equal to the slope of a tangent at a point (B), determining the rate of return for that level of capital accumulation. Of course, the reader is by now certainly aware of our criticism of this approach to understanding production processes in the economy. But we carry on with convention as the usual means to portray the Harrod classification of technical progress.

Now let us be clear about a movement on the production function (f): In a move from B to C it is presumed that the labor input coefficient is unchanged, but that it is now working with a greater amount of capital, and that the addition to these "tools" is technologically very similar to what has previously been part of production. But at some point there are, so to speak, too many tools, reducing the growth in output as labor attempts to work the larger capital stock—if only we could "allow" a greater number of hands per

Figure 8.4

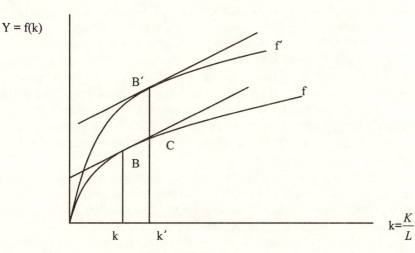

unit of output. Again, the diminishing returns configuration to the f function in the move from B to C is assumed attributable to the labor input and not to the output capability of the machines.

Now at k' we have a technological change that results in one pair of hands being able to produce the output of two, increasing output per unit of labor and shifting the function to f'. What caused this to happen? According to Harrod, technical progress, and as seen in Figure 8.4, it is not attributable to the nature of productivity of the newly accumulated capital, as the marginal productivity of capital remains the same as given by the parallel slopes of the tangencies at B and B'. So this labor-augmenting technical progress must emanate from within the labor input itself. This brings us to a statement about Harrod-neutrality: At a constant capital-to-output ratio, the ratio of the relative shares of profits to wages remain unchanged. Neutrality results from a labor-augmenting change that leaves unaffected the marginal product of capital as it maintains constancy in the ratio of the value of capital to that of output. There are intertwining relationships here resulting in the unchanging relative income shares. Again we look at Figure 8.4.

In the move from B to C on function f there is an increase in the ratio of capital-to-output due to, as we pointed out, the conventional declining productivity of labor in the face of "capital deepening," that is, the higher level of k. Now at k' we have a technical occurrence that "cancels" the increase in the capital-to-labor ratio by adjusting the labor force in terms of efficiency units, which is as if the labor force in natural units were itself growing. To reiterate: It is the increase in the capital-to-labor ratio and associated technical change that is reckoned to enhance the productivity of the "pair of hands" to the degree that it is as if the labor force itself increased at the same rate as that of capital. And with the constant returns to scale assumption, output and capital will then exhibit a common growth rate as given by the slope of the lines at *B* and *B'*. Now with the marginal productivity of capital reckoned to be the same, so that the rate of return (in conventional thinking) is unchanging, profits grow in line with the increasing accumulation of capital and hence reside as a constant proportion of output. With regard to labor, wages grow in line with the productivity of labor, so that total wages increase at the same rate as that of the effective labor force and are then maintained as a constant proportion of output.

This is Harrod technical progress in its neutral stance; to keep matters clear, let us compare this to Hicks-neutral progress. In essence it depends on the classification of points on the original and new function. Hicks compares points with identical input ratios; thus it is the unchanging ratio of the marginal productivity of capital to that of labor in the face of a technical change that defines Hicks-neutrality and maintains the constant ratio of the relative shares of income. Whereas Harrod-neutrality maintains constant relative income shares as a consequence of an unchanging capital-to-labor ratio in the face of technological change that holds the rate constant within the reality of the deepening of capital.

We have evidenced our disquietude regarding the Hicks approach as a way for us to reckon, or appreciate, the role of technical change in a growing economy. As we indicated, the Harrod framework carries more realism, as its effect is quite specific and does not appear as a residual falling evenly over all inputs. Yet Harrod-neutral progress, as well, gives rise to some doubts. There is, of course, the aggregate "disembodied" nature of this labor-augmenting effect; the change that increases the output of a pair of hands does not only impact the new hands operating the newly accumulated capital, but is absorbed by all units of labor working on all ages of machines. Furthermore, the approach that technical change is to be seen or calculated solely in terms of labor enhancement would, as we mentioned, seem to imply that the cause for the increase in labor productivity stems from within the labor input itself. But this runs up against an intuitive belief that, more often than not, it is the new machines, that is, the new investment, that "contains" the technology that is causing the augmentation of the labor force. And if we were to think of this new technology as being disembodied across the capital stock, then why not calculate the impact of technological change as capital augmenting and talk in terms of an "effective capital stock." Why not have the natural (maximum) rate of growth be defined in terms of both the growth of capital and labor in efficiency units? Is the notion of a steady-state growth economy possible within such a context or must technical change augment labor only?

Consider an individual "producing" 3,000 words per hour while operating a word-processing machine; at a later time we find the individual producing 6,000 words per hour. What can cause this "technical progress" to happen?

1. The person at the later time is working the same number of hours, has the same skill, but is now operating a machine with a different technology.
2. The individual at the later time is working with the same machine and the same number of hours as earlier, but has now increased one's skill, say, as a result of practice during off-work time.

Of course, this technical progress is revealed through the increase in production for the same input (as if we were to have two operators working the original number of hours) or via the ability to produce the original output with half the hours worked. And yet when the production function is shifting upward due to the growing efficiency or augmentation of the labor force, whose augmentation is causing the growth in this effective labor force? And if we are to say that the cause is that of effective capital, then are we to presume that operators working on older machines can adapt their machines to incorporate the latest technology so that there is an all-around increase in labor productivity? We would most likely answer, "not really." Harrod-neutral technical progress does not then leave us totally satisfied.

Another (perhaps very obvious) point to bear in mind: As long as we do not envisage total machine-robot production so that some natural units of labor are part of production, there will always be labor augmentation, but the important matter is the underlying causation process and its effect on employment and income distribution in the growth process. It is this conflict over the cause of productivity increases in relation to labor's bargaining clout with management that greatly decides the distribution between profits and wages.

Our classification of technical progress into the Hicks- or Harrod-neutral forms has been an attempt to see the influence of such progress on an economy in the process of steady growth. As it turns out, the only kind of technical change consistent with the characteristic of steady-state growth is Harrod-neutral, or change in the labor-augmenting form. This would answer the question we asked previously, but why should this be so? As Solow puts it: "It is not easy to explain why this special labor-augmenting form of technical progress is necessary for steady-state growth to be possible."[3]

Recalling our analysis of the steady-growth path, we have a constant savings ratio that, as we know, implies the existence of a particular distribution of income, giving rise to a rate of capital accumulation such that the rate of growth in output and demand is equal to that of capital—and we are referring to capital in "natural" units. Thus along the growth path there is a constant capital-to-output ratio in conjunction with an unchanging distribution of income; this, as we know, is compatible with Harrod-neutral technical progress. Now suppose that technological change were both capital and labor augmenting, what happens to the "internal mechanics" of the steady-growth path?

Both capital and labor are growing at the same rate in efficiency units (Hicks-neutrality with a different twist), with output then having to grow at that common rate as well (the constant-return assumption). But this means that capital growth in efficiency units and the growth in productive capacity that it represents, exceed the growth of capital in natural units and the accompanying increase in demand and output that it gives rise to. So what we have is an increase in unused capacity reflected in an increasing capital-to-output ratio that, by virtue of conventional assumptions, will lead to a decline in the rate of profit. And this altered distribution of income reduces savings and thereby the growth of capital in natural units, which may undermine the full employment path itself. If output has to grow at a greater rate than the growth of capital in natural units itself, there can be no configuration to a constant capital-to-output ratio; that is, a state where the capital stock is growing at the same rate as output with a constant distribution of income between wage and profits. Solow comments on this as follows:

> [A] constant savings-rate and a constant capital-to-output ratio are incompatible. If the economy maintains full employment (or a constant unemployment rate) with a constant fraction of output saved and invested, the capital/output ratio will persistently rise and the rate of profit will persistently fall. If the economy wishes to—or thinks it must—maintain a constant capital/output ratio and a constant rate of profit, it must save and invest a persistently decreasing fraction of its output.[4]

And it must be a declining fraction such that the growth in "effective" capital be no greater than that in natural units in the absence of augmentation, and hence be equal to the growth in output as determined by the effective labor force. It is as if the growth in efficiency capital is canceled via the reduction in the growth of natural capital.

Let us look at the situation again. If the economy is in the steady-state mode with labor-force augmentation and it becomes subject to capital augmentation technical change, it will lose its consistent movement due to a change now in the ratio of capital (effective) to output and the related change in the distribution of income thereby altering the heretofore constant savings propensity. What we are saying is that the growth in productive capacity as given by the growth of capital in natural units and the growth of capital in efficiency units outpaces the growth demand and output as determined by the capital-to-(effective) labor ratio, that is, by the growth in output per unit of labor. And this will, after a time, affect the rate of accumulation of the capital stock itself. Thus it would seem that technical change within the steady-state structure must be Harrod-neutral in form.

But this reasoning may put us into a somewhat uncomfortable position. We made the observation that steady-state growth is a good approximation of recent U.S. economic experience, and can serve as a framework to understand the economic reality. However, we also indicated less than total satisfaction with the view that the only way to understand the role of technical change in the growth experience is via Harrod-neutrality. This seemed to ask the observer to place total emphasis on change in the intrinsic quality of labor itself as the cause for the increase in labor productivity, and thereby as the means to account for labor in efficiency units. There is no relating the presence of effective labor to the changing design of the capital stock, as the (natural) capital-to-labor ratio is increasing over time. One would almost intuitively take the position—as we have stated before—that the lower ratio of labor to capital results mainly from the changed technology inherent in the newly accumulated stock that reduces the labor coefficient as it increases labor productivity. Technical progress generally is embodied in new capital accumulation through which it becomes effective, that is, raises productivity. Thus even if we were to accept the conventional production functions in Figure 8.1, the shift of the curve cannot come out of the blue, but must be related to some transmission mechanism for the presence of technical change that comes from within the system itself and brings about the function shift from f to f'. And I would think we would agree that this shift is to a large degree not explainable by learning by doing or by some improvements in organization and work rules.

Thus we accept that over time there will be an increasing effective labor supply, but in conjunction with, and attributable to, capital growth, both in natural and, more importantly, in efficiency units. We are saying that one needs growth in effective capital in order to account for the growth in effective labor. And the reality of this duel augmentation must be handled in a way that does not upset the consistency of the steady-state path.

This can be done if we take the approach that the augmentation of labor in natural units, that is, the rate of increase in efficiency units, is a mirror of the rate of increase of capital in efficiency units. The rate of increase in the productivity of capital, reflective of the technical change embodied in the capital (natural) unit is to be reckoned as having been passed into the hands of the labor unit operating with it. It is as if there is no growth of capital in efficiency units; that is, technical change augments labor only. Note that we are not adding the growth of effective labor to the growth of effective capital, which would raise problems of an increasing capital-to-output ratio and a declining rate of profit.

The Vintage Capital Reality

This understanding opens the way to incorporate technical change through the presence of "vintage capital goods." We begin with some characteristics of this reality. First of all, in line with what we have been suggesting and what seems apparent, is that advances in technical knowledge (i.e., technical change), can only affect production when they are infused or embodied in new capital goods through gross investment. Solow makes the point that "many, if not most innovations need to be embodied in new kinds of durable equipment before they can be made effective."[5] And Kaldor's statement, which reflects his approach to the impact of capital accumulation, is that "the use of more capital per worker inevitably entails the introduction of superior techniques which require inventiveness of some kind"; and, he continues, "most, though not all, technical innovations which are capable of raising the productivity of labor require the use of more capital per man."[6] Two overall observations: The impact of technical change (the bringing of invention to the "production floor") comes through its embodiment in the capital input and is reflected in the nature of the equipment; and its presence is associated with an increase in the capital-to-labor ratio, meaning essentially a decrease in the labor coefficient per unit of output.

Let us revisit the conventional production function in Figure 8.4. Moving along function f reveals gains in labor productivity from increases in capital intensity or capital deepening, though eventually subjecting the "pair of hands" to the diminishing return nemesis. What the production function is referring to, to reiterate, is a deepening in terms of the use of more capital in natural units per worker (measured in terms, let us say, of the increasing value of capital machines at constant prices). Of course, the nemesis can be thwarted by technical change shifting the nature of the labor input growth from natural to efficiency units, thereby shifting the curve from f to f'. Conventional analysis then makes a distinction between gains in productivity from increases in capital deepening (moving along the function) and technological change (the upward shift of the function). However, with our vintage capital approach, this conventional image must be put aside and these two sources of productivity improvements merged into a single functional relation.

And Kaldor does this with the construction of his technical progress function, which is illustrated in Figure 8.5. The progress function is a look-alike

Figure 8.5

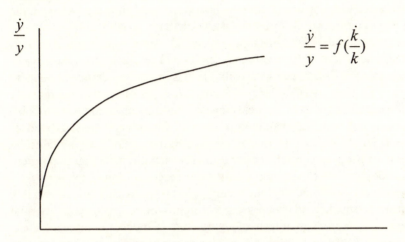

$$\frac{\dot{y}}{y} = f(\frac{\dot{k}}{k})$$

to the conventional production function, but that is as far as it goes. Each point on the progress function reflects the growth in output per "pair of hands," attributable to an increasing rate of accumulation of capital as well as technical change that resides in the new additions to the capital stocks, and which together cause an increase in productivity per unit of labor—labor works with more capital and more technologically advanced capital. Certainly what this does is to remove a cause of concern along, say, the function *f* in Figure 8.4, which is to infer diminishing returns in relation to some level of capital deepening. With the vintage capital approach as mirrored in the progress function, one cannot automatically infer this diminishing returns nemesis. Throughout this book we have argued, in different contexts, that diminishing return is a wrongly applied idea; here we have further reason not to allow our thinking to be held hostage to this "principle."

Some additional observations about this progress function need to be made. It seems that the number of capital enhancing innovations that appear within the production process is related to the pace of accumulation of the underlying capital stock itself. Thus the greater the increase of capital deepening through gross investment that increases output per unit of labor along the output function, the more potent or magnified is the function shift itself with its heightened effect on output "per pair of hands." And each point on the progress function mirrors this duel impact on output growth per capita.

But the way we interpret what the progress function is telling us bears on how we explain the natural rate of output growth with full employment. Recall the definition of the G_n (natural rate of growth): It is that rate of growth that in the presence of full employment is permitted by the growth in the labor force and the rate of technological progress, that is, by the growth of the effective labor force. But which labor force? While the points on the progress function speak to us about the increase in labor productivity of recently hired labor working newly installed equipment, it could be presumed that the different technology embodied in the recent additions of capital can be passed back to modify all existing older equipment so as to increase the productivity of previous employed labor to that of the recently employed. Thus we have the transmission of technical change via gross investment, but with the change impacting all investment—past as well as present. So we are back to Harrod's natural growth rate (the growth of the labor force being absorbed by net investment) but with technological progress now endogenously transmitted via the most recent working capital.

However, this is not what the vintage capital approach is about, and it is not how we should read the progress function. We are not, in all reality, able to transmit the production technology inherent in the new equipment to existing older capital currently in use, which may very well present problems of maintaining full employment for a particular rate of capital accumulation and growth of the labor force. How would we calculate the natural growth rate at a point in time? Supposedly it would be equal to the output growth brought about by effective labor on the latest installed equipment, added to the output of the labor employed on older equipment, and so on. It is as if the net investment absorbs the increase in the labor force with the economy realizing the higher productivity of that addition to the workforce without any effect on the usage of previously installed capital with its particular employment level. But this has to strike the reader as rather odd. Why should we suppose the ongoing operation of older—higher labor cost—equipment to keep pace with the secular growth in sales? We would suppose that gross investment with its related increased capacity will result in a degree of economic obsolescence of older equipment with the release of labor. The increase in labor productivity accompanying technological progress can be expected to have a negative side in terms of technological unemployment. How would this be handled within our steady-growth context?

This brings us back to the essential point of this vintage approach. Of course, by the term "vintage" we are referring to age; at any one time the working capital of the economy, that is, its productive capacity, is composed of capital of different ages, where the capital (machine) of each age (i.e., of each vintage) contains, or is embodied with, the latest technical know-how at the time of its installation with its related impact on the productivity of labor working with it. More modern equipment will contain a different technology that will yield a different (higher) labor productivity than equipment of an older vintage. What is essential in this image is that the technical change embodied in the latest accumulation of capital cannot be passed back to be incorporated in the machines of an older vintage.

What we are then saying is that the economy is composed of qualitatively different kinds of capital with corresponding different degrees of labor productivity; that is, different labor costs per unit of output. It may be that the different technology embodied in the most recently installed machine may require a change in its design; thus the latest addition to the stock may even be of a changed physical form from that of older capital where both are part of a process producing the same output. In this regard it may be easier to visualize this situation if we think of the economy as one megacorp organization whose capacity consists of plants of different vintages.

What has been referred to as the pure vintage model assumes that technical change is embodied in the latest machines only at the time of installation; thereafter, this equipment cannot share in any further technological advances. This has also been labeled the putty–clay capital model. The idea is that prior to installation one can choose from different machine designs or blueprints evidencing different capital-to-labor ratios as reflective of their different embodied technologies—the capital in its putty state. But once installed, as Phelps stated, the putty, so to speak, "takes shape, it turns to hand baked clay"[7]; that is, the productivity of labor mirroring the technical advance built into the machine is baked in or hardened and cannot be altered by later technological changes. As an overall observation, we can say that technical progress takes the form of new ideas to be embodied in new investment that will increase productivity; it does not mean new ideas for the more efficient use of existing equipment.

A related approach is that of a clay–clay capital model. Here there is no flexibility in the capital-to-labor design prior to installation or subsequently. There exists a single technology reflective of the latest knowledge that calls for a particular input ratio—there is "clay" at the outset. There is no choice in the accumulation of capital of adding to the stock equipment of the type already in use; but the megacorp would not look to do this in any event (unless it can only do this because there is no technological change). So the economy (i.e., our giant firm) is presented with a given fixed input proportion production function for increases in its output, which is maintained until further technological advances come onto the scene.

We have championed the use of the fixed coefficient production function to move us away from the conventional malleability model of capital in the production process; with its aggregate uniform concept of capital that instantaneously alters or molds all of itself to be suitable to operate with different numbers of workers (the reader may want to revisit the nature of the orthodox production function as seen in our chapter on income distribution).

Yet aside from this image, which assumes a price-driven freely variable capital-output coefficient, if we are to have technological progress, then all capital goods, old and new alike, are assumed to share equally (to be equally embodied) in this progress. Thus from a technology point of view all capital is alike or homogeneous; but then we cannot account for the reality of capital becoming economically obsolete. Solow puts the matter neatly when he says, "Since all capital was homogeneous, none could become obsolete because all would become obsolete."[8] Of course, we needed to get away from this unreal imagery, and the vintage capital model enables us to do that. Yet interestingly, the vintage approach does give us, one might say, a modified version of capital malleability or variability in the capital-to-output ratio. But this is a variability tied to a heterogeneous capital stock, which yields differences in production techniques tied to advances in technology. Thus some capital can become obsolete without all becoming so, and we want to see how this works out within the context of the full employment growth path.

What is it that we now do not have, which heretofore characterized or "permitted" the steady state? We do not find a uniform increase in labor productivity for the whole of the labor force, and as we are dealing with diverse capital structures operating at the same time, it is no longer meaningful to think of the notion of a homogenous input of something labeled capital that is placed into a production function. This means that there is no operational meaning to the idea of a capital-to-output ratio that is characteristic of a balanced growth path. In reality there is no singular capital-to-output ratio; there exist simultaneously different capital-to-output ratios. Thus we need some other key variable that "accommodates" or moves to permit the steady state. That variable is the economic lifetime of capital that, in Solow's words, is "the length of time that elapses between the moment that investment occurs and the moment at which the capacity laid down becomes obsolete."[9] A particular feature of vintage capital models, of which it is best to think of the clay–clay variety, is the presence of obsolescence of capital of successive vintages. And in the steady state the economic lifetime is constant; that is, each successive age (vintage) of capital becomes obsolete after some constant number of years.

We begin at a point in time with a given labor supply (Lt) that we will assume to be equal to total employment (Nt). There exists a level of capital stock (or, let us say a number of plants) of different vintages in use, each with its fixed but different input coefficient technology. This stock is the result of an investment history and at time t yields full employment. A rate of accumulation now occurs equal to gross investment, which brings new capacity online that carries with it a higher level of labor productivity. We keep in mind that we are considering the increase in output per unit of labor working with the newly installed capital as a function of the technical advance inherent in the new capacity. And this technical advance will, as a general observation, require a smaller number of pairs of hands per unit of output.

Again, it may be helpful to conjure up our megacorp that has brought new capacity into play and must now decide how to allocate its existing labor force over its available total capacity of different vintages. But this is like saying that since a new plant needs to begin production, which of the older vintage plants should be declared obsolete and cut off from operating capacity and maintain the full employment of its labor force. What determines which vintages should be left unused?

With the existence of a markup price and a money wage resulting from a previous negotiation, the most recently added capacity will carry with it a lower ratio of wage costs to total costs since it embodies the latest technical advance. That is, it reflects a level of labor productivity higher than that found on earlier installed capacity. The technology of the newest installed capital means that it will require fewer "pairs of hands" for its operation and thus reduce the labor costs per unit of output. Then the excess of revenue over labor costs will be higher from the operation of this newest capacity than from that of all earlier installed capacity, that is, all earlier vintages of capital. It bears repeating that the latest progress of Harrod-neutrality on new capital cannot be passed back to previously installed capital; all progress affects newly installed capital only.

Now if we assume no change in the money wage, we could see our megacorp operating all its different vintage plants, each yielding a different rate of return on capital. However this will not happen, as the higher labor productivity in the most recent facility will trigger a money wage rate increase, most likely the result of a contractual arrangement that ties higher money wages to increased productivity. Yet the point to be aware of is that a higher wage will be negotiated not only for labor working with the newest capital, but will apply equally to labor working with the capital of existing vintages. Certainly the wage outcome—being generally the result of negotiations—will not be one of discrimination between workers producing the same product.

What will then happen is that for some previous vintage plant—now a number of years after its installation—the higher wage costs, being the result of the particular requirement of units of labor and the higher money wage, will cause the profit on that capital to fall to zero and the capital to thereby be rendered obsolete and scrapped, that is, cut off from the megacorp's operating capacity. And the place of this scrapped capital will now be taken by the next oldest vintage, as being most vulnerable to obsolescence due to technical advances that raise the money wage over time in conjunction with ongoing capital accumulation. Thus the economic life of capital (denote this by T) is a finite number determined by the condition that the excess of revenue over wage costs of capital of vintage (V) falls to zero at T periods after installation.

The release of labor from production as a result of obsolescence of capital is a more realistic way to consider the notion of technological unemployment than how it is customarily handled in the Principles of Economics course. There the emphasis is placed on the erosion or obsolescence of skills that prevent one from being productive in a technologically changed workplace. But workers in a facility of vintage (V) cannot realize the technological progress of the modern plant and hence do not "see" a changed environment that renders them obsolete, yet the facility is cut off and they are unemployed. It is ironic that the growth in the wage rate, which workers of any vintage plant have been receiving over time, may very well be the cause of their unemployment and not their lack of work skills for the particular process in which they are engaged. The root problem is the obsolescence of capital.

We need to keep in mind that the economic life of capital of any vintage varies inversely with the rate of growth of the wage rate and thus with the share of wages in output. We now appreciate that a plant of any vintage cannot alter its input coefficient production process to ward off the negative input of higher wage rates, most visible in terms of "technological unemployment," with this negative stemming from the positive results of technologically driven increases in labor productivity.

Our discussion of the reality of vintage capital causes some reconsideration of the steady-state growth properties. The rate of output growth is not straightforwardly related to the rate of capital accumulation in the presence of a growth rate of Harrod technological progress; since all operating capital does not share in this progress, we then cannot aggregate the increase in labor productivity to the whole of the labor force. Furthermore, the growth of the labor force (perhaps it is best to say the growth in the number of available "natural" units of labor) is more than a matter of demographics, as it is so often thought of. Of course, it is that to a degree, but the growth of available labor will also mirror the pace of capital obsolescence, which is driven by the pace of technological progress, which may itself depend on that fundamental element of the rate of capital accumulation. How is full employment maintained in this context? As we mentioned previously, the presence of a constant overall capital-to-output ratio that permits, or reflects, the presence of steady growth is no longer meaningful within the reality of generally fixed coefficient technology and vintage capital structures.

So we place ourselves within the steady state to understand the properties of full employment growth under vintage capital production conditions. Coming to this at time (t), we find the labor force of a particular size as a result of having expanded at some rate due to population growth; it is a level of production stemming from the operation of a range of existing vintages of plant that provides full employment for the labor force, and a level of savings generated by an existing distribution of income that will produce a rate of capital accumulation, thereby adding to the operating capacity.

To reiterate the important point: All ongoing vintages are associated with different levels of employed labor and yield different levels of production. Say that from time (t) we look over a range of operating plants of different vintages and find that the oldest plant in use is ten years old, so that it came online at $t - 10$. As long as this capital is in operation it will be associated with the same level of employed labor as at its installation, that is, at $L(t - 10)$, and with the same output $Y(t - 10)$. Let $w(t)$ be the money wage rate prevailing at t, which then yields a wage bill associated with production in vintage plant $t - 10$ of $w(t)L(t - 10)$, with profits realized at time (t) being:

$$Y(t - 10) - w(t)L(t - 10) \tag{8.6}$$

Clearly the obsolescence condition is

$$Y(t - 10) - w(t)L(t - 10) = 0 \tag{8.7}$$

which will be brought about by the level of the prevailing wage rate at t that is, to a degree, reflective of the higher labor productivity in the newly operating facility at time t. Again we see the point that the economic life of capital is a finite variable determined by the growth of technical progress.

It is evident that profits of vintage t will be greater than those of the vintage facility $t - 1$, whose own level of profits will exceed vintage plant $t - 2$ and so on. This is because the younger the vintage plant the lower the labor input coefficient and the higher the output per unit of labor. Thus for $w(t)$ there will be an older vintage plant whose revenue over wage cost will be zero—say that equal to $t - 10$—and be scrapped. As we pointed out, its place as the oldest vintage plant is taken by $t - 9$. But this has brought about "released" labor, what we referred to as technological unemployment. Thus at any point in time the younger that the oldest capital in use is, the smaller the level of employment.

So at time t we presume that the operating capital of the different vintages are employing all of the labor force; and there will occur an accumulation of capital that brings online capital of vintage $t + 1$ with its associated technical progress and labor input coefficient, and the labor force will be growing at some rate, thereby increasing available labor in $t + 1$. What is required for the maintenance of full employment growth in this context?

One would, at first glance, look to the rate of growth of capital as the adjustment mechanism to absorb the growth of the entrants to the labor force, except for that uncomfortable observation that the vintage capital of $t + 1$ will require a lesser labor input coefficient than the capital of previous vintage t. Yet the fact that the new capital requires a smaller level of employment due to the growth in labor productivity, as a result of the operation of capital that embodies the most recent technical advance, will cause the obsolescence of some previous vintage capital of age T. This, as we now understand, is due to the growth of the money wage rate that relates to the growth of productivity. It would then seem that for the continuation of full employment in the presence of the two avenues of labor supply availability, the economy would need to realize a labor supply growth as governed by population growth, that is less than the labor requirements as governed by the growth of capital, with the difference being accommodated by the released labor from the cut off capital of vintage T. Hamberg put this another way: "It is that the increment in labor supply at any time t must always match the difference between the labor requirement of new capital and the quantity of labor being released by capital, age T, being scrapped."[10]

As a characteristic of the steady state, we assume the labor force growing at a rate n, the level of gross investment growing at the rate g, and the growth of labor productivity ongoing at a rate λ. The full employment requirement is that

$$n = g - \lambda \tag{8.8}$$

The λ designation is a manifestation of the degree of scrappage of older vintages of capital, as it tells of the money wage increase, and thus the rate at which wage costs are rising for the different operating facilities. With the given g and n growth rates, the rate of growth of released labor to maintain the employment of the total work force must be

$$\lambda = g - n \tag{8.9}$$

Thus as capital is being added to the operating stock at the g rate with the associated labor requirements, older plants must release labor at a particular rate to accommodate the operation of the additional facilities. This implies that a characteristic of the steady state is some regular pace of capital scrappage and hence a constant economic life of capital, that is, at any point in time the age of the oldest operating facility is a constant. That is, each successive vintage of capital becomes obsolete (T) years after its installation— again, for given g and n rates. As an example, say that at time t the economic life of capital T is five years. The addition of a unit of capital in $t + 1$ will cause the scrappage of the older unit of capital of five years; thus in the sixth year, that is, $t + 1$, the previous capital of vintage four years now becomes the oldest capital of vintage $T = 5$.

This image of a constant economic life might be easier to grasp if we assume zero growth of the labor force; then the amount of labor available to work the new capital is entirely supplied by machines of T years of age being scrapped. This is saying that the constant labor force is evenly distributed over all old vintages of capital. Thus at any time the additions to capital will require the services of the labor force of the successive older vintage capital. We keep in mind that the additions to the stock, say at time t, are of a greater absolute number of machines requiring less labor per unit of machine (they embody the latest technical Harrod-neutral advance) than the accumulation of a previous period. But the total labor requirement in this greater number of new machines will be supplied by the obsolescence of the next older vintage capital that utilized a greater amount of labor. The scrappage of the latter releases the sufficient quantity of labor to man the former, and so on in successive periods. Let us now consider some adjustment that society would need to make if it were off the steady-state path. One manifestation of this is the realization of a too rapid rate of population growth leading to

$$n > g - \lambda \tag{8.10}$$

The growth of the labor force (via population) is greater than that required to fill the difference between the quantity of labor required by the additions to the operating capital and the available released labor due to capital obsolescence. Yet in an overall way, regardless of the source of the problem, labor force growth is out of alignment. We can restate (8.10) as

$$n + \lambda > g \tag{8.11}$$

For a labor force growth rate of n, it may be that the rate of labor productivity growth is too rapid, obsoleting too many machines and releasing labor in excess of what can be absorbed by the growth in the number of machines themselves. It is through this vision

$$\lambda > g - n \tag{8.12}$$

that we can appreciate the notion that technological progress causes unemployment via the circumstance that the economic life of capital (T) has been lowered excessively.

The adjustments to achieving full employment would involve a more rapid rate of capital accumulation in conjunction with the additions to the operating stock now embodying a smaller "level" of technical change. This latter change reveals a lesser rate of increase in labor productivity, which increases the economic life of capital and reduces the availability of released labor.

The adjustment via a high rate of accumulation necessitates an increased savings rate through a change in the distribution of income; that is, there would need to be a corresponding increase in the rate of profit. This could very well result from an unemployment condition as seen in statement 8.10, which reduces labor's bargaining power so that the wage rate would grow at a lesser rate than the embodied rate of increase in labor productivity. The result is greater profits: a higher savings rate and a corresponding increased rate of accumulation. There is, as well, a secondary positive effect of reducing the rate of capital obsolescence, thereby increasing the economic life of capital and lowering the rate of released labor.

It bears repeating that lengthening the economic life of capital is, in this scenario, the result of a lower increase in wage costs that is not reflective of the growth in labor productivity on the new accumulation of capital. It is not the result of a switch to new machines that embody a lower rate of labor-augmenting progress. All new capital goods embody the most recent technology; that is, there is no ex ante variability in that capital can be designed to utilize any amount of labor before installation and obviously afterward. The restoration to full employment—given n—must hinge on extending the economic life (T) of old capital to take advantage of the higher labor input per unit of output as a consequence of the lower capital-embodied technical progress. Thus in the clay–clay circumstances the full employment requirement would positively relate the economic life of capital with the rate if growth of the labor supply.

Should the unemployment problem stem essentially from too high a rate of technical progress and hence an excessive rate of increase of released labor (as we discussed in relation to Equation 8.12), the solution does not seem that direct. In the clay–clay model—where we do not find a multiplicity of capital goods in the technical embodiment sense; there is only the "latest" model—increasing the rate of accumulation of capital may carry with it a corresponding growth in labor productivity that, for the usually assumed wage rate adjustment, will only aggravate the unemployment problem. How does one increase the accumulation of capital rate while at the same time keeping a lid on the technology genie? Again, the possible way out of the bind would need to fall on a rather limited increase in the wage rate in the face of the high rate of increases in labor productivity.

Yet some relief would be found should we assume a putty–clay system where the unemployment condition would prompt the construction of new capital that embodies a lower rate of increase in labor productivity, that is, the production progress being more labor intensive. This would have the desired effect of curtailing wage cost increases, thereby decreasing the rate of "technologically released labor."

Once the system ultimately restores the full employment growth path, having adjusted the growth of the labor force, then the maintenance of conditions hinges on the proper rate of capital accumulation, which brings us back to the centrality of income distribution and the resulting savings ratio. In a comparison of growth paths with different savings ratios, the one with the large ratio, that is, the larger rate of accumulation, would correspond to a shorter economic life of capital, telling us of a greater rate of technical advance and faster obsolescence. And the state with a smaller savings ratio would be accommodated by slower obsolescence. The economy will find the steady state appropriate to its savings behavior.

In the steady state at full employment, output grows at the same pace as the accumulation of capital, which is to say at the rate of absorption of the growth labor force "containing" the growth of technical progress that, as we now realize, will itself affect the size of that growing labor supply. Thus with the economic life of capital (T) not changing, total employment will grow at the rate of growth of the labor force (n), and be equal to $n = g - \lambda$ (to restate Equation 8.8). Thus we have $g = n + \lambda$, which is the steady-state growth rate reflecting Harrod's natural rate of growth. So we return to the basic long-run property of a growing economy, and we do so from a real world—multiplicity of (vintage) capital goods—framework.

It will serve us well to step back and look again at what composes this real world. It is the presence of fixed input coefficient technology (no direct substitution of input factors here); a multiplicity of capital goods, each bearing a particular capital-to-output ratio and thereby existence of embodied technical progress with the ongoing presence of economic obsolescence; and a constant savings ratio linked to, one can say, the "micro underpinnings" of income distribution. All that need be said in a most direct and simple way is that the steady-state or long-term growth configuration of the economy is a situation in which output and employment are undergoing constant proportional rates of growth, and the society is saving and investing a constant proportion of its output. There is no dealing here with maintaining the constancy of a capital-to-output ratio, and the hard-to-believe ideas of alike capital and disembodiment of technical progress.

In our aim to clothe models of economic relationships in a frame of institutional-behavioral reality, we have, however, not taken cognizance of and sought to incorporate the presence of money into our discussions (models) of growth and distribution. Modern economics is obviously monetary economics, and it is not likely that money simply acts as a "veil" behind which the real activities of the economy regarding investment, employment, and output growth are taking place. I am not considering this money element as a determining variable; we have intuitively presumed that its existence or, more to the point, a change in its quantity will have no influence on real outcomes. It is as if money is simply there as a facilitator of transactions. In the following chapter we will come to think differently as we learn about the influence of this money element.

Notes

1. Paul Samuelson and William Nordhaus, *Economics*, 14th ed. (New York: McGraw Hill, 1992), p. 557.

2. See the Samuelson discussion of Denison's numbers.

3. Robert M. Solow, *Growth Theory: An Exposition* (New York: Oxford University Press, 1988), p. 35.

4. Ibid., p. 38.

5. Robert M. Solow, "Investment and Technical Progress," in *Mathematical Methods in the Social Sciences*, ed. K. Anow, S. Karlin, and P. Suppes (Stanford, CA: Stanford University Press, 1960), pp. 89–104.

6. Nicholas Kaldor, "A Mode of Economic Growth," in *Essays on Economic Stability and Growth* (Glencoe, IL: Free Press, 1960), p. 264.

7. This terminology was introduced by E.S. Phelps, "Substitution, Fixed Proportions, Growth and Distribution," *International Economic Review* (1963): 265–288. There is a good expository analysis (though somewhat mathematical) in Daniel Hamberg, *Models of Economic Growth*, chap. 5 (New York: Harper and Row, 1971).

8. Solow, *Growth Theory*, p. 47.

9. Ibid., p. 41.

10. Hamberg, *Models of Economic Growth*, p. 179.

9
Money and Economic Growth

Introductory Remarks: Money and Prices

One normally begins the study of money in the Principles course with an introduction to the functions of money, the other side of which is the rationale for holding money. Of course, the most obvious purpose served by money is as a facilitator of transactions; that is, it provides a commonly accepted medium of exchange through which trade takes place. This gives rise to what can be considered as "transactions money," which relates to the M_1 classification of money, consisting of currency plus demand deposits; the latter also are referred to as checking accounts or checkable deposits. And this is typically the means through which households acquire goods and services.

Economic units, that is, households and firms, will want to hold a proportion of their income in the form of cash balances (transactions money). Clearly, a household's behavior is generally not to spend all of its income at one time to purchase what it requires, and then at a later time when income is again received, to spend it all again, and so forth. It is usual to undertake expenditures in a rather smooth flow pattern per unit of time; one holds transactions money to bridge the gap between the receipt of income and the payments that have to be made—for example, to iron out the difference between a monthly paycheck and daily payments.

With slight changes in terminology, we would refer to savings as output minus transactions money, which is reflective of the flow of consumption expenditures as part of aggregate demand. And the equality of saving and investment tells us that the only asset that is held by economic units must be real capital or titles to real capital. The point is that every act of savings is a decision to add to wealth. Solow adds, "It is a decision to buy real capital, to invest, because there is no other asset to buy."[1] And there is no other asset because we do not reckon savings money as being put to any other use; the money supply is "demanded" to be used for the purposes of household transactions and for investment. But what if money were to be put to another purpose, that is, where income less the transactions money balance was not all used to acquiring real capital? We will analyze how this impacts the growth path; but now, let us look closely at the nature of this transactions money.

It is reasonable to assume that the higher the level of nominal income the greater the number of expenditures or frequency of transactions, and the greater the level of transactions balances. We can consider the demand for money balances to be a positive function of the frequency of transactions, which, to reiterate, is itself related to the level of income. So:

$$M_{TD} = k(Y) \tag{9.1}$$

This notion of frequency of expenditures is simply another way of considering the velocity of circulation (V) relating to a given level of income. We can restate 9.1 to read:

$$V \equiv \frac{1}{k} = \frac{Y}{M_{DT}} \equiv \frac{pQ}{M_{DT}} \tag{9.2}$$

We see that in an increase in the income-to-transactions balance (the money supply) ratio, the smaller must be $1/k$, telling us of a higher velocity of circulation or more frequent turnover of money for goods per unit of time. On the other hand, if k is high, then the ratio of income to the money supply is low; that is, $1/k$ is low, signifying a reduced velocity if circulation. Again, we make the point that the money supply, the "liquidity" in the system, is equal to what economic units want to hold in the transactions balance, which at a point in time is a function of realized incomes, but the velocity of which will determine the subsequent level of income. We can see this in Figure 9.1.

The M_D lines are drawn to show different existing velocities. The steeper the curve the greater the money demand at a given level of income and the lower the velocity, that is, a given money supply resulting in a lower level of income. The flatter the curve, the lower the money demand leading to greater frequency of transactions per unit of time, thus a given money supply resulting in a higher level of income.

This view of money in its role as an active circulation agent in relation to the velocity variable has been used to explain movements in the overall level of prices. The mechanism to do this has been the quantity theory of prices or, in its more familiar designation, the equation of exchange. The student may have encountered this initially in its truism form as

$$MV = pQ \tag{9.3}$$

where M is the supply of transactions money and V is its velocity of circula-

Figure 9.1

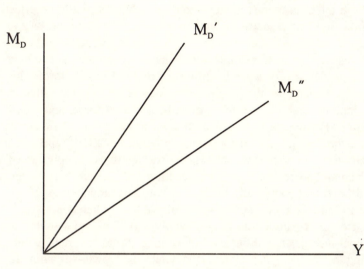

tion. Total spending in the economy is equal to the overall (average) price level (p) multiplied by the quantity of goods sold (Q). And this spending is equal to or financed by the money supply multiplied by its velocity of circulation. But to reformulate the truism into an expression that focuses on the determination of the price level, we would restate 9.3 as

$$p = \frac{V}{Q}(M) \tag{9.4}$$

There are two monetarist assumptions (or beliefs) regarding this price equation. One is that the velocity element is fairly stable and predictable over long periods of time, being the result of the stable pattern of households' receipt of income and habits in the flow pattern of the payment of their bills. It is not to be expected that an increase in the supply of "circulation money" will be offset by a reduction in its velocity; instead, this increase in M will be transmitted to the economy as an increase in total expenditures, that is, a higher $p \cdot Q$ or Y. This leads to the question as to what this higher Y is "composed" of. Is it greatly the result of an increase in the quantity of goods produced at overall stable prices, or is it mainly the result of higher prices with little if any (in the extreme) increase in real production? Is it that the effect of an increase in the money supply is on the price level, with negligible effects on employment and output? This brings us to a related assumption, that an increase in total expenditures engineered via an increase in the transactions money supply will have virtually no effect on real production (the reader may want to translate this as an increase in the aggregate-demand (AD) curve from the Principles text's AD–AS [aggregate supply] restatement of the simple Keynesian income model). The quantity of goods produced (Q) depends on those structural or real forces that we spoke of in maintaining the long-run steady-state growth path—that is, the rate of capital accumulation, the growth of the labor force, and growth of technological change with its effect on labor productivity. These forces, of course, determine the level and growth of productive capacity and output. In the steady-state experience we can visualize the aggregate-supply curve (AS) moving continually to the right in conjunction with an increase in aggregate demand (AD) that continually justifies or warrants the increase in capacity and the full utilization of a growing, effective labor force.

The growth of transactions money supply will be in line with the growth in nominal income as will the level of savings; prices will remain constant reflecting the "proper" markup level that yields the growth-sustaining rate of profit and hence the savings rate and investment. Thus in the long term, by which we mean a state of equilibrium growth at the natural rate, it would appear that money is "neutral" in that it serves as a "veil" behind which real forces are propelling the economy. The money supply is derived from real income growth for the existing distribution of income-and-savings ratio. But we have to keep in mind that in this context we are considering money in its transaction balances role; that portion of income that does not fall into this category has as its only outlet the act of investment, that is, the ownership of real capital.

Certainly if the presence of money balances is to affect the real growth of the economy, it has got to do so via its influence on the rate of capital accumulation. Its existence would somehow have to separate the savings decision from the act of capital accumulation. In this sense, money balances would be active in influencing real income and not neutral or passive.

Money as a Stabilizing Agent

Yet the controversy surrounding the role of active cash balances, regarding its impact on real output and employment, really comes to light when the economy is outside the state of full employment. We revert to the static Keynesian mode using the familiar AD–AS diagram to illustrate the different approaches to money as a short-term stabilizing agent. This will give us a base from which to place money in the growth context and also show how the standard reasoning reflects the difference from our analysis of pricing

Figure 9.2

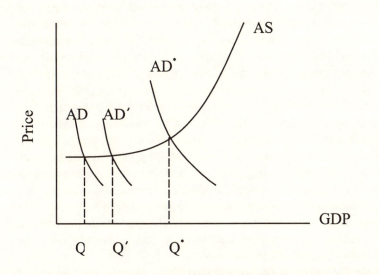

and the technique of production. Figure 9.2 demonstrates the mainstream Keynesian approach to stabilization policy; we assume a condition of under full employment at Q. The policy prescription is to increase the money supply so as to enlarge the level of transactions (expenditures)—there is no offset by a reduction in velocity—thereby placing pressure on inventory levels and motivating higher production and employment. We portray the lower portion of the AS curve as relatively flat (not perfectly elastic as others are wont to do), but the essential observation is that the shift of the AD curve to Q' spills out overwhelmingly in terms of increasing real output with negligible impact on prices.

This mainstream result calls for an explanation on two fronts: One question is, where is this money increase coming from (we are not dropping currency from a helicopter) and what is its link to expenditures? Second, what is the rational for the observation that prices are not moving proportionately (in the extreme, not moving at all) with the money supply? Regarding the first matter: The reader may recall the money and banking discussion in Principles of Economics where it was shown that the Federal Reserve System (the Fed) affects what can be termed "reserve or high-powered money" via open-market operations, which has the dual effect of increasing the banking system's capability to extend loans and lowering the federal-fund rate, resulting in lower interest rates. The assumption is that this reduced cost of borrowing will absorb this increased capability into a higher demand for transactions money widely over the economy; the money supply increases as mirrored overall by the higher dollar amount of checkable deposits, that is, checkbook money. The point we want to make is that the Fed's action does not per se increase the money supply, which must await the "demand to borrow" response (the approach here is that the open-market procedure is a bank-to-bank operation); an analysis of this occurs later in this chapter.

As we can see in Figure 9.2 the presumption is of a sufficiently high-interest elasticity of demand by firms and consumers to crank the real economy forward. Mainstream economics has generally carried on its analysis within the competitive framework, which, in its reasoning, offers an explanation for the lack of a price response here. On the input-cost side of production there is the assumption of an almost infinite supply of resources (essentially labor) at the existing market-determined wage rate; the image being that the monetary policy is reviving the economy from a condition of recession that had led to a rather severe increase in the unemployment rate. There is no impending shortage of labor in the overall sense nor of particular skills; the notion is that labor-market forces will not bring about higher wage rates in the face of an increase in demand.

On the technical production side, firms must be encountering declining marginal costs or increasing returns to labor, which is not the usual assumption of mainstream reasoning when the upward-sloping supply curve is constructed on the basis of increasing marginal costs resulting from diminishing returns, that is, depicted as showing up almost immediately after the onset of production. Thus even if the money wage rate is not increasing, costs per unit of production would be, with their attendant price increases. The reasoning behind the presumed flat portion of the AS curve as depicted in Principles courses is, to an extent, inconsistent.

But from our non-neoclassical vision the rather stable price response is readily explainable. As the reader will recall, the production process with its flat marginal cost curve and declining average costs over a wide range of production levels up to full-capacity operations negates any pressure from the production side to increase prices. On the wage-cost side, it is reasonable we assume that the restoration of higher levels of employment would take precedence over higher money wage rates in the negotiation stance of labor organizations, at least in the early stages of economic recovery supposedly engendered by the increasing money supply.

Thus from the mainstream Keynesian perspective money does matter with regard to its impact on real income and employment, operating through the institutionally administered interest rate changes. This policy would then carry the economy to the full employment (Q^*) position, whereupon subsequent increases in aggregate demand would mainly result in higher prices.

And the rationale for higher price levels can take on different emphases.

In the usually explanation the "culprit" is the growing shortage of resources, causing their prices to rise which, in conjunction with declining productivity as their employment increases, will mandate higher selling prices for finished goods to maintain profit levels and the incentive for increasing output. An extreme view here is that there is literally little or no ability to increase real production due to the physical using up of the given resource base. The higher level of demand must then spill out in the form of higher prices as the market's answer to the unavailability of additional supply caused by the exhaustion of resources.

But we would rather offer up a different perspective. From the megacorp-organization view these increases in demand will at some point require a decision as to whether or not to increase productive capacity and simultaneously a decision as to how to finance this increase in the "capital budget," assuming a positive decision on capacity. Quite possibly the finance answer could be to greatly, if not totally, raise the required capital through internally generated funds by establishing a higher margin over costs so as to increase the average cash flow. But this higher markup or set-price is not without its possible longer-term negative consequences. The reader would perhaps need to remember our pricing analysis in chapter 3, though we would reiterate some points here. An important longest view consideration of a higher markup is an erosion of market share normally achieved as a result of much effect, and the extent of this loss would depend on the particular firm's "monopoly power." A further consideration is the loss of market share industrywide as a result of market penetration by foreign megacorp "competitors" willing to accept lower profit levels to gain access to new markets. In general, what happens to prices as demand growth utilizes greater degrees of capacity depends on the state of excess capacity as the organization overviews what, in current times, is its worldwide production operations. And even if it decides to build additional capacity, it may decide not to change its markup price, but instead to raise the finance "externally" by issuing new securities and/or undertaking bank borrowing. Certainly these decisions would need to be made well before the organization finds itself producing at the limit of what we referred to as its engineered rated capacity.

A distinction should be made between a higher set-price and profit margin, being driven by the need to raise finance capital, and a higher price caused by the increase in unit labor costs, as a response to maintain the existing markup. In the latter situation we have the organization's decision to counter labor's negotiating stance to press for an increase in money wages relative to the growth in output per worker that, at the existing price, is propelling the growth in profits. And with the unemployment rate falling, labor may certainly decide to press for a greater share of the national output. These institutional workings could act to bring about a higher aggregate price index before the economy approaches the textbook notion of "running out of resources" condition, or they could act to keep overall prices constant even late into a cyclical expansion.

There is simply no automatic correspondence between increases in demand and aggregate price levels. The thought process behind the configuration of the AD and AS curves in Figure 9.2 is the orthodoxy of the market-determined price level carried over to the aggregate scene, with the usual technical reasoning underlying the aggregate supply curve. But we are now fully appreciative that the construction of these curves is, overall, not reflective of the workings of the world about us. Whether we are thinking of prices of inputs (basically labor) or of finished consumer goods, these prices are not the result of the anonymity of market forces (as much as one likes to use the term market); they are the outcome of deliberate decisions taken by powerful private economic enterprises (business as an organization rather than an individual, labor as a negotiating collective body rather than an individual decision maker) with particular goals to be achieved (not necessarily the conventional maximization outcome of profits or employment) that may keep the price in place in the face of changes in demand.

So what can we say to the question, Does money matter? We would need to answer that an increase in transactions money does matter with regard to the effect on real output (save for a very nontypical economic circumstance). Its impact on prices must, however, be seen as uncertain. But a question arises concerning the condition that we mentioned previously where the economy has run out of resources, that is, has reached the physical limit to real GDP, and it is still experiencing increasing levels of demand. Would not the demand shift totally come out in the form of higher prices? After all, we are talking about the influence of money changes in the short term, which is a duration over the business cycle where the resource base is presumed constant and there are no increases in technological innovations. Yet the reality of economic life is that in an expansion phase of the business cycle we are not likely to encounter the physical limits to production before the downturn ensues, and all the more so in a world of globally situated operating plants.

What monetarists (that non-Keynesian view) would argue is that in the vicinity of full employment—where the economy is situated more often than not—conditions would quickly arise that cancel the higher profit levels arising from increasing prices, thereby eliminating the profit incentive for increasing production. Firms are seen not to respond to increases in aggregate demand (financed by a higher level of circulation money) because of a lack of profitability of increasing output and employment, and not because of an inability to do so due to a running out of production capability. For monetarists, money supply increases are viewed as the prime determinant of nominal GDP, with negligible effect on real output growth.

This is illustrated in Figure 9.3 where we redraw Figure 9.2, portraying the AS curve in its extreme Keynesian and monetarist positions. Thus the perfectly elastic segment illustrating the textbook "depression range" condition, and the vertical segment illustrating the extreme monetarist perspective that changes in the money supply affect prices only. Considering the reasoning underlying the monetarist conclusion we find (in one version) that it relies on the traditional market construction regarding the behavior of labor and the determination of the wage rate, as well as the determination of prices generally.

We piece together this monetarist story in Figure 9.4 where panels a and b show the labor market behavior and effect on real output respectively. The reader will recall panel a as the conventional labor market drawn from our chapter on distribution but shown here with more elaborate notation with the term $f(N)$ indicating the amount of labor demanded at different money wage rates, given the final good selling price (p), and with the $g(N)$ notation indicating the amount of labor forthcoming. Again, this is the conventional approach to the labor market that we elaborated upon in chapter 7. As we see, the market is drawn with the money wage (W) on the vertical, so that a change in the price level acts as the shift variable for the demand and supply curves indicating the response of the market to a change in the real wage (w) for an existing money wage.

Presume a money supply expansion resulting in a higher level of aggregate demand that, in the traditional link, results in an increasing general price level from (p) to (p'). This will increase the demand for labor at the existing money wage (W) in response to the increasing profitability of production, thereby shifting the labor demand curve from $[p \cdot f(N)]$ to $[p' \cdot f(N)]'$. The result will, at least conceptually, be a very temporary or fleeting opening to higher levels of employment and lower real wage even at a higher money wage (W_0). We say this because of the orthodox stance that the labor market will adjust quickly to avoid a deterioration in the real wage—that sufficient money wage flexibility is forthcoming.

There are different ways to manifest this flexibility. One stems from the conventional reasoning behind the supply curve itself; that is, the work–leisure trade-off as a function of change in the real wage. On this basis labor would withdraw from the market in proportion to the decline in the real wage; that is, to the degree of the shift of the demand curve. We observe this in Figure 9.4 as the supply curve shift to $[p' \cdot g(n)]'$. This creates a labor shortage that, in the usual thinking, will cause the wage rate to rise to the point of eliminating the shortage, that is, to restore the real wage rate. The opening to higher levels of employment may be seen to close immediately as

Figure 9.3

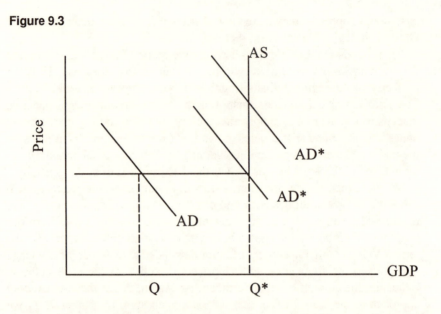

the money wage jumps from (*W*) to (*W′*); or would close soon after to eliminate the higher levels of employment and production that did occur, as the profitability of maintaining such levels erodes in the face of the upward movement in the money wage from (W_0) to (*W′*).

When the economy adjusts to the demand shift, both prices and money wages will be higher, with the real wage remaining unchanged, and thereby also the level of employment and real production. As we see in panel b, nominal GDP has increased by the overall increase in prices from *p* to *p′*. The essence of monetarism, then, is that money can affect prices and real output over the short period after a change in its supply, but over a longer period such a change "mainly" affects the price level or, as in our analysis, will "only" affect prices.

Certainly the logic of this monetarist approach is here, but the reality of the mechanism driving the result is missing. And in this regard the reader may want to review our critique of the labor market construction in chapter 7. We can then take a different tack to the same result by suggesting that organized labor will have as a priority the protection of the real wage over any gain in employment, and all the more so as the economy is operating close to full employment. We substitute the reality of the union institution for the supply-curve shift to support the monetarist conclusion.

And we can bring up an additional (modern) approach to this wage flexibility by relating an expectations element to the supply-curve behavior, though still maintaining its conventional construction. We draw the supply

Figure 9.4

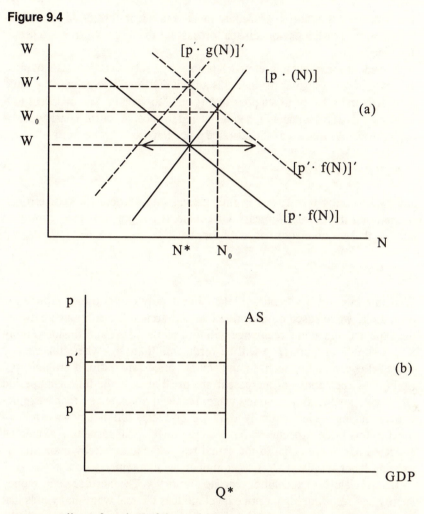

curve as a direct function of the real wage on the vertical; and the real wage is determined by the money wage "negotiation" as related to expectations regarding prices and the actual price level itself.

We suppose that prices expectations are formed adaptively; for example, the expected price level in time t, that is, p^e_t will be equal to that which existed in the period before, that is, p_{t-1}. But should the price level in t exceed expectations, that is:

$$p_t > p^e_t = p_{t-1} \tag{9.5}$$

then price expectations in $t + 1$ will be equal to the "mistaken" higher price in t. Thus in this adaptive procedure there is no error-correction element in the forecast as one does not adjust a forecast for the forecast error of a previous time period.

One could argue that this approach is not very likely, since in a state of price increases in some regular manner, this adaptive way will perpetuate the same error. It is more likely to suppose that if one "fooled" or was mistaken in a regular way, expectations will then be altered to account for the consistency of one's mistake. A more realistic adaptive procedure can take the form

$$p^e_t = p_{t-1} + \theta \ (p_{t-1} - p_{t-2}) \tag{9.6}$$

and by assuming $\theta = 1$, one is fully taking into account the past error in formulating the current forecast. Of course, if the previous prediction was correct, there is no error to account for and

$$p^e_t = p_{t-1} \tag{9.7}$$

With this in mind we "rephrase" the labor-supply curve to read labor's expected real wage based on the price forecast, so that the difference between the expected and actual real wage will turn on the forecast. Consider Figure 9.5. A supply of labor (N_0) will be forthcoming at (W_0) where this money wage reflects an adjustment to an accurate price forecast of a previous period (p^e). Expectations of increase in the price level in the following period $(p_e{}')$ will, for the given money wage, result in an expected real wage decline, reducing the labor supply to (N'). However, a full money wage adjustment to this price expectation (an increase to W') will serve to maintain an expected real wage equal to the actual real wage and thereby maintain the existing labor supply at (N_0), assuming an accurate price forecast.

Let us relate this expectations idea to Figure 9.4. The increase in the money supply and resulting higher price level reduces the real wage and yields that opening to greater production levels and employment. But this will prompt a price forecast equal to the higher (unexpected) existing price level, resulting in a corresponding demand for a higher money wage and a restoration of the real wage level.

The full inward shift of the labor-supply curve is not seen here as a reflection of a sort of withdrawal of labor that creates the necessary labor shortage, but a manifestation of the recognition that the higher price level does reduce one's real wages (labor does not suffer from a money illusion where one's well-being is thought to be related to money income per se) and labor has the power to carry through the necessary money wage increase as determined by expected price changes.

Figure 9.5

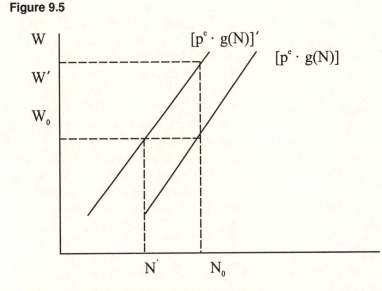

The monetarist's basic claim that increasing the money supply as a stability device to maintain full employment will produce little if any effect, can, as we see, be rationalized in different ways. But what it comes down to is a dichotomy or separability in the understanding of the economy. Employment levels are determined via the adjustment of the labor market to changes in demand; once this is determined, with given technology one then "reads" real output from the traditional production function. Changes in demand are one thing, causing changes in nominal GDP based on the approach that changes in demand will have minimal effects on employment; real changes in production are another, requiring real motivating forces, such as growth in the capital stock and technological change that enhance the productivity of labor. As we know, these are elements driving the economy along the long-term growth path, so we want to focus on the role of money as it impacts these real variables. If we accept that money does not matter in the short term with regard to real income, does it matter within the context of the longer-term steady-growth path?

Before heading out in this direction, we add some additional commentary about money's short-term role, or lack of it, by considering again the other approach. We recall Figure 9.2, which reflects the Keynesian mainstream attitude that changes in the money supply have an important real effect not only in that particular "depression state," but in a general way in that it, together with fiscal policy, can bring about recovery from conditions of recession. They argue that monetarists overplay the idea of wage–price flexibility in the economy; their point being that institutional arrangements, clearly evident on the labor side, convey much wage "stickiness." The supply curve does not fully adjust to price increases, so that a reduction in the real wage and higher levels of profitability of production can be sustained for a period of time as the rate of unemployment declines.

Mainstreamers usually point to the fact that money wages are in many circumstances locked in by long-period contractual arrangements, while final goods prices are free to be demand determined. To which we might add that the money wage adjustment lag, or its "inflexibility," could also be attributable to wrongly formulated price expectations. Or to a weak condition of worker bargaining that prevents the attainment of a contract whereby wage negotiations can be reopened in the event of a certain increase in prices, or a contract that contains an escalator clause whereby wages are automatically adjusted to price changes.

All in all, the end result of this approach is depicted in Figure 9.6 to show the contrast with Figure 9.4.

Yet the entire debate concerning the efficacy of monetary policy as a short-term prescription is carried on within a framework of an orthodox supply-and-demand diagram whether in the analysis of the price of labor or the price of goods. Keynesians usually present their argument with mixed signals; they stress wage inflexibility, normally citing contractual obligations, hence implying an institutional determination of wages, while speaking of competitive market-force determining prices.

The reader is by now well aware that we have taken the position that the conventionally structured supply and demand curves be (finally) put aside as they generally do not explain the price results we see in the operations of the real economic world. This brings us to a look at this money-supply debate with the use of our restructured labor supply and demand curves as presented in the income distribution chapter. We repeat that representation here but drawn with the money wage on the vertical in Figure 9.7, to make it easily comparable to Figures 9.5 and 9.6, assuming a price increase from p to p', lowering the real wage, and increasing the demand for labor at the (W) money wage. Labor's response in this condition of declining real income is an increase in the number of hours worked and/or an increase in the numbers of "hands" working; this is evidenced in Figure 9.7 by the rightward shift of the labor-supply curve associated with price level p'. The "opening" to higher levels of real output and production is maintained due to the greater level of employment at the existing money wage rate.

The Keynesians are right with regard to the real GDP impact of increasing the money supply, but generally on wrong reasoning. It is not so much a result of wrong price expectations or a money illusion; there is no illusion

Figure 9.6

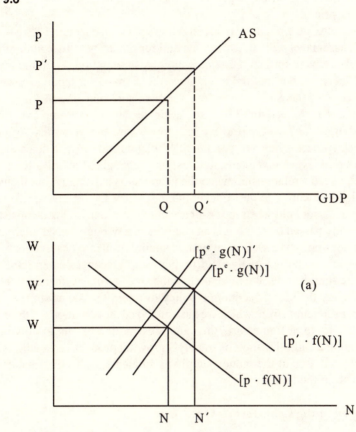

(a)

Figure 9.7

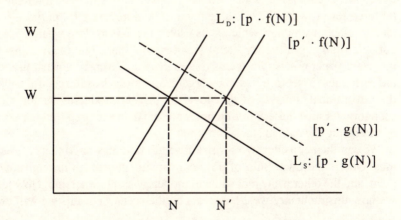

but there is an awareness that more income has to be acquired in the face of higher prices.

To reiterate a point we made in our distribution chapter: The real wage at W is associated with an excess demand for goods, with its counterpart in an excess demand for labor. The conventional assumption is that money wages will increase, but that only heightens the demand for labor, worsening the shortage. If there is to be a "market cleaning" outcome in the realism of Figure 9.7, the economy will see a greater amount of employment at the existing money wage. And we are now aware that, contrary to the usual thought process, there is no "automatic" relationship between demand changes and price-level movements. Interestingly enough, Principles texts usually accept such a relationship when the economy is expanding, but then call the student's attention to the "ratchet effect," where the demand–price relationship does not hold when recessionary conditions exist. This inconsistency is normally passed over, but it is an example of a wrongly based micro analysis that does not serve well in an understanding of macro observations.

Here we end our analysis of money-supply changes as an issue in economic stabilization. We reiterate that the short-term designation to all this is to convey the idea of economic policy to return the society to full employment production, from which we have analyzed the conditions of the economy in its long-term framework, this latter designation having to do with maintaining the full utilization of society's growing productive capability. So we now want look at the money supply as an element affecting real economic growth in the long term.

Money in the Long Term—One View

In this context the presence of a money balance will be seen to affect the rate of capital accumulation, which we have spoken about much as a fundamental force for growth. There is a demand to hold money for a purpose other than transactions money, which is its use as a means to store wealth. We are not here thinking of money literally as cash holdings, but as investment in monetary paper assets. Yet this is not an investment in the normal usage of the term; these assets are issued by organizations (such as the central bank or the government) outside of or above the private producing sector of the economy. As such these assets do not represent debt acquired for the purpose of increasing the capital stock.

We can then consider two forms of wealth holdings or "outlets" for savings. One is the ownership of physical capital (indirectly) through investment, and the other is the real value of monetary asset ownership. Now let us see how this monetary wealth appears on the scene.[2] For this we will bring that outside organization, that is, the government, into an understanding of the steady-growth path and see how its actions via the creation of these monetary assets (bonds) affect the rate of capital accumulation.

The government purchases goods and services that are used for public consumption, and that do not affect the private spending decisions by households; it also levies taxes and makes transfer payments. When expenditures (which includes transfers) exceed tax revenues, the government covers the deficit by issuing bonds, that is, by assuming the appropriate amount of debt. When revenues exceed expenditures, it uses the difference to retire some proportion of its debt. We can consider the offering of these bonds, which, of course, carry a face value, as tantamount to the printing of money that is injected into the system by means of these bond assets. Indeed, the holding of these bonds is in essence the holding of cash balances (M).

Suppose we have government expenditures as a fraction (h) of nominal net national product (pY). The existence of a budget deficit is revealed as $hpY - Taxes$; and this difference is equal to the issuance of a corresponding dollar value of bonds, which then changes the size of outstanding debt. In other words, the financing of the deficit changes the level of monetary assets (cash balances) held "inside" the system at any point. Households (as a unit inside the system) are assumed to save a certain proportion of their disposable income, but in this context, what constitutes disposable income?

If we presume a constant price level, we would define disposable income as equal to national income (including transfers) minus taxes plus the real value of one's monetary assets, that is, M/p. And any change in real value would result from a change in the dollar amount of money balances held. But it is sensible to presume that in a growth context where we are looking at the economy over long periods of time (encompassing many business cycles), the price level will show a trend movement. Notwithstanding the existence of virtually stable prices over the current (historically the longest duration) cyclical expansion, the U.S. experience, say, over the last fifty years, has been one of steady price increases.

What this reality of price-level changes is telling us is that the evaluation of disposable income (for whatever level of national income and taxation) would have to account for changes in the real value of cash balances that now emanate from two sources. There is the change in the dollar value of assets held, coupled with the change in the price level; both determine the change of real holdings of monetary assets, that is, of government debt. For a bond with a face value in real terms of $500, a decline in prices of 3 percent conveys a capital gain to the bond holder of $15. The real face value has increased by $15, and it is reasonable to suppose that the bond holder will reckon this gain as an increase in disposable income. Conversely, an increase in the price level of 3 percent conveys a reduction in the real value of this asset, and it will be realized as a reduction in disposable income. What we are describing is a price-driven change in the real value of existing monetary holdings, where this change is shown as $\Delta(M/p)$. Then:

$$\Delta(\frac{M}{p}) = -\frac{M}{p} \cdot \frac{\Delta p}{p} = -\frac{M}{p^2}(\Delta p) \tag{9.8}$$

We refer to this change as the rate of return on the existing holdings of real monetary assets.[3] But the overall change in real holdings, to reiterate, results from the real value of an increase in the nominal amount of assets held minus the rate of return on the existing level of holdings, which mirrors the rate of change in the price level. Thus the absolute change in real balances is

$$\frac{\Delta M}{p} - (\frac{M}{p} \cdot \frac{\Delta p}{p}) \tag{9.9}$$

which can be stated as

$$\frac{M}{p}(\frac{\Delta M}{M} - \frac{\Delta p}{p}) \tag{9.10}$$

We then have a determination of disposable income; it is equal to net national product minus taxes plus the change in the real value of monetary asset holdings (i.e., money balances). From what we previously said of the government deficit, we have

$$T(\text{taxes}) = hpY - \Delta M \tag{9.11}$$

So disposable income is

$$Y_D = pY - hpY + \Delta M + M(\frac{\Delta p}{p}) \tag{9.12}$$

Real disposable income becomes

$$Y(1-h) + \frac{\Delta M}{p} - \frac{M}{p} \cdot \frac{\Delta p}{p}$$

or

$$Y(1-h) + \frac{M}{p}(\frac{\Delta M}{M} - \frac{\Delta p}{p}) \tag{9.13}$$

Private economic units are assumed to save a proportion out of this real disposable income, which brings up some important relationships. Prices play a role in determining disposable income through its impact on the rate of return on money balances and, in this connection, its effects on savings, and will also influence the disposition of savings as between those outlets of capital accumulation (investment) and of acquiring additional government debt. This disposition is spoken of as the "portfolio balance" in the composition of the wealth held by the public. And the decision concerning this balance will be important in understanding additional properties of the steady growth path.

But now let us overview the character of this "monetized economy." There is a government ("outside") sector explicitly being made a part of output growth, in that the growth of output along the natural growth path is taken up by real consumption on the part of government and by private ("inside") units, with the remainder going to real capital growth. The government collects taxes that, even if we were to presume are its only source of revenue, create, a difference between national income and disposable income. Thus even if this outside entity consumed always within the context of a balanced budget, so that it does not issue any debt and thereby creates no money asset holdings (all money is inside money created as transaction money), the level of savings would obviously be smaller than that suggested by an aggregate savings propensity related to national income, or by different propensities as related to the given distribution of the national income. And it would be smaller by an amount equal to the ratio of disposable income to net national income, which reflects the proportion of national income consumed by government [$(1 - h)Y$] and thereby taxes levied.[4] Thus a way to increase the rate of real capital formation is to reduce government consumption and thereby increase disposable income and real investment; keeping in mind that in this nonmoney wealth vision the only outlet for savings is real capital ownership.

But in the long view of government operations, deficits are normally being incurred, which means the issuing of government debt and the existence of money balances, the value of which, as we know, is incorporated into disposable income. It bears repeating the ingredients of this valuation; there is the effect of a change in asset holdings at existing prices, that is, from (9.10):

$$[\frac{M}{p} \cdot \frac{\Delta M}{M}] \tag{9.14}$$

minus the decrease in the real value of existing holdings as a result of a price increase or, more to the point of an expected price increase, again from (9.13):

$$[\frac{\Delta p}{p} \cdot \frac{M}{p}] \tag{9.15}$$

And depending on this absolute change in value, disposable income will rise or fall with corresponding changes in savings. So the connection to keep in mind, as Solow reminds us, is that "the existence of public debt makes a difference to private savings only if its real value is actually changing, that is, if the nominal debt is changing at a rate different from the rate at which the price level is changing."[5] This real value change may generate an increase in savings, the whole of which may go to a further accumulation of money assets at the "cost" of displacing an equivalent amount of real investment. And this may break down the full employment steady-growth path, as the stock of real capital grows at a rate less than that of the labor force, reckoned in efficiency units.

We seem to have exposed other "internal balances" required to maintain the natural growth rate within the reality of an economy with monetary assets, that is, where there exists an asset demand for money. And the existence of these money balances must not alter the level of disposable income so that savings is not affected; furthermore the portfolio balance (i.e., the disposition of this savings) between investment in physical capital and in real money balances is not changed. In other words, given these two forms of wealth, its form in terms of the growth of real capital must be equal to that of the supply of labor in efficiency units. The very existence of a proper growth of real capital to maintain full employment and yield the constant output-to-capital ratio (thinking here of the simpler growth story of uniformity of capital) is a rather complicated affair in the reality of a money asset framework. It is more than simply locating a necessary distribution of income and corresponding savings ratios.

Let us bring together some points that may have been scattered about. The growth in the nominal stock of "outside" money, or what we recognize as public debt, is the result of a government policy decision, and we assume that this is translated by the "inside" private economic units as an anticipated increase in the rate of inflation, and we will also suppose that anticipations turn out correctly. This increase in the price level is calculated to lower the real yield on money asset holdings, that is, cause an absolute decline in real holdings of government debt. By real yield we mean a decline in the excess of the nominal rate of interest over the inflation rate. As this decline is the negative of the rate of price change, and the paper asset is not currency but an interest-bearing (i) short-term bond, then the yield on money balances is

$i - \pi$

$$\pi = \frac{\Delta p}{p} \tag{9.16}$$

In this circumstance wealth holders can be expected to alter their asset portfolio balance in favor of real investment. The proportion of wealth held in either form depends on the difference between what could have been earned from holding (having title to) a unit of real capital and what will be earned from holding a unit of money assets.

The yield on real capital we term the rate of profit (r), so the opportunity cost of holding a nominal unit of money (seen as a capital loss) is

$$r-(i-\pi)=r-i+\pi \qquad (9.17)$$

We are left with the possibility that a change in the price level will alter investment in favor of increasing the rate of accumulation and hence determine the rate of output growth. It is as if the "effective" savings ratio has been increased by a price-driven diversion of a portion of current savings (wealth) into real asset investment.

Yet there is an additional proviso if the higher price level is to take the form of an "as if" higher savings ratio. The rate of inflation stemming from the existence of a higher public debt must not make a difference to private savings, that is, total private assets. For this to happen, the nominal debt holdings must be changing (increasing) at the same rate as the price-level increase. If the inflation rate were greater, this would result in a negative change in real money holdings, which is reckoned as a decline in disposable income, and thereby lower the savings base out of which the portfolio adjustment is occurring. Quite possibly the price effect would enhance the opportunity cost of holding money assets, resulting in an increased rate of capital accumulation. The rate of price increase, as we know, cannot be set out as straightforwardly related to the increase in the money supply and higher levels of spending. The growth in the nominal supply of money (that is, government debt) is a policy decision, but the growth rate of the price level is an economic result that cannot be ordered.

Yet if the relationships are correct, than we can say (within the confines of the long run) that money matters in adjusting growth rates by altering the savings level and real capital growth and output. As an example, consider the circumstance where the natural growth rate exceeds the warranted rate. Then an increasing price level can increase the warranted rate (increase rate of output) by increasing the effective savings ratio. The scenario for this plausible adjustment follows the mechanism we have been describing.

To make it all apparent,[6] we can presume no change in the nominal stock of real money balance so as to see the effect of price changes only. The increasing price level conveys a capital loss to the money asset holder, prompting a portfolio adjustment resulting in a greater proportion of savings being invested in real capital. This will lead to higher capital-to-labor and capital-to-output ratios conducive to growth at the natural rate. Yet this is not an unambiguous result, should we add an obvious complication that we talked about concerning the capital loss inclusion in the disposable income measure. Furthermore, the higher price level reduces the real rate of profit, thereby reducing the opportunity cost of holding money assets and limiting the move to capital asset investment.

Overall, we come back to our previous point that price changes may be effective in changing the portion of current savings going into real cash balances and thereby affecting the rate of capital accumulation. It is through these "mechanics" that we conclude that money should not be considered as neutral; that in the long term, changes in the quantity of money can be expected to have an effect on real income. And as changes in the money supply rest on deliberate government policy, we have a long-term result that reinforces the short-term Keynesian view of changes in the money supply as an economic stabilizing agent.

But let us now bring together the monetary properties of an economy in the full employment steady-state mode, now that changes in the money supply is a realistic characteristic of such a path. In doing so, we are able to bring government expenditures into the picture as a consumer of real output through its presence as a creator of private wealth (i.e., outside money), with the remainder of output being taken up by real private consumption and real capital formation. The reader will recognize the static (Principles of Economics) aggregate equilibrium condition:

$$Y = C + I + G \tag{9.18}$$

which we place into a growth framework. Thus:

$$C = (1-s)Y_D \tag{9.19}$$

$$I = \Delta K \tag{9.20}$$

$$G = h(Y) \tag{9.21}$$

At every point along the full employment growth path we have

$$Y = (1-s)[Y(1-h) + \frac{M}{p}(\frac{\Delta M}{M} - \frac{\Delta p}{p})] + h(Y) + \Delta K \tag{9.22}$$

With some manipulation this works out to[7]

$$\Delta K = (1-h)\,sY - (1-s)[\frac{M}{p} \cdot \frac{\Delta M}{M} - \frac{M}{p} \cdot \frac{\Delta p}{p}] \tag{9.23}$$

And the rate of accumulation is

$$\frac{\Delta K}{K} = \frac{(1-h)sY}{K} - \frac{(1-s)[\frac{\Delta M}{M} - \frac{\Delta p}{p}]\frac{m}{p}}{K} \qquad (9.24)$$

which comes out to

$$\frac{\Delta K}{K} = (1-h)\frac{s}{v} - (1-s)[\frac{\Delta M}{M} - \frac{\Delta p}{p}]\frac{m}{v} \qquad (9.25)$$

where:

$$v = \frac{K}{Y}$$

$$m = \frac{M}{pY}$$

= ratio of money assets to net national product

In Equation 9.25 we have the generalized Harrod–Domar growth model, now with government expenditures as a proportion (h) of net product, which yields a ratio of asset money–to–net national product.

Were we to assume the straightforward H-D exposition, then $h = 0$ and $m = 0$, and we are back to the basic formulation

$$G = \frac{\Delta K}{K} = s/v \qquad (9.26)$$

And 9.26 is a simple version of a nonmonetary growth economy, of which it bears repeating that we mean that money is not a wealth-holding instrument so that it plays no role in the rate of capital accumulation; indeed, the only wealth that savings creates is the ownership of real capital.

We now overview some points. Assuming that government operations were carried on under balanced budget conditions, then there is no government debt and no stock of money asset wealth. The additions to the real capital stock would be smaller than that presumed by the aggregate savings propensity, as savings comes out of disposable income, which is now below the net national product by the budget-balancing tax levy. Thus the presence of government, even under this seemingly benign budget condition, may do damage to the private sector's ability to accumulate capital at the required rate necessary for full employment growth. This consideration is shown by the first term on the right side of Equation 9.25.

But over the long term it can be expected that the government budget will more often than not be in deficit; this creates government debt that is, so to speak, "transferred" to the private (inside) units of the economy, thereby creating money wealth holdings. Again, we have to keep in mind that money is here created by government budget deficits, so that every unit increase in money is a corresponding increase in private wealth. And this increase in wealth (i.e., holding of government debt) translates to an increase in disposable income that governs the savings of households. Thus we need to see the growth path as characterized by private units being in possession of money-asset wealth, and reckoning a change in the real holdings of this wealth as altering disposable income and subsequent savings levels. Will an increase in savings—reckoned in this way—turn up as an increase in real capital formation, or will it displace this formation in favor of additional holding of government debt? And this question is mirrored in the second term on the right side of Equation 9.25.

Given the rate of growth of the labor force and that of technological change, the amount of savings available for real investment should make capital grow at the natural rate, which, as we recall, will yield the constant capital-to-output ratio. We have here the image of a less sophisticated growth path consisting of the growth of alike capital. The level of this required savings depends on the level of disposable income (given the savings propensity), which is influenced by government expenditures that, when taken with taxes, determine the level of government debt and thereby the change in nominal asset money holdings; it will also be influenced by the capital gain or loss stemming from the change in the value of one's asset holdings, meaning the consideration of a change in nominal holdings minus the change in the price level.

Characteristic of the steady state, we will find a growing level of government expenditures as well as government debt, with both growing at the same rate as national output. But the growth in the level of disposable income now abetted by the increase in nominal money assets is, so to speak, negated by a constant rate of inflation (imparting a capital loss), so that there is no change in the value of total money balances. In this way the existence of government debt will have no impact on private savings. A related condition is that the actual rate of inflation is equal to the expected rate, which is equal to the growth in nominal debt.

A corollary to this is that along the path the proportion (in value terms) of the two forms of wealth (real money balances and physical capital) holdings is constant, telling us that the differences between the return on real capital and the rate of return on government debt (the real yield) is given. The notion is that a portfolio balance holds the stock of money balances as a particular proportion of income, and in doing so will "release" the requisite proportion of wealth for capital accumulation to maintain the natural growth rate. We can represent these related properties of the "steady state with money" path with the following equations.

$$m = m[v, r - (i + \frac{\Delta p}{p})]$$

(9.27)

$$G = (1-h)\frac{s}{v} - (1-s)[\frac{\Delta M}{M} - \frac{\Delta p}{p}]\frac{m}{v}$$

(9.28)

Equation 9.27 is a statement concerning the demand to hold money-asset balances as a proportion nominal net product. There are two influences at work here. One is the shift variable of this demand curve, which is taken as the change in the capital-to-output ratio (v). Given asset yields, the demand to hold money assets is positively related to the degree of "mechanization" of production. The greater the use of capital per unit of output, the greater the income per capita and the level of private wealth, enabling the society to absorb a larger amount of government debt.

The other influence, representing a movement along the curve, is the portfolio adjustment as to the proportion of wealth held in the form of money assets. And, as we indicated, this depends on the change in yields. A lower rate of profit, or a lower rate of inflation (increasing the real face value), increases the demand for money balances, that is, government debt, per unit of net income. However, with a given capital-to-output ratio and no change in asset yields, m is constant, telling us that the demand for the nominal stock of money is proportional to the current value of output.

However, based on our analysis of income distribution, we tend to feel somewhat uncomfortable at this orthodox explanation of money demand. In laying out this demand curve, Solow makes the point that the rate of profit is not to be taken as an independent variable. He tells us that "in fact I have already assumed that r is a decreasing function of v."[8] What we have here is the neoclassical approach, which has the rate of profit being read off of the slope of the conventional production function. Thus for a large v the economy will earn a relatively low rate of profit and will demand to hold a greater proportion of money balances to output.

The upshot is that m is reckoned as being positively related to v, thereby giving its negative relation to r. This makes it "artificial" in a sense, to separate movements on the demand curve from a shift of the curve itself. Well, this is not the first time that we encounter such an "interplay"; the reader will remember our discussion of the Kaldor technical progress function in relating technological progress and the rate of capital accumulation.

However, there is perhaps a greater artificiality in this money-demand curve resulting from the negative relationship between the rate of profit and the capital-to-output ratio. If we adopted the determination of the rate of profit as

$$r = \frac{1}{s_K}(\frac{I}{K}) \tag{9.29}$$

and with the not too unreasonable assumption that $s_K = 1$, we have the rate of profit equal to the rate of growth. In the money-demand equation, we substitute the growth rate (G) as the shift variable, but the accommodation in portfolio balance is now solely in response to a change in real holdings of money balances, essentially the result of a change in the rate of inflation. Once the position of the curve is given, we know the rate of profit. As we will see, the price level will need to increase at a particular rate if the portfolio balance, that is, the m, is to be in support of the natural growth rate.

We can now relate our two growth-property equations to solve for the appropriate asset-money holdings; in doing so, we maintain the conventional money-demand equation. Along the steady state v is a constant, and then so is the rate of profit. To see this latter constancy via the other approach, we have the profits distribution equation as

$$\frac{P}{Y} = \frac{1}{s_K} \cdot \frac{I}{Y} \tag{9.30}$$

And with a constant proportion of profits to income, profits must be growing at the same rate as the capital stock.

Yet this is telling us that the real asset wealth as a proportion of output is constant or, what amounts to the same thing, that m is unchanging. Thus the growth in nominal asset holdings in real terms is equal to the growth in real output; there is no change in yields and no move along the money-demand curve. We can perhaps make this a bit clearer. Along the path the nominal stocks of money assets must be growing at the same rate as the value of current output. So:

$$\frac{\Delta M}{M} = \frac{\Delta Y}{Y} + \frac{\Delta p}{p} \tag{9.31}$$

and

$$\frac{\Delta p}{p} = \frac{\Delta M}{M} - \frac{\Delta Y}{Y} \qquad (9.32)$$

or

$$\frac{\Delta M}{M} - \frac{\Delta p}{p} = \frac{\Delta Y}{Y} = G \qquad (9.33)$$

Along the path, the rate of inflation must be equal to the difference between the growth rate of government debt and that of real output. We are saying that prices must be rising at a rate to reduce the rate of increase in nominal balances to that of real output. The whole point being, to reiterate, that a characteristic of a steady-state advance is a constant m.

So we substitute this characteristic into the growth equation 9.27 via Equation 9.32 to solve simultaneously for the portfolio balance and associated growth outcome. Thus:

$$G = (1-h)\frac{s}{v} - (1-s)[G](\frac{m}{v}) \qquad (9.34)$$

then

$$(1-s)[G](\frac{m}{v}) = (1-h)\frac{s}{v} - G \qquad (9.35)$$

and

$$m = \frac{(1-h)s - Gv}{(1-s)G} = \frac{(1-h)s}{(1-s)G} - \frac{v}{1-s} \qquad (9.36)$$

Equation 9.36 yields a negative sloping line relating the rate of growth of the economy to the level of money-asset balances held as a proportion of output.[9] We reiterate the obvious: An economic system can evidence steady state at different rates, though there is a singular rate that we designate as "natural" or maximum. Every point on the line (which can be referred to as the Harrod–Domar line) is a locus of steady-state growth outcomes reflecting different capital-to-output ratios. Let us consider the extreme points.

We want to reckon the growth rate of the economy within the reality of government expenditures as part of aggregate demand. If, as we have done, we assume government consumption to be a constant proportion (h) of output, but also assume a balanced budget, then taxes will be rising absolutely but in proportion to the increase in output. This obviously reduces the proportion of output available for savings, that is, for capital accumulation. Where we have no government and no taxes, net income is disposable income, which is taken up by private consumption and private investment, we have the usual one-asset "non-monetized" growth system. But with government spending and taxation net disposable income is less than net income; it is out of the former that one calculates the fraction spent on real consumption and, if we may use the term, "spent" on real investment.

Not meaning to belabor the issue, we need only compare the following conditions:

$$v = \frac{K}{Y} = \frac{s}{G}$$

$$G = \frac{sY}{K} = \frac{\dot{K}}{K} \qquad (9.37)$$

compared to

$$v = \frac{K}{Y} = \frac{s - sh}{G}$$

$$G = \frac{(s - sh)Y}{K} < \frac{sY}{K} = \frac{\dot{K}}{K} \qquad (9.38)$$

Solving for the growth solution (the extreme point on the v axis) for $M = 0$, $h > 0$, we have

$$\frac{(1 - h)s}{(1 - s)G} = \frac{v}{1 - s}$$

$$\qquad (9.39)$$

$$v = (1 - h)\frac{s}{G}$$

Figure 9.8

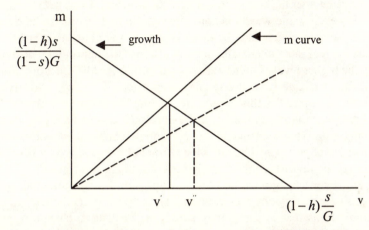

Turning to the demand for money balances, we reasoned that this is considered an increasing function of v; and in Figure 9.8 we have this upward sloping m curve drawn in the m–v space. The point of intersection reflects the interplay of Equation 9.36, telling us that the growth rate of the economy, that is, the rate of capital accumulation, reflects a portfolio asset balance consistent with what the private sector wishes to maintain. Should the society desire to maintain a smaller proportion of net output in the form of money assets, it will give rise to and be consistent with a higher capital-to-output ratio.

We keep in mind that the "outside authority" (i.e., the government) can promote or provide the incentive to alter the portfolio balance through monetary and fiscal measures. Certainly the nominal amounts of government debt are policy parameters to which the economy adjusts. Let us then assume that the authorities run a larger deficit, causing the supply of government debt and hence the money supply to increase at a faster rate. What may be the impact of this on the rate of capital accumulation?

Considering some of the matters that we discussed, we can trace what may happen in a stepwise fashion. Assuming at first no change in the rate of inflation, wealth owners will find themselves with increased nominal holdings of money assets, which increases disposable income thereby effectively increasing the saving ratio—the rate of capital accumulation. We are considering a change in asset holdings at existing prices. But it is likely that the rate of inflation will increase in response to the rate of increase in aggregate demand and the money supply; if it does so correspondingly, it will, in real terms, cancel or neutralize the increase in money asset balances, that is, there will be no change in the real holdings of government debt and no change in disposable income and, through this mechanism, it would seem, no change in the rate of real investment. The point is that the ratio of money balance to money income is the same after the change in government policy as it was before.

However, while wealth is not increasing in real terms, the higher rate of price increase, when taken with no change in the nominal interest, will reduce the real interest rate and thereby increase the opportunity cost of holding the higher level of money assets. This will have the effect of "tilting" the portfolio balance toward a greater proportion of owning real investment assets. In Figure 9.8 this is seen by rotating the *m*-curve downward at the existing *v*, resulting in a new steady-state path that has a higher capital-to-output ratio. Thus a change in the inflation rate brought about by changes in government policy will impact the real side of the economy; it is not neutral or a veil behind which the real elements are being determined.

However, changes in the money supply can be made neutral through a coordination of policy. For example, an increase in the interest rate at the same rate as that of the money supply will cause no change in portfolio balance and leave unchanged the ratio of government debt holding to net national product. The neutrality of money in the long-term growth context will depend on the effect of a change in its supply on that *m* ratio. But this brings us back to our awareness that prices need not rise in a corresponding fashion with an increase in the money supply (i.e., aggregate demand), so that the increase in nominal wealth may not be totally neutralized; the impact of this on the rate of accumulation and the capital-to-output ratio is not at all certain. The real increase in wealth can translate into increasing the effective savings ratio that may take the form of holding more physical capital assets, or it may show up as displacing real capital in favor of a greater proportion of money-asset holdings. We may be belaboring the point, but we want to say again that in a money-asset economy, savings may take the form of either physical capital or an expansion of the real balances of this "outside" money.

Now let us take the positive outcome as shown in Figure 9.8, which then may strike the reader, to use Solow's words, as revealing a "superficial paradox."[10] We see that a more rapid increase in nominal money reduces the ratio of money holdings to income, moving us toward the one (real) asset component of wealth, yielding a value of *v* reflective of the non-money Harrod–Domar steady-state outcome. However, we understand that there is no contradiction here; the higher rate of inflation generates a price level sufficient to prompt a flight from money assets to reduce the *m* ratio.

Money in the Long Term—A Second View

Uncertainty and Endogenous Money

The inclusion of asset money and how it may affect the equilibrium growth value of *v* is itself somewhat paradoxical. We introduce an element that is certainly in keeping with the reality of the operation of the economy, only to find that it yields a lower equilibrium capital intensity and hence a lower per capita output and consumption. One might ask, What are the advantages of the monetary two-asset economy? Are we to conclude that the presence of government consumption invariably linked to budget deficits will, as a long-term influence, simply give rise to a less productive economy? Or is it that we are overlooking some inherent (not obvious) rationale for holding money based on a service-in-kind that it provides, which, if accounted for, will not necessarily lead to a lower output per capita in the steady state. We are thinking here about the role of money balances tied to the enhancement of production, so that we may consider "liquidity" as an input to the production process similar to that of a producer good. We will understand this input as a means to enable the firm to cope with the uncertainty of future outcomes when making economic decisions concerning such matters as undertaking investment expenditures and levels of production.

We begin with a concept of time referred to as "logical" or "mechanical" time, which creates an environment within which decision makers formulate expectations about future events, and which mirrors the orthodox (neoclassical) equilibrium approach to economic relationships. Time, as Davidson so aptly states, "is a device which prevents everything from happening at once."[11] Which means that for most economic outcomes, thinking, for example, in terms of production levels or levels of sales and revenues, a period of actual time needs to elapse between the time when a decision is taken and the time at which its consequences are realized. The question is whether the decision maker, looking to the future, can confidently predict the outcome of actions taken during the current period. Does one possess sufficient current and historical information to forecast the future event with a degree of certainty? We use the word "information" though we could use the word "experience" as well, based on what we would agree is the human trait to assume that past outcomes flowing from a similar decision would provide a reliable basis for judging future results. But we must be careful about what we mean by "certainty" so as to be able to contrast it with "uncertainty."

Let us assume that the decision maker does believe that past events provide a reliable guide concerning future outcomes, and that one has all the relevant information. How does one transmit that knowledge into a basis for a forecast? Without getting into a statistical analysis of probability, we would say that this knowledge reveals the frequency of an outcome flowing from a particular action, which then enables the decision maker to assign a "probability coefficient" to a similar outcome in the future, stemming, of course, from the same action. That is, the assigning of a number that tells about the likelihood or chance of a future event based on a set of observations about

the past behavior of this type of action. In assigning this likelihood of outcome number, the decision maker is taking a calculable risk in engaging a
particular action; we can say that the decision is taken within a "state of
knowledge." The basis for taking the action is an objective probability or
likelihood of a particular outcome. Thus:

$$\text{State of Knowledge} \rightarrow \overset{\text{Probability}}{\text{What Is Likely to Happen}} \qquad (9.40)$$

As an example: Suppose one is thinking of investing in a project that in an
economy under a condition of high inflation will only have a 30 percent
chance of yielding a profit—a probability of success of 0.30; but past knowledge of the same type of investment under government action to keep inflation low yields a probability of a profitable outcome of 0.50. Then if we have
information about how the authorities have responded in the past to high
prices, we can form a knowledgeable estimation of risk in taking this action,
that is, in making the decision to invest in the particular project.

This is what is meant by certainty; it is the taking of an action (making an
investment or starting up production of a line of output) under conditions of
a calculable risk (knowledge) of realizing a particular consequence.

We can distinguish two environments for arriving at a probability. One is
what we have been talking about, where an analysis of past frequencies of
outcomes provides a statistically reliable basis for assigning a probability of
a future outcome. Davidson refers to this as "an objective probability environment."[12] The other, considered a "subjective probability environment," is
a situation where a probability is formed when one does not have past information or decides not to consider it. The likelihood of an outcome then
reflects the best one can do based on current knowledge, perhaps aided by an
expert consultant's opinion or, in the final analysis, simply on the basis of
one's own conviction. We can perhaps assume that the probability assign-
ment formed subjectively will coincide with one drawn from the statistical
analysis of past events.

Yet whatever the environment, the basic point is that one does not profess
ignorance about the future; indeed one professes knowledge in the form of a
probability or likelihood of an outcome. This certainty, however, is not at all
what is usually meant by the word certainty. The important point here is that
future economic events (and events in life generally) cannot be calculated or
predicted with certainty in the normal usage of the word, meaning that one
cannot assign a probability of 100 percent. There is no certainty or determin-
ism about future events, no matter how much data we have about the past
and the present. Only the probabilities of various possible future outcomes
can be determined.

This idea of decision making under certainty underlies the concept of logical time and the framework of equilibrium analysis. Certainly the reader has used equilibrium outcomes in many instances in the Principles course, but what is really being considered? What equilibrium does is to depict an outcome or a position corresponding to one set of conditions, and then compares the outcome to a different set of conditions at a different point in time. And there is the supposition that if one reversed conditions, one could assign a high probability of later redeeming the original outcome. One could go forward in time to a position that existed in a past time period; it is as if time, being mechanical, could be reversed.

But more to the point, if the set of conditions does not change, then the future outcome is a probabilistic determination of past events; this tells us that the future event is knowable. And it is knowable on the basis of supposed "economic laws" that are inimitable with the passage of time. To be somewhat more specific: Suppose market conditions change, say as a result of an increase in incomes; equilibrium (mechanical time) would tell us that the directional change in the price and quantity outcomes for the good in question are known, all that is needed is a study of existing and historical data to assign a probability to the degree of the change. To reiterate the fundamental point here: a knowledge of past events forms a reliable probability guide to future outcomes whether we move forward in time to an outcome that did not exist before or forward in time to a result that existed in the past.

However, there is a different non-neoclassical (post-Keynesian) view regarding economic decision making that claims that decisions are made within an environment of "uncertainty," and that it is historical time with its rejection of equilibrium analysis that is the framework of the decision. In this environment the individual acts with the clear understanding that between the time of the decision and the time consequences emerge there will occur unforeseen events; unforeseen in the sense that one could not have expected them as a result of consulting history. Of course, the future is "uncertain" (again we need to be careful about the meaning of words); it always is. The uncertainty here is that history and/or current events do not provide a sufficient guide to the future, so that one cannot even venture probabilities about outcomes—one cannot project historical statistical averages to forthcoming events. The economic world is one in which the laws of probability generally do not apply.

Davidson tells us:

> Our knowledge of economic events occurring through time is, however, asymmetrical: although we know the past we cannot be sure that we have any reliable knowledge about the economic future. The future remains to

be created by human actions and is not merely determined by some immutable economic laws.[13]

And a word from Hicks: "[P]eople do not know what is going to happen and know that they do not know what is going to happen."[14] Time, or outcomes flowing through time, moves in one direction—forward. There are no past guides to the future and no future guide to reclaim the past. All we know is that each point in time proclaims its own result, with the future left to work out its own outcome. This is the idea of decision making within a framework of historical time where the future is unknown and unknowable.

Assuming that this is the context of economic decision making, then what is the role of money balances in this process? Actual economies are, of course, monetary economies, not only in the obvious sense of needing to hold money for normal personal transactions, but as well, in the less obvious sense, that producing units do hold money or need to have clear access to the availability of money, in order to reduce the amount of uncertainty in carrying on the business activities of production and exchange. It is in this latter understanding that money holdings become an indispensable part of the production process, similar to other inputs.

Let us briefly review some earlier analyses. In terms of the long run (structured as a steady-state path) we saw that money is not neutral; that the ratio of real balances to output determines the net amount of liquidity that remains for real investment. But the proportion of output that serves as this store of value in the form of money assets is best understood as a response to this world of uncertainty. We talked in terms of individuals managing a portfolio consisting of money in the form of government debt (bonds) introduced via fiscal policy and that of real investment with the uncertainty dealing with expected rates of return. We are aware that an absolute increase in the real holdings of money assets affects the individual's disposable income and conveys a degree of "utility," since the holding of this asset, easily convertible into cash, enables the individual to quickly take advantage of the reasonable expectations concerning changes in the difference between the rental rate and the real yield in monetary assets. In this sense we can think of money assets as a consumer good.

Now we want to broaden our understanding not only with regard to how money is introduced but how it serves as an instrument in production. Entering into a production process normally involves a reasonably long time between the organization of inputs (to begin and maintain the process) and the product outcome and sale; production does usually involve a long gestation or carrying-out period of time. Whether we think in terms of a single unit of output (e.g., the construction of a building) that will be completed and sold at an estimated future time, or in terms of a flow output per unit of time over a future span of time, what is required to fulfill these production plans is some assurance of a flow of material and labor inputs into the future, thereby setting up an associated stream of cost expenditures.

Let us think of our megacorp organization with a given productive capacity, and of being able to form some estimation as to the cost of output as a result of a particular level of production (utilizing the plant at some degree of capacity) based on a forecast of future demand. The organization undertakes this production with some target rate of profit in mind, so that it has an expectation of sales proceeds in relation to cost, and hence of the markup at which it will sell its output. In our "uncertain" world (and the reader now understands the particular usage of this term) there is the ever present possibility of disappointment on the sales revenue side, against which there may be no protection. But there are, as well, unpredictable circumstances arising on the cost side, against which the organization believes it can put up a defense so as to greatly reduce if not eliminate those production uncertainties.

The company would need to be able to count upon, in essence to guarantee, the required flow of material and labor input over a span of time and to have some money cost control over the entire process. We are talking about some control over unit cost of production. Certainly expectations regarding these costs could be based upon existing price arrangements; but given our world of uncertainty, the organization cannot assign any value to future unit cost based upon existing or past knowledge. To remove itself from this state of "not knowing," the organization will enter into "forward contracts" with input suppliers. Such a contract is a legal obligation between the contracting parties that specifies a future date (or dates) for both delivery and money payment.

Of course, negotiated wage contracts are "forward" in that they obligate labor to perform certain hours of work at a stipulated cost per hour, with all sorts of contractual provisions covering overtime pay, pay for hazardous work, sick leave compensation, and so forth. The point of the forward contract is to remove, as far as one can, the uncertainty governing labor cost per unit of output. We say "as far as one can" since unit labor costs depend as well on labor productivity aside from objective money costs. Clearly one cannot "forward" disturbances in technical change or changes in workplace arrangements due to a merger of organizations.

Overall, what we find as an indispensable tool of production is the presence of a forward money contract. As Davidson puts it:

> Since production takes time, the hiring of labor and the purchase of materials to be used in any production activity must precede the date when the finished product will be available to the entrepreneur for delivery to buy-

ers. For any lengthy production process, hiring and raw material purchase transactions will require forward contracting to permit entrepreneurial control of the production operation and the efficient sequencing of labor, capital and raw material inputs in producing the final product for sale.[15]

In the absence of these types of contracts, firms would be quite hesitant to begin a long-duration production process; for they provide knowledge of, and thereby control over, future costs. Such contracts are modern institutional arrangements that permit economic agents to reduce the uncertainty in their operations, and to deal with and limit liabilities in the event of a negative outcome.

The parties entering into a production process are presumed to be willing to abide by the provisions of the forward contract. Should one party be unable or unwilling to fulfill one's obligation, then it is the legal enforceability of the agreement under civil law that gives the aggrieved party the assurance of a just monetary compensation. Thus a seller of material inputs, for example, is given the confidence to enter into a long-term relationship with the producing unit, being assured of a future cash flow even if unforeseen events cause the organization to be unable to meet its obligation, say, with regard to payment and/or acceptance of delivery of a quantity of goods.

The reader at this point may wonder why we spend this time in describing an obvious and pervasive relationship between economic units, but as we will see, it is the presence of these contractual arrangements that draws money balances into an active input role throughout the production process. Let us recall a point made much earlier in this chapter where we made reference to the view that money was seen as a "veil" behind which the real characteristics of the economy were worked out. And in terms of the steady-state analysis, that money did not matter for long-term real growth. We demonstrated that this is not so by the way in which we introduced money balances into the system and its role in the composition of wealth (it is not merely a transactions device).

Yet a support for the orthodox view that money does not matter may be seen in the introductory analysis of the marginal revenue–marginal cost behavior of the firm. The firm is supposed to know its wage cost over a production process, because they are "market-determined," which means that they are known based on past and/or current events. This permits the firm to purchase all input needs at known prices at the onset of every production period. There is no uncertainty here and no contractual obligations due at a future date; that is, all contracts are settled at the same moment that they are entered into. Thus money balances in the economy are simply active transactions balances resulting from previous realization of sales. There would seem to be no other function of money, say, as an "inactive store of protection" against unforeseen circumstances, that would exist in the orthodox world of certainty. Of course, we want to leave behind this make-believe orthodox framework and show the role of money as an active ingredient in the real outcome of the economy.

It would seem that the producing unit through these contractual agreements can greatly assure its costs of production; however, it is on the sales revenue side that most of the uncertainty prevails. The understandably basic concern is whether it will be able to sell its production at the end of the process so as to cover its costs and yield the expected level of profits. Here it can greatly assure its future cash flow by forward contracting to sell its output at a stipulated cost–markup price, as well as contracting the quantity delivered and paid for per unit of time.

So we come to the main point, which is that our organization will not undertake long-term production projects unless it can be assured of an appropriate flow of liquidity (i.e., money balances) to meet its contractual obligations. Quite possibly this needed finance will be provided entirely with internally generated funds; failing this, the organization must be able to borrow the necessary "debt money" to finance its production operations. The presence of this money cannot be considered as neutral, as the flow of credit is mirrored in the myriad of forward financial contracts that serve to intertwine economic agents and that reflect ongoing levels of economic activity.

Money as an input to the production process comes to the economy along with the accumulation of debt, which is a reflection of the generation of credit to facilitate production. The money supply, one might say, is in a respondent position to the change in the demand for credit flows, which is related to the level of economic activity as a result of production plans entered into by firms in accordance with their expectations.

Let us set out the basic image here. The emphasis is not on money as such (defined, as the reader will recall, in terms of the different M's) but on credit (or loan money), which enables the producing unit to bridge the time gap between necessary spending and the cash flow. The essential relationship is that money is credit driven; indeed, one can think of money balances as an output of the economy in response to the input of credit, essentially by banking institutions, where the demand for this credit is governed by the borrowing needs of firms. When firms expand production, they will normally be increasing their wage bill as well as other costs. And as we said, production does take time, so until the output is sold and the cash flow begins, firms will need an increased credit flow to bridge this gap. We will presume that the banking institution will satisfy this credit demand by bringing about an increase in demand deposits and through this an increase in the money supply. Hence changes in the money supply are caused by changes in production plans on the part of firms rather than the reverse. Of course, the reverse is what is espoused in Principles of Economics texts where the line of reasoning runs from the money supply (determined by the monetary authority outside the production system) to economic activity, usually via interest rate changes. Our point of view is that the money supply should be considered as endogenous to the economy in the sense of being determined by its demand, which is itself conditional on output, prices, and interest rate levels. The supply and demand for money (i.e., credit money) are interdependent; there are no free standing money supply and money demand curves that are brought into balance with one another through a change in the interest rate price in a so-called money market. As with other facets of economics, this market image has been a source of misunderstanding.

Before going on to some necessary elaboration concerning this idea of endogenous money and its role in determining the level of real economic activity, let us take a brief overview as to how money is employed in introductory texts, so that we can see where the misunderstanding lies as to what "type" of money is or is not endogenous.

As the reader may recall, the usual exposition is that the Federal Reserve System has at its disposal monetary tools (essentially the open-market operation) that it can employ to determine the "monetary base." This base consists of currency in circulation, that is, federal reserve notes, and member bank reserves or deposits that are all found on the liability side of Fed's balance sheet. This base money is referred to as such because it acts like a base in support of the money supply. What may at times get lost in the definitions of money and the analysis of monetary policy is the need to keep separate a change in the money base from the influences determining a change in the money supply. One introduces money in Principles courses with the *M*-definitions of money and then goes on to monetary policy, where one is talking about the money base. And it is all too easy to lose the distinction; one text by Parkins, in its introduction to the Fed monetary policy, begins with the statement: "The Fed constantly monitors and adjusts the quantity of money in the economy."[16] Well, not really so; what is meant here is the adjustment of the money base and the interest rate.

These "kinds" of money relate to each other via the money or deposit multiplier, which is a formula showing the amount by which a change in the money base (i.e., bank reserves) is multiplied to determine the aggregate change in the money supply, given the banking systems' reserve requirements against their deposits. We see this multiplier as:

$$\text{Money Multiplier} = \frac{\text{Change in Deposits}}{\text{Change in Reserves}} \tag{9.41}$$

If the multiplier is four, then a one million increase in reserves can potentially create four million in deposits, with the multiplier linked to the required reserve ratio by

$$\text{Money Multiplier} = \frac{1}{\text{Required Reserves Ratio}} \qquad (9.42)$$

The reader who may have studied the simple Keynesian expenditure model with the related expenditure or income multiplier will immediately notice some similarities here.

Recall that the simple income multiplier occurs as a result of the expenditures of one economic unit becoming the income of the second, with the subsequent expenditure of the second becoming the income of the third, and so forth, as one calculates the totality of income created through the system as a result of some exogenous change in expenditure. The aggregate income created depends on the successive levels of income received, which depends on what we may think of as the positive attribute of the marginal propensity to consume, or on the negative aspect or "leakage" as given by the marginal propensity to save.

The money multiplier operates along similar lines. The Fed injects a level of base money or reserves into the banking system, which then permeates through all of the individual banks of the system, as each bank is presumed to create demand deposits (an increase in the money supply) equal to its lending capability as measured by its excess reserve position.

Let us look at several banks in an operation that is similar to those expenditure "rounds" or "steps" in the exposition of the income multiplier. Trace the flow of reserves through the three banks in Table 9.1. From our money ratios we know that with a required reserve ratio of 0.25, the money multiplier is four, so that

$$4 = \frac{x}{100}$$
$$x = 400 = \text{increase in money supply} \qquad (9.43)$$

We have gone through this exercise to show how easy it is to slip into the attitude of the money supply as an exogenous variable. The Fed increases the base money with each bank, which is then assumed to create deposits up to the limit of its reserve capacity. And there is the assumption that at the determined interest rate as an offshoot of the open-market operation, the

Table 9.1 (in $)

Bank	Acquired reserves	Required reserves	Excess reserves	Lending capability
A	100.00	25.00	75.00	75.00
B	75.00	18.75	56.25	56.25
C	56.25	14.06	42.19	42.19

And so forth, with the total amount of deposits created equaling 400.00.

totality of consumer and business loan demand will equal the banking system's lending capability. And thus we find the overall observation found in Principles texts, that as long as the currency-to-deposit ratio and the reserve ratio do not change, the Fed can control the money supply by adjusting the monetary base—the whole money supply is built on the monetary base.

But we would argue that focusing on deposit creation in a sort of automatic way in relation to lending capability obscures the real economic forces. The starting point should be the demand for credit, which consists of the demand for business and consumer loans as governed by the level of real economic activity (involving forward financial contracts) and the rate of interest. One needs to relate the demand for credit with the bank's deposits—and through this its excess reserve position—as a measure of the liquidity pressure on banks. If this pressure is high (we are talking about the ratio of bank loans to bank deposits), then it will play an inhibiting role, say, in the financing of capital accumulation and thus in the level of real economic activity.

Let us be certain about this ratio; the top of the ratio reflects the demand for credit, while the denominator measures the lending capacity of the banking system. When the former increases relative to the latter, the commercial banking system will become less liquid and thus less capable of providing credit that is tied to those forward money contracts. Thus when we refer to the presence of money balances in this context, we mean the state of bank liquidity to finance the demand for credit.

Now let us tie all this to our notion of endogenous money. Certainly the money supply or the level of bank deposits is determined by production conditions inside the system. Seeing this from the bank's balance sheet, we would have the causation run from the liability side to the asset side; banks extend credit, thereby creating deposits (increasing the money supply) and then look to obtain reserves. Or to put the matter differently: Banks first make loans (appearing on the asset side) and then seek the required reserves to cover the increase in their assets. Banks may then find themselves under heightened liquidity pressure, as the rise in deposits will at the same time lead to an increase in the banking system's required reserves, which may place a constraint on additional supply of credit financing. These reserves will be provided; in doing so we observe a core principle of central bank operation, which is a "policy of accommodation." In reality, reserves pose little if any constraint; the Fed as "a lender of last resort" will provide the reserves required to accommodate the increase in the money supply. What is clearly a misunderstanding is the assumption that banks create loans only after the central bank has increased the money base, that is, put reserves into the system. Of course, this gives the impression that the central banks control the change in the money supply. But in reality, as a matter of general policy the Fed accommodates to the already determined loan demand—it acts to provide an elastic currency (reserve) supply. In fact, in the workings of the banking system, the amount of reserves required to be maintained at the end of a given statement week is predetermined by the level of deposits created weeks earlier. Since banks have to meet their reserve requirements, which are not alterable, being based on previous deposit activity, the required reserves will simply have to be made available. Certainly the central bank will have the freedom to decide how these reserves are to be acquired, and they can be supplied through a combination of ways. But to suggest that open-market operations would be used as a means to prevent a rise in reserves is illogical in the face of this predetermined requirement. To state a point in contrast to what is assumed in conventional banking analysis, the change in the money base is not to be viewed as a tool to directly affect a future change in the money supply; it is to be viewed as a required response in support of an already existing change in some money aggregate. This brings us to a summary view of the reality that the money supply in a credit money economy is endogenous: Money is credit driven; loans make deposits; deposits make reserves.[17] Yet if we do need to have in mind an exogenous relationship, it is that this money supply, that is, this creation of credit finance tied to those forward money contracts, is exogenous with respect to reserves. Indeed what is instrumental on the part of the central bank in influencing real output is not a monetary aggregate or a quantity, but its price; that is, the rate of interest. Placing this discussion within our steady state growth path, would have us "visualize" an accommodating central bank policy that thwarts bank liquidity pressure as the banking system meets the growing credit finance needs along the natural growth trajectory (we think of the growth rate of this money supply as being equal to the G_n rate). Money, as we see it in terms of available debt financing, joins those other supportive forces sustaining long-term growth.

Now let us get back to that exogenous variable, the rate of interest, which the central bank can determine through its open-market operations. Given the "price" of its choice, the Fed is prepared to supply the reserves necessary to support whatever the amount of bank loans demanded at that price; in other words, the supply of "money" is infinitely elastic, giving us a horizontal curve with respect to the given interest rate. Thus the ability of the central bank to control the growth of monetary aggregate depends on the ability to control the rate of bank lending (credit demand) via the rate of interest and not, to reiterate, through control of the monetary base. What is normally lost sight of, to repeat an operational point, is that when reserve requirements come into effect, the loans inducing such requirements have already been made.

We illustrate our discussion in Figure 9.9.[18] In panel i we find an administered interest rate $(\bar{r})$ on the vertical, with a corresponding level of credit finance demand (C_d) on the horizontal, that translates into a level of the money supply (M') in panel ii. At the given interest rate the banking system will supply the amount of bank credit demanded (again note the interdependence of the demand for and the supply of money), while the central bank provides the money base induced by this increase in deposits. In panel iii we find the reverse (nonconventional) causality, where the money base is shown endogenous to the money aggregate (M'), with base money being equal to the reciprocal of the money multiplier (M_m) times the money supply, which can be worked out from Equation 9.41.

As this book is asking the reader to consider a different reasoning to various tried or trustworthy economic principles, we would suggest in this context that one adopt a "horizontalist" stance in an analysis of the role of money. Yet we do not mean some general notion of the money supply, but one in terms of an aggregate that has direct influence on real production and employment, which is, as we have been saying, that supply of credit finance that fundamentally is tied to those forward money contracts inherent in the production process, and that is a mirror of the demand for such finance at its institutionally determined (politically influenced?) price, that is, the rate of interest. Let us finally put aside the conventional market mechanism with regard to the determination of this price, as we have argued for its nonapplicability in an understanding of the prices of finished goods or, indeed, of that of labor. This may be a good place to reinforce our overall observation made in a different context in this work. Certainly it may be useful to talk in terms of the factors influencing demand from those influencing supply, but as Eichner tells us, "One should not assume that the two will automatically be brought into balance with one another through a change in the market price."[19] He goes on to stress that it is the latter error that permeates the entire body of conventional theory of which our Principles texts are all about, and which has "led to the present intellectual bankruptcy of economics."[20]

Recall our analysis of commodity pricing and the realization that it is in fact not demand-determined over a wide range of capacity utilization. The analy-

Figure 9.9

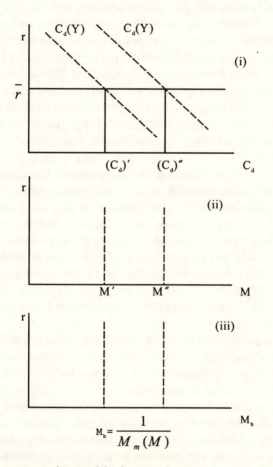

sis finds its counterpart in panel i of our endogenous money diagram, where increase in income and the associated demand for credit financing does not normally lead to an increase in interest rates. The miseducation inherent in the orthodox supply-and-demand framework applies in more than one context.

On a grander scale, our analysis would cause us to abandon the quantity theory of money, with its essential principle embedded in the causal arrow running from the money supply to nominal income to the price level. Indeed, given the reality of the endogenous money supply, the causal relationship runs in reverse. Interestingly enough, the standard Keynesian approach would have the effect of the central bank's change in the money supply run through the interest rate "market," which is a misspecification to say the least. In the workings of this market, the conventional thinking would have the central bank increase the money supply (shift that vertical exogenous money-supply curve to the right), thus creating a level of the money stock in excess of what the system desires to hold (i.e., demand) and driving down interest rates.

But the quantity of the money supply is always determined by the demand for credit money finance; there can never be an excess supply of money. Of course the Fed can target a particular lower interest rate; but then the banking system will supply whatever liquidity is demanded at that price. The control variable is the interest rate, not the stock of money itself, which is, to reiterate, always demand-determined at any short-term interest rate. So much then for the money-market equilibrium diagram that students are imbued with in the Principles discussion of money.

In fact, it has been suggested that we eliminate the idea of the money supply or money stock from the lexicon of monetary policy. For an increasing money supply is merely a reflection of the pressures for increasing credit demand, which is supplied by the banking system, with this supply capability guaranteed or accommodated by the central banks' provision of additional reserves. It is this accommodating policy that prevents liquidity pressure with its retarding effect on real production. In our steady-state context this policy keeps the rate of interest from rising and thereby provides an important ingredient to keep output growing at the required rate. Of course money matters for real economic growth.

If such a policy were not forthcoming, banks would need to ration credit with accompanying higher short- and long-term interest rates. This would have a negative effect on real production via an inability to finance forward contracts. One can explain a cyclical downturn in real economic activity through a nonaccommodating monetary policy. Again, we make the point that the essential element is not bank deposits (and thereby lending reserves), but the change in bank deposits relative to bank loan demand (liquidity pressures) that central bank operations respond to, fully or otherwise.

However, orthodoxy (monetarists) will object to eliminating the money stock from a money macro model, claiming that this removes the variable to explain the secular increase in prices. Let us quickly review the usual linkages here. An exogenous increase in the money supply operating on the money market lowers interest rates; this will stimulate increasing aggregate demand, which spills out in the form of increasing real output with corresponding (indeed necessary) higher prices and nominal wages.

At various places in this book we have shown that there is very good reason to doubt the operations of these links in the reality of the way the economy works, and these relationships should be jettisoned. There is much evidence suggesting that the long-term rise in prices is best explained by the growth of money wages in excess of productivity. When this happens, credit demand increases, which the central bank will either accommodate or, if it does not, will force a decline in real output and employment (as a means to limit wage increases). Parenthetically, if we think back to our discussions of production mechanics and markup pricing, we realize that for "technical" and organizational reasons, prices are, in the main, not demand-driven. Should the central bank in its quest to reduce the rate of inflation (or the expectations of increasing prices) reduce the money base and engineer higher interest rates, the result will be a diminishing of real output and employment with little impact on aggregate price level changes. This is a very quick explanation for the U.S. economy's recent experience with "stagflation." Even people in positions of having much economic power may be wedded to accustomed or traditional economic principles that give a misreading of reality.

This book has been an experience in traveling the road of nonorthodox economic reasoning. At this point we bring our trip to an end, though we are far from having completed all the journey. Yet insofar as we have gone—that is, given the ideas and topics that we have analyzed—it would be satisfactory if the reader is now in a position of doubt, questioning many of our standard Principles of Economics. For the intent of this book was to bring the reader to such a posture and to offer alternative economic reasoning. Yet for this book to fulfill a more basic purpose requires that the professor not be timid, but begin to fuse this material into the body of what is customarily the Principles of Economics and beyond. For what we all desire is a more exciting and certainly a far more realistic explanatory experience, as economics confronts real-world issues and institutional arrangements.

Notes

1. Robert M. Solow, *Growth Theory: An Exposition* (New York: Oxford University Press, 1988), p. 59.

2. The basis for this analysis is Solow's "A Model with Two Assets," in *Growth Theory*.

3. Suppose we have a $1,000 bond and a price level (p) of $10, which gives a real face value of

$1000/$10 = 100

Now assume that the price level falls by 5 percent, so that $0.5/10 = \Delta p/p$. The capital gain is

$$\frac{\$1000}{\$100}(0.5) = 5$$

$$\text{as} \quad \frac{1000}{9.5} = 105$$

4. Assume $Y = 20$, $h = 0.4$, then government consumption is

$$20(1 - 0.4) = 8 = \text{Tax}$$

with the ratio of Y_D (disposable income) to Y being

$$\frac{12}{20} = 0.6$$

Should h be reduced to 0.2 we have

$$20(1 - 0.2) = 16 = \text{Taxes}$$

with the ratio being

$$\frac{4}{20} = 0.2$$

5. Solow, *Growth Theory*, p. 62.
6. The working out of this apparent case is as follows:

$$\Delta K + \Delta(\frac{M}{p}) = sY \qquad (9.\text{i})$$

and let the change in the stock of real cash balance be stated as DM_r so

$$sY - \Delta M_r = \Delta K \qquad (9.\text{ii})$$

The rate of capital accumulation is

$$\frac{sY}{K} - \frac{\Delta M_r}{K} = \frac{\Delta K}{K} \qquad (9.\text{iii})$$

which can be stated as

$$\frac{\Delta K}{K} = (s - \frac{\Delta M_r}{Y})\frac{Y}{K} \qquad (9.\text{iv})$$

now

$$\Delta M_r = -[\frac{M}{p} \cdot \frac{\Delta p}{p}] \qquad (9.\text{v})$$

then

$$\frac{\Delta K}{K} = s + [\frac{M}{pY} \cdot \frac{\Delta p}{p}]\frac{Y}{K} \qquad (9.\text{vi})$$

7. From (9.22) we go to

$$Y = Y - hY + [\frac{M}{p} \cdot \frac{\Delta M}{M} - \frac{M}{p} \cdot \frac{\Delta p}{p}] + hY + \Delta K - sY + sYh - s[\frac{M}{p} \cdot \frac{\Delta M}{M} - \frac{M}{p} \cdot \frac{\Delta p}{p}]$$

which gets us to

$$\Delta K = (1 - h)sY - (1 - s)[\frac{M}{p} \cdot \frac{\Delta M}{M} - \frac{M}{p} \cdot \frac{\Delta p}{p}]$$

8. Robert M. Solow, *Growth Theory*, p. 66.

9. If m = 0, we have:

$$\frac{(1-h)s}{(1-s)G} = \frac{v}{1-s}$$

Then solving for v

$$v = \frac{(1-h)s \cdot (1-s)}{(1-s)G}$$

$$= (1-h)\frac{s}{G}$$

and with

$$v = 0, \quad m = \frac{(1-h)s}{(1-s)G}$$

10. Robert Solow, *Growth Theory*, p. 69.

11. Paul Davidson, *Controversies in Post Keynesian Economics* (Aldershot, UK: Edward Elger, 1991), p. 46.

12. Ibid., p. 46.

13. Ibid., p. 35.

14. J.R. Hicks, *Economic Perspectives* (Oxford, UK: Oxford University Press, 1977), p. vii.

15. Davidson, *Controversies*, p. 58.

16. Michael Parkins, *Economics*, 8th ed. (Reading, MA: Addison Wesley), p. 517.

17. One can obtain more involved analysis from Marc Lavoie, *Foundations of Post-Keynesian Economic Analysis* (Aldershot, UK: Edward Elgar, 1992), pp. 169–181. Also one might want to consult the analysis in Stanley Bober, *Recent Developments in Non-Neoclassical Economics*, chap. 8 (Brookfield, VT, and Aldershot, UK: Ashgate, 1997).

18. Taken from Bober, *Recent Developments*, pp. 428–429.

19. Alfred S. Eichner, *Toward a New Economics* (Armonk, NY: M.E. Sharpe, 1985), p. 7.

20. Ibid.

Index

About the Author

Stanley Bober received his Ph.D. from New York University in 1962, and was a member of the economics faculty at Colby College from 1960 to 1964. He is currently professor of economics at the A.J. Palumbo School of Business and Administration at Duquesne University. He also serves as a professor on the graduate economics faculty. His areas of research are business cycles and economic growth in relation to alternative (non-neoclassical) paradigms of economic analysis. Professor Bober is on the editorial board of the *Eastern Economic Journal* and is the author of seven books. His latest publications are *Modern Macroeconomics: A Post-Keynesian Perspective* (1988), *Pricing and Growth* (1992), and *Recent Developments in Non-Neoclassical Economics* (1997).